D0408866

WILD
BLUE
YONDER

WILD BLUE YONDER

Money, Politics, and the B-1 Bomber

NICK KOTZ

PANTHEON BOOKS

NEW YORK

For all the brave American fliers
who have defended their country.

LIBRARY OF CONGRESS CATALOGING-IN-PUBLICATION DATA
KOTZ, NICK.
WILD BLUE YONDER.
1. B-1 BOMBER.   2. UNITED STATES. AIR FORCE—
PROCUREMENT. I. TITLE
UG1242.B6K69 1988   358.4'2   87-43057
ISBN 0-394-55700-X

DESIGNED BY ROBERT BULL DESIGN

MANUFACTURED IN THE UNITED STATES OF AMERICA

FIRST EDITION

CONTENTS

Is Anyone in Charge Here?   vii

ONE:
The Politics of National Defense

1 But Will It Fly?   3
2 The Best Bases Politics Can Buy   10

TWO:
The Rise of the Military Economy

3 Dwight Eisenhower and the Politics of Fear   27
4 Curtis LeMay and Strategic Air Power   37
5 Dutch Kindelberger and the New Defense Politics   48
6 Politics and the Missile Gap   59
7 The Whiz Kids and the Bomber Generals   67
8 Vietnam and the Test of Air Power   79

PHOTO SECTION AFTER PAGE 86

THREE:
The Parable of the Born-Again Bomber

9	The Greening of California	89
10	The Goldplated Bomber	107
11	Who's on Who?	123
12	Jimmy Carter and the Anti–B-1 Coalition	139
13	The Politics of a Nuclear Engineer	158
14	The Secret War to Save the B-1	180
15	The Democratic Bomber and the Republican Bomber	200

FOUR:
Hooked on Defense

16	But Does It Fly Well Enough?	221
17	Out of Control	234
	The Defense Network, 1957–87	251
	Major B-1 Contractors	258
	Acknowledgments	261
	People Interviewed	264
	Source Notes	268
	Bibliography	297
	Index	304

IS ANYONE IN CHARGE HERE?

Almost every American holds deep patriotic convictions about the defense of our country and its freedoms. We support a strong military that will deter aggression and protect our national interests. Yet we don't want war. We dread the cost and we fear the results of an out-of-control arms race. We recognize that a nuclear war would be an immeasurable horror.

And yet American defense policies and practices too often clash with our professed values, as we the people seek to govern ourselves in the world's strongest democracy. We are puzzled by revelations of the Defense Department paying outrageous prices for coffeepots, toilet seats, and simple bolts. We are indignant at the news of billions spent to build weapons that fail to perform. We don't feel any safer, even after massive buildups. We have spent a trillion dollars on defense from 1982 through 1987—and when we need a simple minesweeper in the Persian Gulf, none are available. We constantly seek newer and more powerful nuclear weapons, even when we already possess the power to destroy all civilized life on earth, many times over.

We live, of course, in an irrational and dangerous world, in which we have adversaries who do not wish us well. To consider our own frightening buildups and mixups without assessing those of the other side would be worse than naïve. But even so, our own actions are themselves often irrational; they do not match our professed beliefs in an effective defense, in getting our money's worth and avoiding waste, in seeking a safer world.

In national defense, we seem to be caught up in the vortex of political and economic forces that have run amok. The compass that guides us to wise decisions of broad national interest has swung widely off course, with sensible priorities being twisted badly askew. We manufacture weapons that are not needed, that cost too much, and that don't work, while we fail to meet other, more basic, defense needs.

The influence of politics on national defense is so pervasive, so deeply embedded at every level, that it becomes difficult even to identify. Virtually every American is involved, directly or indirectly. Selfish political and economic interests in military affairs are often carefully wrapped in the American flag, and defended with the most elegant, sophisticated, and technically complex rationales.

The dynamics of national-defense politics are far more complex, fragmented, and disturbingly erratic than many of us acknowledge—or even recognize. Politics influences literally thousands of decisions that constantly must be made to create the treaties, strategies, forces, bases, and weapons that collectively make up our national defense.

Is there any way to understand what is going on within this tangled defense web? Can we find out how these decisions are made, who exercises the most influence, and why we seem to make the same mistakes over and over again? Why are we constantly beset with contradictions in our military programs? Who is really in charge here? Or is no one in charge—is the system really out of control?

In explaining our defense woes, we either defer to the experts or glibly blame powerful, impersonal, and autonomous forces that are beyond our control. But to a great extent, these are evasions, ways to justify our passivity as citizens and to avoid taking responsibility for our own actions, or lack of them. We need to take a much harder look at the system, to see how it really works.

In seeking to understand American defense decision-making,

I have examined a perennial centerpiece of the U.S. defense debate for the past thirty years—the question of whether to build a new strategic bomber of the U.S. Air Force. The political battle over the bomber finally led to production of the controversial B-1. The story illustrates many of the recurring problems of American national defense.

My hope is that with greater knowledge, we can begin to bring the system under control. Only thus can we fulfill our responsibilities as citizens, protect our nation and its precious freedoms, and strive for a more peaceful world.

N.K.

Washington, D.C.

October 1, 1987

ONE

The Politics of National Defense

1

BUT
WILL
IT FLY?

On October 1, 1986, the U.S. Air Force proudly hailed a victory for which its generals had valiantly fought for thirty years: A new strategic bomber called the B-1 was taking its place in the American nuclear arsenal. Precisely on schedule, the first squadron of fifteen sleek planes stood poised for action at an airbase in the mesquite-covered hills of north Texas. Over the next sixteen months, eighty-five more B-1s would roll off production lines in the desert near Palmdale, California. At a cost of more than $28 billion for the hundred-plane force, the B-1 was the most expensive airplane in aviation history.

The Air Force thought the bombers were worth every cent. General Lawrence Skantze, whose Air Force Systems Command had shepherded the plane through production, praised the B-1 down to its last rivet, calling it "the best, most capable manned penetrating bomber in the world." Carrying twenty lethal nuclear missiles, each bomber could wreak two hundred times as much destruction as the bombs that leveled Hiroshima in World War II. The Air Force, it seemed, had finally prevailed.

Taking Air Force spokesmen at their word, anchorman Dan Rather declared on the *CBS Evening News* that "a big new element of the U.S. nuclear weapons force went on line today." Pictures showed a breathtakingly beautiful airplane: The 127-foot span of its slim wings flowed into a long, narrow fuselage nearly half the length of a football field. A needle-sharp nose sloped downward from the cockpit like a beak. In its dark camouflage paint, the B-1 bomber loomed in the sky like a graceful bird of prey.

Months later, however, a different story began to unfold, tarnishing the luster of the Air Force's achievement. Prodded by congressional investigators, the Air Force admitted that, despite the fanfare, not a single bomber had been battle-ready that October day. The B-1 was instead snarled in technical problems—problems the Air Force had known about for more than a year. The most serious malfunction would take at least four more years to correct—handicapping the B-1 precisely during the critical period for which the Air Force had contended the plane was most needed.

The American public had been misled; so had the Congress and Secretary of Defense Caspar Weinberger. Even the National Military Command Center at the Pentagon, responsible for the nation's secret war plan, was unaware that the B-1s were not ready for battle.

Some glitches and growing pains are inevitable in developing any complex weapons system. But the B-1 had more than its share, and they were more serious than mere glitches; if they were not remedied, the plane would be hamstrung in its principal mission—to penetrate the Soviet heartland and deliver a devastating nuclear attack. The B-1's credibility as a deterrent to war, not to mention its success in battle, would depend on more than the skill and bravery of bomber crews. Equally essential were a dazzling array of state-of-the-art computerized devices, including the plane's systems for flight control, defensive avionics, and terrain-following radar. If these critical systems failed, how could the bombers overcome sophisticated Soviet defenses and reach their targets? The bird could fly, but could it reach its prey?

"It's got limitations which we would rather not have," conceded Major General Peter Odgers, the Air Force officer directly responsible for overseeing the bomber's construction. "But we

4

have a high degree of confidence we can correct those limitations."

Revelation of flaws in the plane revived the partisans in a battle that stretched over the entire history of the Air Force's quest for a new bomber. After conducting its own investigation, the House Armed Services Committee reported in April 1987 that the B-1 bomber's chances of completing a wartime mission were only half as good as intended. "Frankly, the Air Force screwed it up," said committee chairman Les Aspin, a Wisconsin Democrat and longtime B-1 critic. "They screwed it up and didn't tell us about it." Aspin predicted it would take more than $3 billion and four years to deal with the problems, "some of which are correctable at a price and more are question marks, where a solution isn't in sight at any price."

Some defense analysts labeled the bomber the Flying Edsel, alluding to the highly touted 1950s Ford car that flopped; others called it a "lead sled," since the 230-ton bomber was said to be hard to maneuver and unable to cruise fully loaded above a modest 20,000 feet. "An awful lot of that money [spent on the B-1] is down the tube," said Senator Sam Nunn, the Georgia Democrat who was chairman of the Senate Armed Services Committee. Retired Air Force Colonel James Boyd, an innovator of fighter aircraft and critic of Pentagon procurement practices, sardonically told a fellow officer that the best use for the B-1 was "to paint it yellow and use it as a line taxi," to carry equipment and crews from hangars to aircraft. When an Air Force general declared that the B-1 was "the best war plane in the world today," Democratic Congressman Sam Stratton of New York, normally a strong military supporter, responded, "That's a lot of baloney."

Stung by a devastating barrage of what it considered politically motivated and grossly exaggerated criticism, the Air Force counterattacked. A stream of Air Force officers testified that the defects were being remedied rapidly, that even with its faults the B-1 could carry out its doomsday mission. Pilots who flew the plane, including Air Force Chief of Staff Larry Welch, issued testimonials to the B-1's remarkable performance and superiority to the aging B-52 it would replace.

Who was right—the Air Force or its critics? In one way, it didn't much matter. It was too late to turn back—the government had already spent billions, committing the nation to the B-1 bomber.

The bomber dispute raises a host of perplexing questions: How did a thirty-year effort on a major weapons system manage to produce a $28 billion plane that didn't seem to work very well? And why do such problems in military procurement recur so often? The B-1's technical malfunctions and cost overruns were not unique. The Army's Divad antiaircraft gun and its Bradley Fighting Vehicle, the Navy's Trident submarine, the Air Force's C-5A transport and its TFX fighter—all are weapons whose failures and overruns provoked political controversy and even scandal.

But the B-1 bomber story raises fundamental issues that go well beyond overruns and malfunctions. It is a telling example of the defense process at work. It highlights troubling questions about national security and the arms race: How does America make decisions on critical national-defense issues? Whose influence counts the most? Are decisions to build new weapons based on real national-defense needs? Or are they governed by narrow political, economic, and military special interests?

Perhaps the most basic question is: How much nuclear weaponry is needed to safeguard our nation? Some believe that a nuclear standoff exists between the United States and the Soviet Union, that more nuclear weapons are militarily superfluous, and that only arms control can produce greater safety. At the other end of the spectrum are those who believe that American safety lies only in maintaining nuclear superiority—a "first-strike capability" plus the means and determination to fight and win a nuclear war if deterrence fails. This latter view is seldom candidly voiced, because it frightens American voters. Yet it has long been the thinking of influential military leaders and nuclear-war strategists, and it is a basic part of U.S. defense planning.

The dispute over how *many* weapons involves another: Which are the right weapons? Besides the B-1, the Air Force is developing an even more expensive advanced-technology bomber. This airplane, called the Stealth, is shrouded in greater official secrecy than any weapon since the atom bomb. The bill for developing, producing, and operating the two bombers will come to well over $100 billion.

Advocates insist that both new bombers are needed to complement land-based and sea-based missiles as part of the strategic nuclear deterrent, and would also serve as vital weapons in fighting a war, whether nuclear or conventional. Yet a host of critics, including four presidents, have questioned the need for both bombers—indeed for *any* new strategic penetrating bomber—in the age of intercontinental ballistic missiles. At root is a historic argument about the importance of strategic airpower in the nuclear age.

Each military service is of course dedicated to meeting needs of national defense. But each has also zealously promoted the weapons that best advance its own special interests—on which billions of dollars, thousands of jobs, and countless careers are staked. For the Air Force this has meant pursuit of the strategic bomber; for the Navy, a determination to build more super aircraft carriers; for the Army, a desire to have its own helicopters to carry its troops into battle and provide them with close air support.

When the president or Congress has denied service requests, uniformed military leaders have often aggressively carried their advocacy into the political arena, as with the B-1 bomber. This raises still another question: What is the proper relationship between military and civilian authority? Few Americans disagree with the constitutional principle that clearly subordinates military to civilian rule. The country expects its generals and admirals to provide the president, the secretary of defense, and Congress with their candid military judgments—and to go no further than that. Yet it is not uncommon for military officers to cross the line, to become active combatants in defense power struggles, sometimes undermining the orders of presidents and the laws of the land.

As in other major weapons acquisitions, the bomber controversy has swept over vast areas of the American political and economic landscape. From Dwight Eisenhower to Ronald Reagan, seven presidents have faced key decisions affecting the fate of the

B-1 and its experimental predecessor, the B-70. Often clashing with the current president, Congress has acted on the bomber during each of the past thirty years. Hanging in the balance have been huge economic benefits—for defense contractors, for labor unions, and for communities where the bombers would be built or based. At stake in building this plane were tens of thousands of jobs and contracts with fifty-two hundred companies in forty-eight states. A sustained effort to kill the bomber project was mounted by thousands of peace activists, who made the B-1 their principal concern for four years after the Vietnam War. Political candidates have used the bomber both to appeal for votes in communities that would benefit from it, and to show where they stood on national defense.

The tangled and controversial history of the bomber leads straight to the heart of defense politics. The story of those politics reveals how national-defense programs have been buffeted back and forth over the years—not only by an evolving Soviet threat, but also by myriad special interests competing in the political and economic maelstrom of American democracy. These special interests have grossly distorted defense priorities and needlessly exacerbated the arms race.

The bomber has become a highly visible symbol in an endless political, military, and economic struggle over the shape of national defense. Responding to constant shifts of political power, government policy on developing a new bomber has careened erratically for years, often guided by promises made in the most recent election campaign. As a result, the bomber project has been started and stopped half a dozen times, confusing friend and foe alike.

Throughout this checkered history, the Air Force and its allies in science, industry, labor, and politics have relentlessly pursued their goals—and other groups have opposed them. On both sides, the motives of patriotism, financial gain, career ambition, political aggrandizement, and loyalty to an institution or idea were often so mixed that it is hard to tell what was narrow self-interest and what was concern for the national good. American leaders have been faced with the perplexing challenge of sorting out the conflicting interests and charting a path that would assure the nation's defense without squandering national resources or further inflaming the arms race. The challenge has not been met.

When President Eisenhower warned of the dangers of a "military-industrial complex" in his farewell address of January 1961, what he had in mind was the tangled, possibly inseparable roles of industry, the military, science, education, and government in maintaining a permanent military establishment in the nuclear age.

Critics of national-defense policies often refer to the military-industrial complex as if it were a conspiracy imposed from above against the will and desires of the American people. But Eisenhower actually suggested a subtler, more insidious meaning. The "conjunction of an immense military establishment and a large arms industry is new in the American experience," he noted; "the total influence—economic, political, even spiritual—is felt in every city, every statehouse, every office of the federal government. . . . Our toil, resources, and livelihood are all involved; so is the very structure of the society."

In short, the military-industrial complex is ourselves. The ways we influence the defense process—and are influenced by it—can be seen in the development of any major new defense enterprise; the B-1 is only one of many. There is no sign that it will be the last.

It is hard to measure the full effect of the military network—the complex web of interests that stretches all the way from the local chamber of commerce and union hall, to huge industrial conglomerates and the Pentagon, to Congress and the White House. But a good place to start looking is at the grass roots.

2

THE BEST BASES
POLITICS
CAN BUY

On the Michigan shores of blustery Lake Huron, summers quickly fade and winter is a way of life. Sustaining the economy of the rural communities two hundred miles north of Detroit are two important industries: tourism and the U.S. Air Force. The tourists go home at Labor Day, but the Air Force stays forever.

At least that had always been the assumption of the hardy people of the towns of Tawas, Oscoda, Greenbush, and Harrisville. The flat, wooded land, clear trout streams, and deep blue lakes immortalized in Ernest Hemingway's stories of boyhood are still much the way they were fifty years ago. Summer can indeed be idyllic. In winter, the giant Wurtsmith Air Force Base turns out the payroll that keeps business humming in the banks, beauty parlors, auto lots, and Big Boy restaurants. The sprawling 5,200-acre base houses the 379th Bombardment Wing, whose B-52H bombers stand poised to strike at the Soviet Union.

But on June 23, 1983, local business leaders received jolting news about their economic mainstay from an old friend, Air Force Lieutenant General Earl O'Loughlin. O'Loughlin, a decorated combat veteran, brought pride to his boyhood fishing companions in East Tawas. In his thirty-year career he rose from enlisted man to vice-commander of the Air Force Logistics Command. He had come home to address a luncheon meeting of the chamber of commerce at the Waban Inn outside Oscoda.

O'Loughlin delivered an ominous message: Wurtsmith Air Force Base, with its 3,600 jobs and $78 million annual payroll, faced an uncertain future. As the new B-1B bombers came on line in the next few years, most B-52 squadrons would be retired. If Wurtsmith were to close down, the local economy would lose more than $100 million a year, including money spent by Air Force families, federal aid to schools with children of service personnel, and local construction contracts. "If you're not on the list to get the B-1," said O'Loughlin, "you're in trouble." The businessmen bombarded the general with questions. What should they do? What were their chances of getting one of the proposed B-1 squadrons for Wurtsmith?

In the year and a half since President Reagan decided to build the B-1, an alleged list had caused confusion and competition in Congress and in Air Force communities around the nation. The list would name the three or four bases chosen as homes for the 100 new B-1 bombers. Competition for those bases had been intense—particularly among the communities near the thirteen bases already housing the Strategic Air Command's 349 B-52s. Many of these communities felt they faced economic ruin if their SAC bases were to close down instead of receiving another military mission when the B-52s retired. Even before the general's speech, rumors had been swirling in northern Michigan business circles that Wurtsmith had recently been removed from the number-two position on the B-1 base list.

Politics counted, O'Loughlin told his audience. "We have legislators in Michigan who have not defended the B-1 program— and those states with B-1 opponents will be the first to be cut!" Michigan's political problems, the general suggested, were its two U.S. senators, Democrats Carl Levin and Donald Riegle. Both men had opposed building the B-1, but Levin had been particularly outspoken, calling the plane "an unneeded waste of national resources."

General O'Loughlin urged the chamber of commerce to sponsor a letter-writing campaign to Levin and Riegle protesting their positions on the B-1, calling on them to support continuation of

Wurtsmith and K.I. Sawyer, a base on Michigan's Upper Peninsula that the Air Force was considering closing. The letter-writing campaign must be statewide to be effective, O'Loughlin told them. "Even 100 percent of the local community probably won't have that much impact."

On that sunny June day, the Michigan business leaders assumed they were just getting some helpful inside information from an old friend. They had no idea they were viewed as lobbying objectives in a well-orchestrated campaign the Air Force had been waging across the country for at least ten years to build and sustain support for the B-1 bomber. Lobbying pressure was applied at the grass roots as well as in Washington to win approval for the project from both the president and members of Congress. When an elected representative stood in the way of the B-1, the Air Force sometimes applied pressure through his or her constituents. Air Force generals were booked to speak at gatherings of community leaders, such as the chambers of commerce, or at meetings sponsored by local Air Force Association chapters. Earl O'Loughlin may have been visiting his old home on his own time and for purely personal reasons, but his message was vintage Air Force: Support the Air Force's goals and it will support your community; oppose it and your economy might suffer.

Although production was under way on the B-1s in the summer of 1983, the Air Force was taking nothing for granted. Many senators had criticized the B-1 as money wasted on outdated technology. In the same week as O'Loughlin spoke to the businessmen in Michigan, Levin was urging the Senate to cut $800 million from the B-1's 1984 funds; he pushed for building the Stealth bomber, designed to be almost invisible to radar, instead. But the Air Force desperately wanted both planes. Since the long history of the B-1 already included one cancellation of the project, the Air Force would not feel safe until the hundred scheduled bombers had rolled out of the factory.

In the hardball game of Washington politics, it is not unusual for the executive branch to menace the defense assets of a state or community if its elected representatives fail to cooperate with Pentagon requests. Nor is it unusual for members of Congress to support military projects in return for obtaining an installation for their region. However, the political pushing and grabbing usually occurs behind the scenes, not in broad daylight. No one wanted it to appear that such grave issues of national defense as the location of strategic bases could be decided on narrow, selfish political grounds. But the Michigan fight took place in the open. O'Loughlin's blunt remarks, as reported in the weekly *Oscoda Press*, galvanized the asssembled businessmen into action.

Before long, Bob Davis, the Republican congressman representing the region, prepared to go after Senators Levin and Riegle for endangering Wurtsmith by opposing the B-1. Word of the chamber meeting and Davis's impending political attack was relayed to Washington by staffer Chris Jewell in Levin's Alpena office, near Wurtsmith. The message was simple: "We've got trouble up here."

Levin's trouble included a tough reelection fight in 1984. His opponent, Jack Lousma, a former Marine pilot and astronaut, ardently supported the B-1. Levin's opposition to the B-1 could unseat him if it jeopardized thousands of jobs and the economic health of northern Michigan.

Carl Levin tried to reassure his constituents that "the Pentagon makes its decisions based on national security, not on how an area's representative votes." The *Detroit News* replied in an editorial, "That's just plain naïve. The Air Force generals who decide where new planes are to be based aren't likely to favor the home heath of their most strident opponents."

Levin, a Harvard-educated civil-rights lawyer from Detroit, served as city-council chairman before his election to the Senate in 1978. He was a member of the Senate Armed Services Committee, where the Pentagon viewed him as a typical antidefense liberal, sympathetic to nuclear freezes and arms-control agreements, and instinctively hostile to new strategic-weapons systems, whether the B-1 or the MX. The only time Defense Department officials felt they could count on Levin's active support was when major interests of his Michigan constituents were involved. Levin, for example, had been a vigorous advocate of the M-1 tank, which was being built by General Dynamics in the Detroit suburb of Warren.

From his own base of power on the Armed Services Committee, Levin launched a counterattack. He persuaded the Air Force director of legislative liaison to write a letter flatly denying that General O'Loughlin had tied the fate of Wurtsmith to the Michigan senator's votes on the B-1. Not entirely satisfied with the tenor of the Air Force apology, Levin dictated the changes he wanted. He then convened a congressional hearing for the benefit of several hundred Michigan business and community leaders. A parade of Defense Department and Air Force officials, coached by Levin and his aides, reassured the home folks that Wurtsmith *was* being considered for a B-1 base and that neither Wurtsmith nor K.I. Sawyer would be closed.

In press conferences and committee hearings, Levin sent his own message back home: "I may have been against building the B-1s, but they are being built and Wurtsmith is the right place to base them."

The entire episode was a combination of campaign theatrics and serious power politics. In the back rooms of Washington and at the grass roots, the Air Force sought to bend members of Congress to its will, and the congressmen fought alongside their communities to save their prized military assets. But in public, the professionals in the Pentagon and Congress accommodated each other with whatever polite rhetoric was needed to pacify a constituency worried about how national-defense decisions would affect its own economy.

The only thing missing from that political process was any serious debate about what would be best for the national defense.

In the end, Wurtsmith did *not* get its B-1 squadron, although the furor following General O'Loughlin's speech mobilized the Michigan congressional delegation to demand other benefits. Levin steered a resolution through Congress making it virtually impossible for the Air Force to close down K.I. Sawyer, and the Air Force added $100 million in new facilities there and at Wurtsmith.

The outcome demonstrated how national-defense politics can

produce results that make little sense in terms of real defense needs. Michigan has no B-1 squadron, even though Wurtsmith actually filled the bill admirably: its far-north-central location would have been strategically ideal for basing nuclear bombers aimed at the Soviet Union. Yet Michigan did get to keep a fighter base at K.I. Sawyer—which, along with countless other military bases across the country, probably would have been closed but for congressional and grass-roots pressures.

The politics of the B-1 basing left the northern-Michigan businessmen with a lingering cynicism about how the system works. "There was a list," insisted Robert McIntosh, a car dealer in East Tawas. "We were on it, and they crossed us off. Carl Levin was the problem."

"Even though they say those bases are not political," said Ed Dodson, president of the Michigan Bank—Huron and leader of the "Save Wurtsmith" Chamber of Commerce effort, "they are political."

When the Air Force finally unveiled its bases "list," the cynicism of the Michigan businessmen seemed justified. The story of the base selection revealed how powerful political considerations were weighed against strategic priorities in selecting the B-1 bases.

Far to the south of Michigan, the first B-1 arrived in a well-staged production at Dyess Air Force Base in Texas on June 29, 1985. The bands were playing, the sun was shining, and as a galaxy of Washington political and military stars applauded in the reviewing stand, the dark needle-nosed bomber suddenly appeared out of the northern sky. It roared over the welcoming crowd of 45,000, turned sharply over the mesquite-covered hills around the base, and made a perfect landing. The pomp and ceremony at Dyess, outside Abilene, marked the delivery of that first bomber to its new home base. General John W. Vessey, Jr., chairman of the Joint Chiefs of Staff, read a letter from President Ronald Reagan praising the patriotism of the local citizenry, who lined the sides of the twelve-thousand-foot runway, cheering and drinking soft drinks from plastic cups emblazoned with a picture of the B-1.

One small, little-noticed incident marred the perfection of the day at Dyess. The plane that roared into Dyess was actually not the first production model of the bomber, as intended, but one of the research and demonstration planes. The first B-1 had sucked part of an air inlet into one of its jet engines on its flight from California to Texas, and had to turn back.

More than anything else, the ceremony at Dyess was an Air Force "appreciation day" for former Republican Senator John Tower, the recently retired chairman of the Senate Armed Services Committee. Senator Tower had always fought for the B-1. When President Carter canceled production of the B-1 in 1977, Tower helped keep the plane alive with continued development funds. In 1981, with the Reagan administration debating whether to bypass the B-1 in favor of the Stealth, the Air Force took no chances on keeping Tower's vital support: while the decision hung in the balance, an Air Force emissary told the committee chairman that Dyess, the base closest to his home town of Wichita Falls, would be the first B-1 base. He was also promised that another Texas base would get the first B-52 squadron outfitted with cruise missiles. (Neither basing decision was made public; nearly two years later the Air Force would still insist to Senator Levin and his Michigan constituents that the B-1 bases had not yet been selected.)

Many in the Air Force and Congress believed that Dyess was chosen as the first B-1 base to please Tower. Politically, that may have been justifiable. But a north-central Texas site for a B-1 base was considerably harder to justify on strategic grounds.

The Air Force's stated criteria for the B-1 bases were: "prelaunch survivability, wartime considerations, facility availability, access to training routes, weather, community support, encroachment, and environment." In finally announcing the four bases selected—Ellsworth, in South Dakota; Grand Forks, in North Dakota; McConnell, at Wichita, Kansas; and Dyess—the Air Force stressed that all were aligned along the center of the American land mass. That way, each would have maximum warning (though only a few minutes at that) to escape a sneak Soviet submarine-missile attack from the Atlantic or Pacific.

But Dyess was vulnerable on the most important criterion, "wartime considerations." Although all four bases are far from the oceans, Air Force officers noted privately that the Texas base would be vulnerable to short-range attack if Soviet submarines were to penetrate the Gulf of Mexico. The B-1's mission is to attack or threaten to attack the Soviet Union in a strategic crisis, and basing it in Texas would add several hours of flying time to the mission. Bombers taking off from Dyess would need an additional complex aerial refueling to carry out their mission, according to officers at Strategic Air Command headquarters. From a wartime strategic viewpoint, other SAC bases—including Wurtsmith in Michigan—made a lot more sense.

One point in Dyess's favor as a training base for B-1 crews was its good weather. And Dyess met the criterion of "community support." Business and community leaders in Abilene and elsewhere in north Texas did everything in their power to convince their congressmen and the Air Force of their solid credentials to host the bombers. But then, every other SAC base in the United States had good community support, too.

Politics also outweighed strategy in the selection of McConnell Air Force Base on the outskirts of Wichita, Kansas. Kansas Senator Robert Dole began lobbying for McConnell in 1981 when he chaired the Senate Finance Committee, which controlled President Reagan's top legislative priority—tax reform.

McConnell had served as home base for personnel staffing a wing of aging Titan missiles. One of the Kansas Titans developed a leak in 1979, and one stationed in Arkansas exploded in 1980. The Kansas citizenry wanted the Titans removed immediately— but they also wanted to keep their base with twelve hundred Air Force personnel, an economic resource worth about $100 million a year. The Wichita chamber of commerce pressed the Kansas congressional delegation to get one of the B-1 squadrons.

Despite Dole's entreaties, the Air Force equivocated. A number of Air Force officials bristled at the notion of "rewarding" Kansas, because the state's other senator, Republican Nancy Kassebaum, not only had opposed the B-1, but as chairman of the Senate's Military Reform Caucus was a constant thorn in the side of the Defense Department. The congressman from Wichita, Democrat Dan Glickman, also had opposed the B-1.

During the protracted tug-of-war over the B-1 bases, Dole played some slick politics of his own. He delighted in displaying his independence, taking swipes at the president on taxes and at the Defense Department on the B-1 and other issues. He prominently cosponsored legislation calling for a critical study of the B-1's astronomical costs. Appearing on the television program *Meet the Press*, he made page-one headlines across the country by suggesting that perhaps the B-1 should be canceled to help combat the huge budget deficit.

The Air Force finally got the message, particularly when it became almost certain that Dole would become Senate majority leader in 1985, after Senator Howard Baker retired. McConnell got its squadron of B-1s. Announcing the prize, Dole stressed that the decision meant "that the employment and economic impact" of losing the Titan missiles would be neutralized, and "better yet, could be improved" with $115 million in new military construction coming to the base.

From both the strategic and economic points of view, however, McConnell had several serious drawbacks, according to informed Air Force officers. The base shared its crowded runways with the Boeing Company plant—not the ideal setting for an instant launch of bombers in an emergency. The site, on the edge of a crowded city, created problems for base security, and did not satisfy the Air Force's own standards for "encroachment" or "environment" nearly as well as the more isolated SAC bases in rural Michigan, Montana, Wyoming, and the Dakotas. Finally, the Kansas base entailed extra costs of at least $40 million, since it had no facilities for storing nuclear weapons for bombers. The General Accounting Office cited the extra expense in recommending against McConnell as a B-1 base.

But McConnell got its B-1s.

Unseemly jockeying among the White House, the Air Force, and Congress on basing decisions has a long, inglorious history. When Dwight Eisenhower was president, he ordered the Air Force to reopen the Smokey Hill Air Force Base near Salina, Kansas, because he wanted to do something for his home state. Glasgow Air Force Base in Montana was opened and kept operating to please Senator Mike Mansfield, the Montana Democrat who served as Senate majority leader from 1961 through 1976. Seeking votes for a debt-limit extension in the 1960s, President Lyndon Johnson, through Secretary of the Air Force Harold Brown, pointedly warned several congressmen about the possible shutdown of bases in their districts.

As a senator from Texas in 1955, Johnson had helped Abilene businessmen win approval of Dyess for an Air Force base. Abilene had been hard struck when an Army base closed down after World War II. "People lost their livelihood almost overnight," recalled Abilene banker Fred Lee Hughes, who led the chamber of commerce effort to win the B-1 basing in 1981. "Business leaders decided not to let that happen again."

Arkansas got its Little Rock Air Force Base in 1955 because of the combined power of that state's two senators, Democrats John McClellan and J. William Fulbright. Thirty years later, the base apparently became a political pawn in a still-unsettled battle between the Air Force and Arkansas senators who had opposed the B-1.

After a Titan missile exploded, Arkansas citizens wanted to get rid of the aging missiles based at Little Rock. But removing the Titans would mean losing base personnel; and the base also could lose its wing of seventy-six C-130 troop carriers. If it didn't get the new C-17 carriers as a replacement, the base might be closed, devastating the local economy. Base personnel and families comprised a population of almost twenty-five thousand. The annual base payroll of $250 million (providing seventeen thousand accounts in local banks) was the mainstay of the central Arkansas economy.

The well-organized Little Rock Community Base Council implored Arkansas Senators David Pryor and Dale Bumpers to help the base get a squadron of C-17s. The council, led by Pat Wilson, president of the First Jacksonville Bank, was one of the most effective grass-roots base-support organizations in the country—it had raised the money to buy land for the base in the first place. Over the years, Wilson and his indefatigable band had befriended secretaries of the Air Force, congressional committee chairmen, and virtually every Air Force officer who had ever served at the base. Ever alert to shifting military currents, Wilson and his group began lobbying for the new C-17s when the plane was little more than a glint in the eyes of defense planners. Describing his group's long relationship with the Air Force, Pat Wilson said, "It's a question of mutual support."

In Senator David Pryor, the council found a ready ally. Both Pryor and Bumpers, however, had antagonized the Air Force not only by opposing the B-1 but as advocates of arms control who also opposed other defense programs. In addition, Pryor raised hackles in the Pentagon as he became an effective leader of the congressional movement to reform Defense Department procurement practices.

On May 15, 1984, Pryor met in his office with Brigadier General James P. McCarthy, the Air Force's congressional director of legislative liaison, and Colonel Kenneth Anderson, the legislative liaison officer responsible for the Senate. For General McCarthy, who had flown 152 missions as a fighter pilot in Vietnam and commanded a strategic bomber wing, the meeting was just another encounter in a day's work. "Legislative liaison" was his job —seeking support for the Air Force from senators, and dealing with senators who wanted something from the Air Force.

Senator Pryor began by carefully spelling out why Little Rock should get the C-17s: Not only was the base already the principal training facility for the airlift command, it enjoyed broad community support and was important to the local economy.

Finally he got to the point. "Well, general, how do our chances look on the C-17s?"

"You know, senator," McCarthy said, "there are a lot of members of Congress interested in getting those planes."

"General, do you mean that politics are involved in these base decisions?" Pryor seemed shocked by the very idea.

"Well, you know, senator, your positions in many quarters are considered antimilitary," replied McCarthy.

"General, why don't you give me some examples of what you are talking about?" said Pryor.

The general hesitated, then observed that Pryor had opposed construction of the B-1 bomber.

"We've been over that before," said Pryor. "You know that I've supported the Stealth bomber. What else?"

General McCarthy paused, then turned to Colonel Anderson,

who was sitting next to him in a rocking chair. "Colonel, give me the senator's vote sheet," he ordered.

Anderson's face reddened as he reached into the inside pocket of his blue blazer and handed the general a thin folded document.

General McCarthy began ticking off issues on which the senator had differed with Defense Department policy.

"Let me see that thing," said Pryor.

What the general reluctantly handed him was a two-page computer printout titled "Senator Pryor: Floor Statements and News Items." It contained seventeen separate items. It noted that he had opposed the B-1 bomber, had "led the fight against nerve gas production," had been "critical of defense contractors for hiring former Defense Department personnel," had criticized President Reagan for violating the War Powers Resolution, had voted against the MX missile, and had supported an amendment to increase competition in defense contracting. From a narrow and partisan Defense Department viewpoint, the only "prodefense" items on Pryor's report card were his support for the Stealth bomber and three speeches in favor of the C-17.

Pryor was astounded at what he read. "This sort of reminds me of an FBI dossier," he said.

When the meeting ended, the base issue was still not settled. What Pryor had gained was a deeper appreciation of how seriously the military plays defense politics.

General McCarthy had broken the rules of the game: Exert pressure subtly, but never let a member of Congress know he or she is being "graded" by the Pentagon. For a general to tell a senator he had failed the test of Pentagon loyalty was a breach of etiquette, contrary to the military's smooth lobbying technique.

But the Defense Department does keep careful track of its allies and opponents in Congress, and it examines their records as it bargains for support and reaches basing and production decisions. At times it has rated members of Congress on a point basis, much as labor unions or business groups rate the support of congressmen on issues they deem important.

The rating system, lobbying of Congress by the military, and trading support for bases—all have gone on for years. The military, just like other executive departments of the government, routinely violates Title 18 of the U.S. Code, which forbids officials of the executive branch from lobbying members of Congress. In the pristine purity of the law, military officers, just like officials of the Agriculture Department, should only supply information requested by Congress. In reality, though, presidents and members of their administrations, including those in uniform, routinely engage in a mutual game of arm-twisting with Congress, trading favors and votes.

Much less well known is the extent to which uniformed military officers are involved in politics. We expect officers to give their candid opinions to Congress on military issues. But we have also expected, perhaps naïvely, that when operating in the political arena, officers of the Air Force, Navy, Army, and Marine Corps would adhere to higher standards than politically appointed officials. The Constitution makes the military clearly subordinate to the civilian authority of presidents and Congress.

But in reality, high-ranking military officers in Washington are embroiled almost daily in high-stakes politics. They are pressured, for example, by White House officials and members of Congress to make procurement or basing decisions that will serve political interests. Because they advocate a strong national defense and want to advance the programs of their individual services, military officers have not remained passive observers while others attempt to sway defense programs.

On no question in recent years have members of Congress been monitored more closely by the Air Force or lobbied more fiercely than on the B-1 bomber. The Air Force battled presidents, secretaries of defense, and members of Congress for more than thirty years to build a new bomber. Every congressional vote was critical, and the Air Force—along with the defense contractors who would build the B-1—counted those votes closely, always calculating how to woo and win those not yet committed to their support.

The politics of national defense is played by just about everyone. As in a poker game, the players with the most chips can promise, bluff, cajole, and deceive. After the B-1 bases were announced, the Air Force claimed it had actually picked them out

long before the Wurtsmith incident. Why then, asked Senator
Levin, had the Air Force reassured him and his Michigan constituents that Wurtsmith was still in the running? "If we told everyone the decision was made, then everyone would want to know
what the decision was," replied Air Force Major General Martin
Russ at a Senate hearing. And if everyone knew what the decision
was, the game would be over. No more bluffs, no more favors. No
more concessions.

In this defense game, the Air Force obviously held the high
cards. It was dealer's choice, and the Air Force could expect the
other players to place their bets according to its decision. It could
make a militarily sound decision, or it could use the bases as
political bait. Maybe, just possibly, it could do both. But it was
not likely.

Dedicated Air Force officers would much rather locate B-1
bases where prudent national-defense strategy, not politics, dic-
tates. When they can speak anonymously, they rail against the
unhealthy pressures of defense politics. They say that nothing
undermines high standards of military leadership more than the
pressures to make basing and procurement decisions on political
grounds rather than on true military need. But they seldom speak
out, even in the private councils of the Air Force. To question a
decision can hurt, even ruin, one's career. It is easier to rationalize: There's not much difference in the military suitability of the
different base sites . . . One voice will not be heard . . . These political cases are isolated . . .

But they are not isolated. They are part and parcel of the politics of national defense. Communities grown used to military
largesse are hostages to the game—and active players. Defense
contractors pursuing lucrative contracts stand to win billions—or
lose them on the outcome of a congressional vote. Military officers feel trapped in a game they desperately want to control; senators and representatives feel trapped as well.

So do presidents of the United States. Every president since
Eisenhower has sought to put his stamp on defense policy, to
bring the game under control. As we shall see, the ones who went
along with the game were the ones most likely to succeed.

TWO

The Rise of the Military Economy

3

DWIGHT EISENHOWER
AND THE
POLITICS OF FEAR

The last four years of Dwight Eisenhower's presidency—1957 through 1960—pitted the former Supreme Allied Commander in Europe against many of the same military officers he had led to victory in World War II. At issue were profound disagreements about the size, shape, and purpose of the nation's defense and the nature of the Soviet threat it was designed to meet. American generals and admirals, backed by congressional leaders and scientists, demanded far more weapons and troops than Eisenhower thought necessary. For the U.S. Air Force, this dispute with the president marked the beginning of its effort to build a new strategic bomber.

Eisenhower had first come to office in 1953 with a dramatically different perspective. His defense strategy waged the Cold War by threatening "massive retaliation" with nuclear weapons whenever and wherever American vital interests were threatened by communist aggression. The new Republican president backed up his threat by building a massive bomber force that indeed could destroy the Soviet Union or China with little danger of nuclear retaliation against the United States. In warfare, the president warned, nuclear weapons would now be used "just exactly as you would use a bullet." Twice he threatened to unleash the American nuclear arsenal against communist China. "If you are scared to go to the brink [of nuclear war], you are lost," said Secretary of State John Foster Dulles, and "brinksmanship" became the administration's foreign policy. The New Look military strategy permitted Eisenhower to skimp on the Navy and the Army, and to achieve his goal of a limited and tight government budget, which he thought was vital to the nation's economic strength. He worried that an outsize military would turn free, capitalist America into a "garrison state."

By late 1956, however, Eisenhower had changed his mind about brinksmanship. The Soviets now had enough bombers and hydrogen bombs to devastate America. Efforts to maintain American nuclear superiority, he decided, would lead only to a futile and increasingly dangerous arms race, which would sap the nation's economic vitality. The best either side could achieve was "sufficiency"—enough secure strategic nuclear weaponry to convince each other there could be no victors in war. He warned there could be "no possibility of victory or defeat."

But the military neither shared his conclusion nor wanted to give up its "superiority."

Eisenhower's overriding goal became an arms-control agreement that might lessen the threat of nuclear war and lead to peace with the Soviet Union. Writing to Dulles, the president said: "To my mind this transcends all other objectives we can have. Security through arms is only a means (and sometimes a poor one) to an end."

On October 4, 1957, a single dramatic event heightened the conflict between Eisenhower and his critics over the adequacy of American national defense. On that day, the Soviet Union launched a spherical artificial satellite called Sputnik. The Soviets had taken a small but significant step toward the conquest of outer space.

Five days later President Eisenhower felt Sputnik's political sting. Merriman Smith, a gruff-spoken White House correspondent, bluntly challenged him at a press conference: "Mr. President, Russia has launched an earth satellite. They also claim to have had a successful firing of an intercontinental ballistic missile, none of which this country has done. I ask you, sir, what are we going to do about it?"

Dwight Eisenhower, former general of the armies, calmly and candidly tried to explain to the nation why America was militarily secure, why it had nothing to fear because the Soviets "had put one small ball in the air." But Eisenhower had grossly underestimated the psychological and political impact of the event, which overwhelmed any rational analysis of Soviet and American strength.

Sputnik jolted America's confidence in U.S. supremacy in space technology, science, and military might. After emerging from World War II as undisputably the most powerful, affluent nation in history, Americans assumed that no nation could challenge them in any field. Suddenly, experts claimed we trailed the Soviets in everything from missiles to the quality of grade-school math.

The trauma was heightened by Soviet bluster and threats. Soviet Premier Khrushchev claimed that American bombers were useless in the face of intercontinental ballistic missiles (ICBMs) and "might as well be thrown on the fire." Acting with new boldness, the Soviets stirred trouble in Berlin, the Middle East, and the emerging nations of Africa and Asia.

At the time of Khrushchev's boast, we know now, neither nation had a single nuclear-armed ICBM, and the U.S. had a far larger and more powerful force of nuclear bombers. Nevertheless, the secrecy surrounding actual and potential Soviet military capabilities provoked genuine fear and uncertainty. And these feelings developed a dynamic of their own.

Sputnik did not start the Soviet-American arms race, but it established a pattern in the politics of defense that has been repeated, in different settings and with different players, for three decades. Sputnik "became the crucial psychological landmark in the course of postwar arms development, affecting almost every aspect of defense operations," concluded Dr. Herbert York, science and military adviser to Presidents Eisenhower and Kennedy. "Of all the symbols in the mythology of terror which has propelled the arms race, Sputnik is the most dramatic."

The fact that the "backward" Russians had been able to put up the first satellite, and to test the first successful ICBM, prompted a wave of national hysteria. Arms proponents and politicians were quick to ride the wave. All may have been motivated by patriotic concern, but the Democrats jockeying for the presidential nomination in 1960 lost no time turning Sputnik to their political advantage. Less than two weeks after the launch, an aide told Senator Lyndon Johnson of Texas, the Senate majority leader, that Sputnik, "if properly handled, would blast the Republicans out of the water, unify the Democratic party, and elect you president." Quickly joining the fray, Senators Stuart Symington of Missouri, Henry (Scoop) Jackson of Washington, and John F. Kennedy of Massachusetts all sounded their own alarms, warning of weaknesses in America's defenses. The terms "bomber gap" and "missile gap" became political shorthand for the country's purported military weakness.

Eisenhower, supremely self-confident about military matters, rejected the view that Sputnik had revealed any weakness. He refused to panic. Nevertheless, he yielded ground to the combined pressures from leaders in the military, Congress, science, and industry who said the country needed to increase its military spending, particularly on strategic nuclear arms, including missiles and bombers.

The first concrete effect of Sputnik on American defense came as Eisenhower reluctantly approved an extra $2 billion in defense spending for 1958, raising the military budget to nearly $39 billion. Meeting on December 5, 1957, with his military aide, General Andrew Goodpaster, and Defense Secretary Neil McElroy, the president told them that "about two-thirds of the supplementary funds are more to stabilize public opinion than to meet any real need." (Later presidents followed suit, protecting their political flanks by making concessions on defense issues.) He signed the appropriations bill.

The extra funds made a critical difference to a number of new military programs, one of which held special importance for the generals who commanded the U.S. Air Force. They wanted a new strategic bomber. What they had in mind was not just another airplane, with modest improvements over the B-52s then rolling off production lines at the Boeing Company in Seattle. They wanted a new bomber that would fly much faster, farther, and higher than had ever been conceived.

Operating under the top-secret code WS-110, the Air Force had been working on the project with little success since 1954. The best design that aircraft manufacturers had come up with was an unwieldly, overweight monstrosity that Air Force General Curtis LeMay disgustedly said looked like "a three-plane formation." In 1956, the Air Force officially canceled the design project.

Still the Air Force persevered in the quest, and in the summer of 1957 both Boeing and North American Aviation of Los Angeles achieved stunning aerodynamic breakthroughs toward building a supersonic bomber. The most important was the aeronautical equivalent of a speedboat riding almost out of the water or of a surf rider getting just ahead of the crest of a wave and being propelled at a high speed. The new plane would ride atop its own sonic waves.

Taking advantage of the sonic-wave discovery, the Air Force acted quickly. Two weeks after Eisenhower approved the budget increase, the Air Force awarded a research-and-development contract to North American Aviation, one of the nation's most successful manufacturers of war planes. A month later, the contract was extended to include production of 12 test models and delivery of a wing of 50 bombers to the Strategic Air Command by August 1964. They would represent the first installment on a force of 250 planes, estimated to cost $6 billion.

The Air Force was in a big hurry. Under normal procurement procedures, the military carefully required development of prototype test planes before making a major commitment to build a new fleet. But in its urgency to catch the Sputnik funding wave at its height, the Air Force authorized North American to research, develop, and produce the bomber even before its details were fully worked out.

The specifications called for a bomber that could travel 2,000 miles per hour (Mach 3, or three times the speed of sound) at an altitude of 70,000 feet for distances of 7,000 nautical miles while carrying a devastating load of nuclear weapons. It would be called the B-70 Valkyrie, named after the war maidens of Norse mythology.

The Valkyrie certainly would not look like any other bomber. With its wide delta-shaped wings in the rear, tiny front fins, and long, pointed, drooping nose, the B-70 technically was described as a "canard-shaped" airplane. And in a way, it did resemble the ducks and geese that migrate over a north-south flight path that the B-70 might someday follow into battle.

Air Force officers began referring to the still-secret new airplane as their "manned missile." General Thomas S. Power, commander of the Strategic Air Command, called it "the Savior." These nicknames had a special significance. Both the Soviet Union and the United States were developing their first ICBMs. Missiles were the future, but the bomber represented the heart of the Air Force's guiding military doctrine, the overriding importance of strategic air power. General Power and his fellow officers hoped that the B-70 would "save" bombers from being made obsolete by the missile.

The generals had good reason to push ahead rapidly with the plane while they could: time was running out. Scientists working on ICBMs began scoring impressive breakthroughs, and bombers were looking less essential. Trying to revolutionize the bomber in one mighty leap, North American ran into predictable technological snags. And just as important, President Eisenhower decided to dig in his heels against what he considered excesses in American nuclear weaponry.

In 1958, Eisenhower sought congressional authorization to reorganize the Pentagon, in an effort to keep the individual services from independently pursuing their own parochial needs. He created a Scientific Advisory Committee, seeking a broader range of views than he received from the nuclear scientists who always opposed arms-control proposals and advocated more nuclear weapons.

The military resisted reorganization and fought back, requesting a 25 percent increase in the defense budget—another $10 billion. An astounded Eisenhower told his newly appointed science adviser, Dr. James Killian, that "he found it hard to retain confidence in the heads of the services when they produce such proposals as these."

He repeatedly rejected a proposal to build a nuclear-powered aircraft, urged on him by the Defense Department on grounds that "it was scientifically possible to achieve." The next proposal, he scoffed, would be "to take the liner *Queen Elizabeth* and put wings a mile wide on it and install enough power to make it fly."

Indeed, even as they struggled with the problems of developing the supersonic B-70, Air Force planners were spending other Sputnik-inspired funds to design even more visionary airplanes. Beyond the nuclear-powered bomber was a Mach 5 bomber that would fly at 100,000 feet. That would be followed by the bizarrely named Dyna-soar, a bomber to be shot into a path in space at almost satellite speed, then to glide to earth on aerodynamic wings. And beyond Dyna-soar was Lace, an even more futuristic hypersonic bomber. Excited by the first breakthroughs in conquering space, the nation's military, scientific, and industrial leaders felt there were few limits to what mankind could achieve in weaponry, given the time and resources.

Meanwhile, Congress and the Air Force pushed for more ICBMs and for more B-52 bombers. Eisenhower reluctantly agreed to a hundred more planes, but observed, "If six hundred won't do the job, certainly seven hundred won't." Pressed still again for more B-52s, Eisenhower retorted: "I don't know how many times you can kill a man, but about three should be enough."

In the fall of 1959, the Pentagon for the third consecutive year requested $10 billion in new arms. Eisenhower examined U.S. retaliatory capacity of the bombers, submarines, and ICBMs in production and concluded that it was more than adequate. In denying the funds, he questioned again, "How many times do we have to destroy the Soviet Union?"

Eisenhower felt that the arms race was spinning out of control. When the chairman of the Atomic Energy Commission requested a new nuclear reactor to make more atomic bombs, Eisenhower complained that the list of Soviet targets had grown from 70 to 1,500. He felt that the U.S. stockpile of nuclear bombs had increased beyond all rational need—growing from 1,500 bombs when he took office to at least 5,000 by 1959.

Nearing the end of his second term, Eisenhower made his boldest move for peace, inviting Nikita Khrushchev to visit the U.S. in the fall of 1959, as prelude to a Paris summit meeting in May 1960, after which Eisenhower would visit the Soviet Union. When criticized for offering to meet with a communist leader, Eisenhower shot back, "We are talking about the human race and what's going to happen to it."

. . .

Two years after the Sputnik panic pushed him to approve defense expenditures in which he did not believe, Eisenhower set out to put a lid on new weapons. The B-70 Valkyrie was a major nuclear-weapons system whose future was at stake.

In mid-November of 1959, at his favorite vacation haunt, the Augusta National Golf Club in Georgia, Eisenhower met for three days with his defense advisers to settle the fate of the B-70 and other weapons. In the club's stone-and-wood clubhouse, with a fire roaring in the fireplace, Eisenhower debated the bomber issue with Secretary of Defense Neil McElroy; General Nathan F. Twining, chairman of the Joint Chiefs of Staff; Dr. George Kistiakowsky, who had replaced Dr. Killian as science adviser; and the service chiefs, including the B-70's strongest proponent, General Thomas D. White, the Air Force chief of staff.

Contending that the B-70 development could serve many needs besides its weapons role, McElroy cited reconnaissance, military transport, and civilian transport. Predictably, budget-minded Eisenhower retorted that he was "allergic" to the idea of spending military funds to develop a civilian aircraft.

Taking another tack, General Twining, a former Air Force chief of staff, argued that the Air Force needed the B-70 to penetrate the Soviet Union to search out and destroy mobile ICBMS on railroad tracks. "If they [the Air Force] think this, they are crazy," replied Eisenhower. "We are not going to be searching out mobile bases for ICBMs; we are going to be hitting the big industrial and control centers."

Finally, General White presented the Air Force's case for the B-70: The nation could not rely wholly on missiles, none of which had ever been fired in combat. Missiles could not be recalled, as airplanes could. Bombers could lift off and remain airborne while awaiting orders, thus giving the president a range of options in a crisis. Bombers would complicate the enemy's problem, forcing it to defend against several different kinds of attack. Finally, bombers as a demonstration of military might had a powerful psychological effect on friend and foe alike. The Air Force would repeat White's arguments, with embellishments but few variations, for decades to come.

Eisenhower respected General White, both for his leadership in World War II and for his wide-ranging intellect. But the president also knew that White was pressing him as the official representative of a large bureaucratic institution with its own interests at stake. And the president did not accept White's military rationale for the B-70. He told the Air Force chief of staff that the bomber role was served adequately by the B-52, and by the time the B-70 was ready its role would be filled by missiles. He agreed with Dr. Kistiakowsky that the B-70 would be very vulnerable to radar detection and attack by Soviet surface-to-air missiles (SAMs). Delivering the cruelest cut to an Air Force man, Eisenhower said, "We are talking about bows and arrows at the time of gunpowder when we speak of bombers in the missile age."

Like an attorney making his final emotional plea for a client facing the gallows, White asked the President for the B-70, based not on its military value but on its importance to the institution to which he had devoted his life. "There is a question," he implored, "of what is to be the future of the Air Force and of flying. This shift [to missiles] has a great impingement on morale. There is no follow-on aircraft to the fighter and no new opportunity for Air Force personnel."

At the moment that General White lamented the decline of the Air Force, the service possessed 1,895 bombers, including 243 brand-new B-52s with several hundred more scheduled to be built. The Air Force had control of all three land-based ICBM systems. It was hardly about to go out of business. Tommy White's protests represented the Air Force's fear that strategic air power, the core of Air Force purpose, would vanish in the coming missile age. To keep the bomber alive and competitive against the missile, the Air Force thought it needed a much faster, more capable plane than the B-52.

A few days after the Augusta meetings, the president virtually killed the B-70 bomber. He reduced it to an experimental program, consisting of a single airplane without any weapons systems.

Celebrating New Year's Eve with Christian Herter, his new secretary of state, Eisenhower had his mind on peace. Khrushchev's fall visit had been a success, and an arms-control agreement looked possible. "If we cut back our armaments to where only a retaliatory force is left," said the president, "war becomes completely futile."

At the very moment Eisenhower dreamed of peace, however,

his Air Force generals were preparing for a political battle against their commander-in-chief. On January 11, 1960, General White served notice that he would fight the president on the B-70. Appearing at the National Press Club, he announced that the Air Force would take its case to Congress.

Eisenhower was furious. After White asked Congress for the B-70, the president telephoned his brand-new secretary of defense, Thomas S. Gates, Jr. "In earlier times, there was no question that once a decision was made, the officer carried it out without question," he said. "Discipline has been lost in the high-ranking officers of the armed services." The president asked Gates how long White still had to serve as chief of staff. He seriously pondered firing him.

Still angry, Eisenhower told Republican leaders, "All those fellows in the Pentagon think they have some responsibility I can't see. . . . I hate to use the word, but this business is damn near treason."

4

CURTIS LeMAY
AND
STRATEGIC AIR POWER

A group of civilian defense advisers to President Eisenhower gathered in Colorado Springs on September 16, 1957, at the headquarters of the North American Defense Command. They came to find out how quickly the Strategic Air Command (SAC) might react to a surprise Soviet bomber attack.

The demonstration did not go well. The defense advisers expressed alarm about the "alert" readiness of the bomber force—which at that time constituted the entire U.S. nuclear deterrent.

But General Curtis E. LeMay, the SAC commander, seemed quite unconcerned. Top-secret American spy planes would alert him to any Soviet preparations for an attack, he explained. "If I see that the Russians are amassing their planes for an attack," he said, "I'm going to knock the shit out of them before they take off the ground."

Shocked as they were by the revelation about secret spy planes, the civilians were even more stunned by LeMay's readiness to order a preemptive attack.

"But General LeMay, that's not national policy," protested Robert Sprague, an electronics manufacturer from Massachusetts.

"I don't care," LeMay replied. "It's my policy. That's what I'm going to do."

The declared U.S. policy at that time was that the nation would never strike first. In truth, the massive preemptive strike described by LeMay was exactly what the top-secret national war plan called for. Whether LeMay would have ordered a nuclear attack in violation of a presidential order is doubtful. LeMay fully appreciated the need for military officers to follow orders and respect the constitutional principle of civil supremacy over the military. He was angered by repeated accusations that he disobeyed orders and flouted civilian authority. Yet his career was marked by controversies with presidents, by advocacy of his own views before Congress, and by a bold independence in the way he led his Air Force commands. LeMay believed that professional military officers, not civilians, had the responsibility to determine how to wage and win wars. As SAC commander, he held awesome responsibility, and wielded enormous authority.

LeMay's apparent contradictions reflected the frustrations of a bomber warrior in the nuclear age—a time of fearsome new weapons and doubts about war as a viable means to an end.

In the late 1950s, it was Curtis LeMay, promoted to Air Force vice chief of staff under General Thomas White, who led the Air Force's fight for the new B-70 bomber, even over the objections of President Eisenhower. It was LeMay who determined that missiles would not displace bombers, and thus reduce the Air Force to being "the silent silo-sitters of the sixties."

LeMay was one of the small group of generals who emerged from World War II as genuine fighting heroes. Unlike such legendary figures as Eisenhower and General George Marshall, whose fame came from their managerial ability and leadership finesse, LeMay earned his stars in battle. His experience as a battle-tested bomber pilot shaped his vision of warfare. His entire career was inseparable from the concept of strategic air power. LeMay was both its embodiment and its spokesman.

The Air Force demands for a new bomber had their origins in the earliest struggles over the role of the airplane in war. During and after World War I, the theory of strategic air power was propounded by Sir Hugh Trenchard, a British aviation leader; Italian Colonel Giulio Douhet; and Brigadier General William (Billy)

Mitchell, commander of air forces in the American Expeditionary Force of World War I. They theorized that the key to victory in war lay in quick destruction of the enemy's "vital center," its war-making industry and large cities. Essential to this strategy were preemptive strikes to destroy the enemy's air forces while they were still on the ground. The compelling assumption was that wars could be won quickly by destroying an enemy's military potential, while avoiding the prolonged and costly infantry campaigns that had characterized warfare for centuries. Strategic air power would revolutionize warfare.

The strategic-bombing concept, however, was fiercely resisted after World War I by the Army and Navy, and also by Army Air Corps fighter pilots, who argued that fighter planes could defeat bombers and dominate the battlefield. Army aviators found themselves at the bottom of the military pecking order, their numbers plunging in one year from twenty thousand officers to two hundred. Mitchell returned home to lead a crusade for strategic air power. His aggressive public attacks on the Navy and War Department led to a sensational courtmartial and his dismissal from the Army in 1925.

Nevertheless, the dedicated officers of the Army Air Corps Tactical School painstakingly persevered to develop the tools and techniques needed for strategic bombing: the navigation system, the Norden bomb sight for accurate high-altitude bombing, and in 1937, the B-17 bomber, with its range of two thousand miles. To dramatize their skill, in 1938 a group of B-17s flew six hundred miles out into the Atlantic, located the Italian luxury liner *Rex*, and "bombed" it with photographs. That mission's navigator was a lieutenant from Columbus, Ohio, named Curtis LeMay. The son of an itinerant laborer, he had worked his way through Ohio State University and joined the Army Air Corps in 1928.

World War II gave the strategic-bomber men a chance to prove their theory. That Douhet and Mitchell had overstated their case was soon apparent. The Army Air Corps entered the war with a detailed plan for achieving victory in Europe in six months by knocking out 154 targets with 6,834 airplanes. It was not so simple. Germany's war-making capacity was not eliminated until near the end. Victory came on the ground—a mile, sometimes a foot, at a time. Some argued that aerial bombardment actually increased the will of both Britons and Germans to resist their attackers.

Beyond any question, however, strategic air power played an important role. Total Allied air supremacy provided cover for the critical Normandy D-day invasion in 1944, and air supremacy tied down the German forces, which were already overextended on two fronts. And the German war machine was gradually ground down by bomber attacks.

Brigadier General Curtis LeMay of the Eighth Air Force was the toughest, most demanding, and most resourceful commander leading those attacks. Broad-chested and stocky, with a cigar stuck in the side of his mouth, LeMay was a rough-and-ready man of stern visage and few words. "You can do better," was LeMay's brief message of both reprimand and encouragement. LeMay's knowledge of the B-17 was awesome. He could fly and navigate it, bomb with it and man the guns, take the plane completely apart and repair it. He ceaselessly trained his crews, giving them the skills, confidence, and discipline to fly through murderous anti-aircraft fire and swarms of German fighters. Despite enormous losses, many American airmen got through to destroy or damage their targets and made it home. After he repeatedly flew the lead bomber deep into the hostile skies of Nazi Germany, his airmen with grudging respect called him Iron Ass.

LeMay proved his tactical genius as well. Turning conventional wisdom on its head, he grouped his bombers in tight formations for mutual protection and attacked on a steady, straight course without taking evasive action. As a result, LeMay's bombers reached their targets faster, achieved more accurate bombing, and lost fewer planes and men.

After victory was gained in Europe, LeMay again displayed daring as commander of the 20th Air Force, which flew B-29 raids against Japan. Given high winds and bad weather, the planes had trouble both finding their targets and hitting them with precision bombing. Without informing his superiors, LeMay tried a bold and risky new tactic. Stripping his bombers of their armament and gunners, he loaded them with incendiary bombs and achieved surprise, attacking by night at perilously low altitudes of 5,000 feet. The explosions and the waves of heat from the fires below tossed the B-29s thousands of feet into the air. In the first raid on

Tokyo, 83,000 Japanese died—about as many as died in the atomic blast at Hiroshima—and 16 square miles of downtown Tokyo were leveled. Hundreds of small factories and shops were destroyed and a million people were left homeless. The Air Corps lost fourteen B-29s. Before they ran out of bombs, LeMay's B-29s had destroyed 106 square miles in six major cities.

The much-debated Strategic Bombing Surveys of World War II were equivocal about the effectiveness of Allied bombing. Critics asserted that bomber raids were notoriously inaccurate, cost an unacceptable number of men and planes, and inflicted barbarous punishment on the civilian populations of such cities as London, Coventry, Dresden, Hamburg, Tokyo, and Hiroshima.

But LeMay drew a very different lesson. He believed that the fire-bombings of Japan shortened the war and would have ended it without a costly invasion, even if the atomic bomb had not been used. The fire-bombing had destroyed thousands of shops vital to the Japanese war effort. LeMay thought the nuclear bomb only confirmed the lesson: "Once you make a decision to use military force to solve your problem, then you ought to use it, and use an overwhelming military force. Deliberately use too much so you don't make an error on the other side and not quite have enough. And you roll over everything to start with and you close it down. You save resources, you save lives—not only your own but the enemy's too—and the recovery is quicker."

Because only the Air Force could deliver strategic air-power, it finally won its independence from the Army in 1946. But because the nation had hastily dismantled its military might after the war, LeMay faced a new challenge: rebuilding the strategic Air Force from the ground up, giving it the ability to attack the Soviet Union with nuclear weapons.

When he took command of SAC in 1948, it was short of trained pilots, planes, fuel, and spare parts. LeMay rapidly reformed SAC to give the United States some credible strategic striking power. His goal was to bring the entire command up to a level of wartime readiness. He trained his squadrons endlessly, showing up for surprise inspections. He instituted on-the-spot promotions to reward air crews for meeting his high readiness standards. He improved base security, fought for higher salaries and better housing for his men. Teamwork, esprit de corps, readiness to fight and win were his goals. In a remarkable achievement, LeMay quickly built SAC into what was generally considered the most powerful, best-trained, most alert fighting outfit in the world.

Skillfully implementing President Eisenhower's New Look defense strategy, LeMay had readied SAC to deter Soviet aggression, and to defeat an enemy if deterrence failed. Until 1956, SAC could destroy any nation with impunity. Only after the Soviets developed the capability to attack the United States did LeMay and Eisenhower part company: The two warriors disagreed about the importance of strategic bombers in the missile age. And they were on opposite sides about the nature of warfare when two superpowers were both armed to face—and produce—Armageddon.

In 1959, Eisenhower established the nation's highest defense priorities: development of the ICBM and launching the Vanguard satellite to compete in the space race. LeMay's quite different priorities were acquisition of more B-52 bombers, development of the B-70, and development of the nuclear-powered bomber. ICBMs ranked at the bottom of LeMay's list.

Aside from the Air Force's own self-interest, LeMay made compelling arguments for the bomber: Missiles were still in development and untested in war. At a time of revolutionary changes in weaponry, LeMay was looking ahead seven to ten years, when Soviet defense capabilities would be far greater. LeMay saw the B-70, more than three times faster than the B-52, as a first-strike weapon, capable of reaching targets anywhere in the world in a few hours. Bombers provided flexibility to meet different situations, he insisted. Furthermore, LeMay believed it imperative to maintain human command at the scene of battle—"human crews who could exercise judgment"—and not relinquish control to a total faith in pushbuttons and computers. To keep "man in the loop," one needed a mixed nuclear force, including strategic bombers. They could stand on air alert, or penetrate to the Soviet heartland, where pilots could decide what or where to attack, or could be recalled. LeMay, as one who had made critical decisions in the heat of battle, could speak with authority.

The general made an appealing argument for "human control" in a frightening, dehumanized era of pushbutton nuclear war. A more difficult question—one that divided LeMay and civilian leaders—was, *Who* would exercise that control, and under what circumstances? The president, or the generals?

The question could well be asked. It was not always clear the president was in control. Testifying before Congress from 1957 onward, LeMay often disagreed with the president's budget, calling for the B-70 and more B-52s. Although Eisenhower and his successors were infuriated by that independent testimony, LeMay said that it was his duty to express his candid military judgments to Congress. Congress was a coequal branch of government with the constitutional duty "to raise and support armies," he would stress. Caught in disputes between Congress and the executive branch, LeMay though he was unfairly "accused of disrespect for civilian control."

What LeMay did not add was how he and other officers constantly played the Congress off against the president to further their own favorite military programs. LeMay worked assiduously at building alliances with key members of the congressional Armed Services Committees. He would bring an entire committee out to SAC to see the planes perform—or fly to the Texas ranch of Senate Majority Leader Lyndon Johnson for the weekend to argue for a pay raise for his airmen. In these power struggles, LeMay won a new nickname—the Diplomat, a satirical reference to his tactless bluntness.

After 1957, the most fundamental disagreement between LeMay and Eisenhower concerned the adequacy of American nuclear forces and their use in war. Once the Soviet Union achieved the capability to destroy American civilization, Eisenhower decided that nuclear war was unwinnable. "What you want is *enough*," said Eisenhower. "A deterrent has no added power once it has become completely adequate." Seeking "nuclear superiority" meant only a futile arms race.

LeMay's contrary views, which were legitimate military opinions about nuclear war-fighting, have remained at the heart of the defense debate for three decades. "Military men think deterrence is possible only in an atmosphere of strategic superiority," LeMay declared in his book *America Is in Danger.* "And superiority advocates assert that a failure of deterrence need not be fatal under conditions of nuclear weapons preponderance."

Furthermore, LeMay believed, "Our general war policy should be designed to prevail and defeat the enemy under a variety of circumstances, and not rule out a first strike." For LeMay the military professional, it was almost a contradiction in terms for his orders to preclude trying to develop the strategy and means to prevail. For the military man of action, strategic deterrence seemed an exceedingly passive concept.

Dismissing arguments about the futility of the nuclear-arms race, LeMay believed "it is the same kind of arms race mankind has been running since the beginning of time." Either the U.S. or the Soviets could win it. If the Soviets held nuclear superiority, he told Congress in 1958, "they may feel they should attack." Watching the Soviets seek superiority, believing they detested us as much as he detested communism, LeMay felt they would attack, given the chance.

LeMay also opposed the efforts of Eisenhower and other presidents to achieve arms control. Testifying against a limited test-ban treaty, he said, "I would never be happy with a situation where we had parity with our enemies." He thought strategic-arms modernization and arms control were irreconcilable objectives. Quoting one of his generals, LeMay asked, "How can we dress and undress at the same time?"

As commander of SAC from 1948 to 1957, LeMay held incredible power not only over the execution of the nation's war plan, but also in deciding which forces would comprise that plan. Known after 1960 as the SIOP (single integrated operating plan), the war plan designated which Soviet targets would be hit by which services with which weapons. LeMay jealously guarded the war plan as SAC's private preserve. With that control, SAC dominated the Air Force, and the Air Force dominated the other armed services.

In 1951, SAC Commander LeMay opposed efforts from Air Force headquarters in Washington to change the war plan to include Soviet targets that were not on his own list. Saying "my hands were being tied," making it impossible to exercise tactical control, LeMay fought off the proposed change. During the Korean

War, he resisted efforts to involve SAC. As he explained in his diary, "SAC was the USA Sunday punch and every effort must be made to make sure that it stayed intact and able to strike, and not be pissed away in the Korean war." In 1955, LeMay refused to share the SAC war plan with the commanders of the Army, Navy, Marine Corps, and Air Force. Although he still withheld important details, LeMay finally divulged the plan only after General Twining, chairman of the Joint Chiefs of Staff, directly and unequivocally ordered it.

At the heart of this tug-of-war was a fierce interservice power struggle. Eisenhower's policy of "massive retaliation" meant that the role each of the armed services played in the grand strategy of the nuclear war plan largely determined that service's importance, its power, and its share of the national defense budget. Because SAC bombers dominated the deterrent until the late 1950s, the Air Force commanded almost 50 percent of the total military budget. From the end of World War II onward, the Army, Navy, and Marine Corps fought the growing power of this brash newcomer.

The services battled fiercely for nuclear capability, often neglecting their conventional war role. The 1948 decision by President Harry S. Truman to build a new B-36 Air Force bomber, rather than the supercarriers sought by the Navy, led to an admirals' revolt in which the Navy decried strategic bombing as "barbaric." But when the Navy finally began to develop carrier-based nuclear weapons, its admirals competed ferociously for a role in the war plan. One gambit was to add new targets. The Navy dreamed up dozens of targets, some little more than cornfields in southern Europe, which its F-4 fighter-bombers could barely reach from their carriers in the Mediterranean.

Rivalry was often overt and more often petty.

The Navy's liaison admiral assigned to the SAC command post also acted as an undercover agent to inform the Navy high command about the latest Air Force ploy to enlarge its own role. The bitter rivalry was played out as LeMay met in his SAC command post with a Navy admiral to assign nuclear targets. The admiral representing the Pacific fleet repeatedly refused to agree to anything. An exasperated LeMay asked if the admiral's orders were to agree to nothing. "Yes," the admiral replied. "Those are my orders."

When two missile-firing tests by the submarine USS *Patrick Henry* failed in 1958, there was celebrating at SAC headquarters. In the same competitive spirit, an Army general expressed glee to an astonished President Eisenhower when a Navy Vanguard satellite launch mission failed. The Army had its own missile for the same job.

The Air Force and Navy competed fiercely over whether the B-70 or the Polaris submarine would get priority. Admiral Arleigh Burke, chief of naval operations, argued that building more bombers and land-based ICBMs was "the prescription for an arms race." Instead, he contended that nuclear war could best be "deterred" by an invulnerable fleet of Polaris submarines. Strategic forces should be adequate for deterrence alone, said Burke, not for the Air Force's unceasing search for nuclear victory. When Polaris and land-based ICBMs became an inescapable reality, LeMay argued that their primary mission should be to blast open a path for his B-70 bombers.

Each service genuinely believed in its own unique capabilities and special weapons; they did not promote different nuclear strategies solely to advance their own narrow interests. In fact, the competition led almost willy-nilly to a multiple strategy with safety features built in. What emerged became known as the strategic nuclear "triad" of bombers, Polaris missiles, and land-based ICBMs. If one part of the triad failed, the theory went, the other two would still offer a formidable deterrent to a potential attacker. Out of their rivalry, it could be argued, the different military services provided "checks and balances" on each other's power.

Nevertheless, President Eisenhower felt the interservice rivalry was propelling the arms race even further out of control. Concerned about the multiplying Soviet target list, the president in 1960 sent Dr. Kistiakowsky to SAC headquarters on a fact-finding mission. Even though Kistiakowsky carried written authorization from the president, SAC Commander Thomas Power (who succeeded LeMay when the latter became vice chief of staff in 1957) treated Kistiakowsky and his aides as if they were security risks. Kistiakowsky reported to the president that there was little coordination in the war plan. Both the Air Force and Navy, for example, had targeted the same militarily insignificant provincial Soviet city with four times as much nuclear power as needed to obliterate it.

And in the early days of 1960, while the president sought ways to hold down the target list and eliminate unneeded new weapons, General LeMay and the B-70 industrial team headed for Capitol Hill to fight for the new bomber.

5

DUTCH KINDELBERGER
AND THE
NEW DEFENSE POLITICS

When Dwight Eisenhower canceled production of the B-70 Valkyrie, he shattered North American Aviation's dream of a $6 billion contract to build a 250-plane bomber fleet. With its aircraft division in jeopardy, North American's president J. Leland Atwood quickly headed for the White House. Meeting with presidential science adviser Kistiakowsky on January 7, 1960, Atwood said that North American had made "tremendous breakthroughs" in its B-70 design. "It would be tragic for the country" not to build the bomber, he insisted.

Unconvinced, Kistiakowsky again recommended that the B-70 should not be built, and Eisenhower concurred. In his diary, Kistiakowsky noted that "Mr. Atwood seemed a sad-looking gentleman, notwithstanding a good rate of compensation."

Atwood's reserve was deceptive. As one of America's preeminent aeronautical engineers, he had led his company to conceive and produce some of the most successful airplanes of World War II. Among students of flight, Lee Atwood's planes were considered brilliant achievements. Nor was Atwood entirely naïve about how Washington worked. Dr. Kistiakowsky had measured only the scientific and economic value of bombers versus missiles. Others in Washington might find the B-70 important for different reasons.

No one received Atwood and his colleagues more warmly than Senator Robert Kerr, the flamboyant Oklahoma Democrat whose power rivaled even that of Senate Majority Leader Lyndon Johnson. Kerr's influence flowed from his position as chairman of the Senate Finance Committee. His wide-ranging interests included the defense of the nation, the well-being of Oklahoma, and his own prosperity—not necessarily in that order, some would say. The senator's Tulsa-based Kerr-McGee Company had made millions in oil and uranium, as had his ventures into banking. As he surveyed the landscape of financial opportunity, Senator Kerr was drawn to the burgeoning new field of aerospace.

Bob Kerr was shrewd enough to foresee that the arms and space races with the Soviet Union would feed the development of a vast new multibillion-dollar growth industry in which government and private corporations would necessarily be partners. Previously, the United States had armed itself only when wars broke out, and disarmed as soon as they were over, but the fast-changing technology of the atomic and space era would lead to nothing less than a permanent defense industry. Never reluctant to capitalize on his inside knowledge, the senator made sure he was appointed to the new Senate Aeronautical and Space Sciences Committee. (When Majority Leader Lyndon Johnson became vice-president in 1961, Kerr succeeded him as the space committee's chairman.)

Kerr's multifarious interests were no secret to the group of executives, engineers, and lobbyists from North American Aviation who briefed the senator on their company's capabilities. They stressed its unique position to meet the challenges of the dawning space age.

Kerr listened without comment, then told the North American team, "Gentlemen, everything you say makes pretty good sense. The space and defense challenges to this country are enormous. You've got a good company, and I'm sure you can help with the job. But there's one thing missing."

"What's that, senator?" asked a North American engineer.

Kerr paused for dramatic effect, then replied with a wide smile, "You haven't told me what's in this for Oklahoma!"

• • •

That conversation in Bob Kerr's Senate office symbolized the emergence of a new high-stakes politics of national defense. With contracts involving billions of dollars, the fate of entire companies, the economic welfare of communities, and the careers of ambitious politicians all hinged on winning key defense projects. Demonstrating the new defense politics in action, Kerr helped gain congressional funds to keep the B-70 bomber alive. Beyond that, he built a relationship with North American Aviation that benefited the company on other projects while it advanced Kerr's personal and political interests as well.

Whether for public works or military contracts, dividing the spoils is an age-old custom, and it has flourished in the United States since the Revolutionary War. What was different in the aerospace age was not the existence of the political pork barrel itself, but its new size and permanence. Now that the stakes in profits and jobs were far higher than those of any government program in history, dividing the spoils ensured that the game of politics would be played on a grand scale. Parochial political interests could determine the direction of nuclear strategy and the fate of giant companies.

North American Aviation quickly learned to play. It opened two plants in Oklahoma—one in Kerr's home town of Tulsa, the other in McAlester, home of Democratic Representative Carl Albert, the House majority leader who soon would become Speaker of the House of Representatives. North American's first reward was the contract to build the Apollo space capsule. Using his power as chairman of the Senate space committee, Kerr ordered the director of the space agency—James Webb, a former Oklahoma business associate he had picked to head the space program—to declare North American the contract winner over its main rival, the Glenn Martin Company.

Kerr's constituents benefited—North American's new Oklahoma plants provided thousands of jobs and helped to establish a new industrial base for the state. Kerr and his friends received their rewards, too. Demonstrating further regard for the senator, North American opened a company account in his Tulsa bank. And at Kerr's insistence, North American even awarded vending-machine contracts in its plants to a company created by two Washington influence peddlers, Fred Black and Bobby Gene Baker. Black was a high-flying Washington lobbyist whom North American hired to help win government contracts, including the B-70 and Apollo. Baker, whose title was Secretary to the Democratic Senate Majority, was an ambitious errand-runner for both Lyndon Johnson and Bob Kerr. Kerr thought these cronies might as well make a little money too.

For North American's top executives, especially Lee Atwood, the relationship with Kerr was an eye-opener. Atwood's success was based on his experience as a brilliant design engineer and production man, but now he realized that this was not enough. North American would have to build stronger bonds with Washington politicians. He began hiring lobbyists like Black, looking for men who could trade on the knowledge and contacts they brought from previous careers in politics or the military.

The exchange of favors between Kerr and North American vividly illustrates how the space and nuclear defense programs began to be carved up to suit the interests of the most powerful members of Congress—particularly the southern Democrats who, because of the seniority system, controlled most of the Senate committees. The space program was carefully scattered over the "southern crescent." For Senator and soon-to-be Vice-President Lyndon Johnson there was the space center in Houston; for Florida Senators Spessard Holland and George Smathers, the launch site at Cape Canaveral; and for the venerable senators from Alabama, Louisiana, Georgia, and Mississippi, a cornucopia of space contracts to benefit companies in their states. Still firmly in command of Congress in the 1950s and 1960s, the southern oligarchs shaped the military-industrial landscape to a new geography. North American plants popped up in dozens of obscure places such as Neosho, Missouri, the home town of Republican Representative Dewey Short, briefly chairman of the House Armed Services Committee. After Mendel Rivers became chairman, Lockheed opened a plant in his home town, Charleston, South Carolina.

In 1960, congressional power over space and military contracts was still tightly exercised by the key committee chairmen. The fate of an Air Force weapon, the choice of a contractor, or the location of a base would often be settled over lunch by Richard

Russell, the Georgia Democrat who chaired the Senate Armed Services Committee, and Air Force General Joe Kelly, dean of congressional liaison officers, whose skill at trading favors with congressional barons became legendary.

Congress by no means monopolized the arms and space programs, however. The power of a determined president and his secretary of defense could still be decisive. In practice, the two branches of government shared power and made political trades. At another level in the government, the entire procurement process was influenced by civil servants and military officers who conscientiously tried to design worthwhile projects and select the best-qualified companies to execute them.

The new demand for high technology in war and space spawned dozens of new companies. TRW, for example, was formed to pioneer in ICBMs. In the midst of all this economic change, the older companies fought for survival. These corporations, still controlled by the bold pioneers who created the American aircraft industry, had a tradition of meeting impossible challenges. In World War II, they had delivered—in record time, through improvisation and brilliant feats of production—the machines that defeated Germany and Japan.

Among those pioneers were James Howard Kindelberger, North American Aviation's board chairman, and John Leland (Lee) Atwood, its president. They belonged to a remarkable group of Americans that included Glenn Martin, Donald Douglas, and Jack Northrop, each of whom created an aircraft company bearing his name. Friends and competitors who learned from each other and fought each other for economic power, they were all rugged individualists, romantics in love with flight, seat-of-the-pants innovators, tough-minded entrepreneurs, and patriots.

Kindelberger and Atwood were classic examples of opposites who perfectly complemented each other. The gregarious Kindelberger, known to everyone as Dutch, was a beefy, salty-tongued West Virginian who dropped out of a Wheeling high school at fifteen to learn the airplane business, starting as an apprentice draftsman with the Glenn L. Martin Company in Baltimore. A man with a quick wit and an even quicker temper, he loved ribald stories and Scotch whisky. Above all, he was a dreamer and a gambler, always searching for the next big project. After moving to Douglas Aircraft, Kindelberger developed the passenger plane whose durability has been one of the most amazing success stories in aviation history, the DC-3.

At Douglas, Kindelberger met Lee Atwood. The Kentucky-born son of a Baptist preacher, Atwood was as reticent as Kindelberger was ebullient, playing the lean ascetic to Kindelberger's rotund, rosy-cheeked reveler. Atwood was the cautious engineer, respected for his powers of incisive analysis, an objectivity that at times seemed almost inhuman, and an ability to express his thoughts with enviable lucidity. He jealously guarded his private life and his solitary pursuits: skindiving, skiing, and reading Shakespeare.

When Kindelberger left Douglas in 1934 to become president of North American Aviation, a moribund little company outside Baltimore, he took Lee Atwood along as his chief engineer. The partnership was an immediate success. Atwood was the ideal engineering manager, and Kindelberger the adventurer who could seize a business opportunity by thinking fast on his feet. (According to one often-told story, Kindelberger presented the design for an observation plane to the Army Air Corps only to be told by a general that money was available only for fighters. "Precisely, general," Kindelberger responded without missing a beat. "The beauty of this observer is that it *is* a fighter." He got the contract.) They soon moved the company to California.

On the eve of World War II, when Atwood and Kindelberger won the competition to produce the principal military training plane, they designed and built the prototype in just nine weeks. This was an astonishing feat, but one they would soon surpass. In 1940, the British desperately needed a high-performance plane to supplement their Spitfires, which were lost in large numbers during the Battle of Britain. Atwood met with British officials in New York, and convinced them that North American could produce the plane they needed. In exactly 127 days, the plane Atwood had conceived was actually flying. His P-51 Mustang turned out to be the most successful Allied fighter of World War II. North American also built the B-25 medium bombers, which gave the country its first morale boost after Pearl Harbor when Colonel Jimmy Doolittle led sixteen of them off an aircraft carrier and bombed Tokyo in April of 1942.

Between 1939 and 1945, North American cranked out 40,984 planes, more than any other company—15,670 Mustangs, 15,498 trainers, and 9,816 B-25s. North American's results were achieved through incredible productivity, sacrifice, and teamwork. Driving that effort was the charismatic Dutch Kindelberger, who encouraged his workers and mingled with them on the factory floor.

In 1945, with peace at hand, the company's backlog of orders plummeted from eight thousand to two dozen. The payroll shrank from ninety-one thousand employees to less than five thousand. Many other war-production companies closed down or retooled to produce consumer goods, but Kindelberger and Atwood determined that North American should keep serving the nation's military needs. The company soon secured a large defense project, the F-86 Sabre, which became the most successful jet fighter plane of the Korean War.

Perhaps the greatest genius of Kindelberger and Atwood lay in their resiliency in adapting to the new aerospace era. No longer could new airplanes be invented in a few months and then cheaply manufactured by the thousands. With nuclear weapons, missiles, and computers, the technological problems were more difficult, the risks greater, the costs astronomical. Production lead times were far longer, and the opportunities to win contracts for big projects far less plentiful. Atwood set up separate divisions to specialize in the major fields of nuclear and space technology. As the space and arms races heated up the Cold War, North American won a piece of most of the major military and space projects.

When Kindelberger died in 1962, Atwood succeeded his friend as board chairman. At that time, North American had in hand $1.3 billion in contracts, including the prime contracts for the Apollo spacecraft, the rocket boosters for Apollo and several of the ICBM programs, the guidance and control system on the Minuteman ICBM, inertial navigators on the Polaris submarines, and the controversial B-70 bomber.

Atwood's new challenge was to keep bringing in the contracts. Losing even one contract could mean disaster. When the company first won the B-70 contract in 1957, North American was in a slump. The national recession had hit the southern California airplane industry with particular force. When the government canceled the F-108 fighter and Navaho missile in 1959, North

American lost twenty-five thousand jobs. Saving the B-70 became critical.

At the time when North American and Boeing were competing for the B-70 contract, Boeing was busy making its B-52 bombers, while North American was in trouble. North American badly needed the work. In a policy never stated publicly and implemented quietly, the government helped the major defense contractors when they experienced economic distress. The rationale was to maintain the defense-industrial base.

In winning what could be a $6 billion prize to build a highly experimental bomber, Atwood and Kindelberger realized they would need lots of help, both technological and political, for the project to succeed. In a shrewd, pioneering effort to build broader political support for the B-70, North American carefully parceled out roles to other major aircraft builders. They selected Lockheed Aircraft Corp. of Marietta, Georgia, Chance-Vought Aircraft of Dallas, and the Seattle division of Boeing to build parts of the plane—parts that North American could have built for itself. Atwood then reminded Congress that hundreds of companies would share in the program, creating sixty thousand jobs in addition to those at North American's own plants.

That decision to share the B-70 work with these major companies provided North American with vital political support in 1960 to fight President Eisenhower in Congress. When Boeing, for example, lost a $200 million subcontract to build the B-70's wings at its Seattle plant, Washington's Senator Scoop Jackson bitterly criticized Eisenhower's decision. He spoke not only of the blow to national defense, but also of the loss of jobs for twelve hundred Boeing workers just before Christmas. The themes blended well.

Another constituency found its voice when California Senator Clair Engle, in whose state North American would build the B-70, called the Eisenhower decision "a blunder that might have grave national security consequences." He was quickly joined by Senator Barry Goldwater of Arizona.

Engle and Goldwater belonged to yet another special-interest group: the two senators held commissions as Air Force reserve officers. At the time, few asked if they might face conflicts of interest when they voted on a bomber project that the president didn't want and the Air Force said it couldn't do without.

Not all the fighting was between the president and the Congress.

In the late 1950s and early 1960s, rival congressional delegations fought monumental political battles over defense projects for companies in their states. Three sets of contractors and their congressional allies, for example, wrangled bitterly over which missile—the Atlas, the Titan, or the Minuteman—would become the nation's principal ICBM.

Sometimes service rivalries became enmeshed in the competition within the weapons industry and in Congress. In the case of the intermediate range ballistic missile (IRBM), the Air Force and the Army each set out to produce its own weapon. The Army's Jupiter missile was backed by the Alabama congressional delegation and the Chrysler Corporation, which would produce it in that state. The Air Force's Thor missile was just as fiercely supported by the Douglas Aircraft Company and the California delegation. Neither project was a notable success.

"The interservice game extends right down through the corporations, depending upon which branch their contracts flow from, and it even goes into the academic institutions, depending from where their research grants flow," adviser John J. McCloy reported to Eisenhower. Concurring with the critique, the president noted that it was "these vested interests" in the military-industrial-congressional-educational alliance that opposed his Pentagon reforms to control defense excesses. Dr. Herbert York, the director of weapons procurement at the end of the Eisenhower administration, estimated later that political, interservice, and industrial rivalries resulted in funding twice as many nuclear missile programs as were actually needed.

The state of the American economy also became a factor in the arms race. The defense and space industry had become such an important segment of the nation's economy that its health had to be considered in administration decisions about weapon systems. Eisenhower did not believe in priming the economy through military spending, but even he yielded to the combined political, military, and economic pressures that conspired to produce weapons he opposed. A case in point was the Air Force's B-58 Hustler.

Aside from its Mach 2.5 supersonic-dash capability, the Convair Corporation's B-58 had been a disappointment. As a "medium" bomber, it could not reach Soviet targets from bases in the United States. It was too small to carry more than a few nuclear weapons, and it could not carry missiles. Finally, it was unreliable. In 1959, the Defense Department wanted to cancel the plane.

Nevertheless, Secretary of Defense McElroy explained to Eisenhower that shutting down the plant in Fort Worth, Texas, where Convair was building the plane for the government, "would cause grave local unemployment." At a time when the national unemployment rate was higher than 7 percent and growing, with corporate profit rates down 25 percent, the president registered concern. Eisenhower suggested that the government-owned Fort Worth plant might be used to build a new Atlas ICBM, but Dr. Kistiakowsky ruled out that solution as uneconomical. (As part of its effort to promote defense projects, the government builds and owns a number of defense plants, and leases them to defense contractors at nominal fees.)

The B-58 issue was debated at the same November 1959 meeting at which Eisenhower decided to cancel B-70 production. If both the B-70 and the B-58 were canceled, the Air Force would be without any supersonic bomber, argued Joint Chiefs Chairman Nathan Twining. Eisenhower reluctantly agreed that the Air Force could build forty-two more B-58s at a cost of $1 billion.

In fending off the B-70 by agreeing to more B-58s—neither of which he thought were needed for the nation's defense—Eisenhower had made a pragmatic, if costly, defense tradeoff. It became a frequent practice as he and his successors sought to balance conflicting pressures and national needs. In this case, the Air Force was mollified and an economically vulnerable and politically sensitive area was protected. Resisting all the pressures and meeting all the needs would be impossible. At best, a president measured out his power to serve his concept of the national interest.

As Eisenhower pushed his peace initiative in 1959 and 1960, some Americans worried that arms reductions would damage the already shaky U.S. economy. "I see no reason why the sums which now are going into these sterile, negative mechanisms that we call war munitions shouldn't go into something positive," the president replied. But he refused to endorse government-supported "peace conversion" as a means to change war industries to domestic needs. With a conservative's aversion to government economic tampering, Eisenhower wishfully assumed that business lost through disarmament "would be an almost imperceptible decline," and would be picked up without any trouble.

However, business was not given a chance to decline through disarmament. Once a gigantic arms program such as the B-70 started rolling, nothing must be allowed to get in its way—least of all internal criticism. Only with great reluctance would either the Air Force or industry raise any issues that might upset its progress. With so much at stake, any doubts could provide ammunition to sink the program.

When skeptical views came from a military officer, the reception was likely to be icy. Early in 1960, Glenn Kent, a young Air Force general known for the intellectual courage with which he presented unorthodox ideas, went to North American's headquarters in Los Angeles to raise questions about the B-70. Kent told North American officials that according to latest Air Force intelligence, Soviet SAM missiles soon would be able to shoot down bombers flying at high altitudes. The B-70 had been designed to attack at 70,000 feet. He suggested that the design team think of modifications to give the plane capability of low-level attack as well.

North American's executives were outraged, as were General Kent's Air Force colleagues. The president already wanted to cancel the program; Kent's notion would only raise new doubts about the B-70s.

When the acrimonious conference ended, it was raining heavily outside North American's offices. No one offered Kent a ride back to his hotel. He walked blocks through pouring rain before finally hailing a taxicab. Within six months, Kent's predictions about Soviet antiaircraft missiles were verified—with important consequences both for the B-70 program and for Dwight Eisenhower's search for peace.

6

POLITICS
AND THE MISSILE GAP

Even as the Air Force and the arms industry turned toward Congress in what he considered revolt, Dwight Eisenhower moved hopefully toward the greatest goal of his presidency: an arms-control agreement that might lessen the chance of nuclear holocaust.

The president walked a tightrope toward a summit meeting. Abroad, acts of Soviet intransigence in Berlin, Cuba, and trouble spots in Africa and Asia hindered every step. At home, Eisenhower faced politicians seeking the presidency, scientists who warned that the Soviets would cheat on a proposed nuclear-test ban, military chiefs who pushed hard for more ICBMs and production of the B-70—and special pressure from the CIA, which yielded the data that made Ike so confident of U.S. military superiority.

This confidence derived in part from secret flights over the Soviet Union. Since 1956, single-engine high-altitude jets, developed in great secrecy by the Lockheed Corporation and codenamed U-2, had gathered valuable photographic information. The U-2 pictures reassured the president that the Soviets were a long way from mounting an ICBM threat. With the summit approaching, however, Eisenhower wanted the intelligence flights stopped.

In February, meeting with his Board of Consultants on Foreign Intelligence Activities, Eisenhower explained his "soul-searching concern" about the provocative nature of the overflights. "I have one tremendous asset in a summit meeting," said Eisenhower. "That is a reputation for honesty. If one of these aircraft were lost when we are engaged in apparently sincere deliberations, it could be put on display in Moscow and ruin the president's effectiveness."

Despite the obvious peril of running yet another U-2 mission on the eve of the summit, the CIA persuaded Eisenhower to permit one more flight. On May 1, fifteen days before the most important U.S.-Soviet meeting since World War II, a young CIA pilot, Francis Gary Powers, was shot down by a Soviet surface-to-air (SAM) missile near Sverdlovsk in the Ural mountains.

The incident caused an international scandal and national embarrassment. As Eisenhower had predicted, the Russians milked the event for every ounce of propaganda value, placing the wrecked airplane and its dazed pilot on display for all the world to see. The Soviets also flaunted a military capability the United States had not taken seriously—the ability to shoot down a plane flying at high altitude. The Air Force's jewel, the B-70 Valkyrie, had been designed to fly at 70,000 feet because the United States assumed Soviet antiaircraft missiles could not reach that high.

The summit conference in Paris was brief and nasty, as Khrushchev stalked out, shattering the president's last hopes to achieve accommodation with the Soviets during his administration. The president complained bitterly to George Kistiakowsky that his scientists had failed him. The scientists, Dr. Kistiakowsky reminded him, had consistently warned that eventually a U-2 would be shot down. The ones who had failed, said Kistiakowsky, were the bureaucrats responsible for managing the spy program.

Eisenhower had complained for five years that the CIA and the Air Force repeatedly violated his orders regulating spy flights over Soviet territory. The Air Force, using observation balloons, competed with the CIA's U-2s in gathering information on Soviet military activity. Even though the information was invaluable, Eisenhower felt the spy flights were excessive and unduly provocative. Though he threatened to discipline officers who violated his orders, he refrained; he felt he could not afford many confrontations with the Pentagon.

As Eisenhower feared, the U-2 incident escalated the arms race and the Cold War, just as Sputnik had three years earlier. The military pressed to accelerate nuclear-arms production and to resume nuclear testing, breaking a year-long moratorium the United States had been observing with the Soviet Union. The Soviets used the U-2 affair as a pretext for aggressive behavior in half a dozen world trouble spots, including Cuba.

The U-2 affair also gave a new boost to the moribund B-70 Valkyrie bomber, even though it should have called into question one of the plane's main features—its presumed invulnerability to avoid Soviet radar and missiles.

The B-70's boost came from 1960 presidential politics as candidates from both parties criticized the defense policies of the still-popular Eisenhower, who could not run for a third term. Democratic Senator Stuart Symington warned of an alarming "missile gap." (Four years earlier, Democrats had spoken of a "bomber gap"—which, as it turned out, did not exist. Then, as now, their information came from the Air Force.) General LeMay and other officers now repeatedly predicted that the United States soon would trail the Soviets in nuclear weapons.

In each instance, the Air Force and other intelligence agencies quite properly drew a conservative worst-case scenario of Soviet capabilities, since it is wiser to overestimate than to underestimate an enemy's strength. Besides, it was difficult to forecast Soviet production potential or intentions. Furthermore, in the late 1950s and early 1960s, bravado disguised Soviet strategic inferiority.

Based on his own military experience and the U-2 intelligence, Eisenhower was convinced that the Air Force and other services repeatedly exaggerated the Soviet threat for another reason—to build pressure for more weapons. The president complained to his aides that the Democratic candidates "were getting away with murder" on the missile-gap issue, but he never shared the secret intelligence information to set them straight.

Lyndon Johnson used his chairmanship of the Senate Preparedness Subcommittee as a bully pulpit for his own presidential candidacy. He shared the platform with military leaders bent on reversing President Eisenhower's decisions on defense spending.

In the spring of 1960, Johnson held hearings that highlighted support for the B-70 Valkyrie by Congress and the military. Disputing President Eisenhower, General Twining urged construction of the B-70 to maintain a flexible "mixed force" of bombers and missiles. "What bombers would the United States have in 1967, if the B-70 is not built?" Twining was asked. "None," he replied—even though the Air Force was then engaged in manufacturing a total of 660 B-52s in addition to 140 B-58 bombers.

Twining based his dire prediction on the assumption that the technological revolution in the weapons of the space age would soon make the B-52 obsolete. The military thought it would take an endless succession of new weapons to stay ahead of the Soviets. No one accurately predicted the success and incredible longevity of the B-52, still a potent weapon almost thirty years later.

To boost his fading presidential hopes, Johnson timed the announcement of his committee's B-70 report for the eve of the Democratic National Convention. Predictably, the report called for building the B-70, stressing both its economic benefits and its strategic necessity.

On July 13, John F. Kennedy, the young senator from Massachusetts, won the Democratic nomination, and Lyndon Johnson became the vice-presidential candidate. Both men then fully embraced the defense rhetoric of the Democratic platform. "The Communists will have a dangerous lead in intercontinental missiles through 1963," the platform stated. It went on to say "that the Republican administration has no plans to catch up. . . . Our military position today is measured in terms of gaps—missile gap, space gap, limited-war gap."

During the ensuing campaign, Kennedy repeatedly endorsed the B-70 bomber, attacking the Eisenhower administration for abandoning it. Wherever he spoke, Kennedy appealed for votes by touting the local weapon product. He told an audience in San Diego, "I wholeheartedly endorse the B-70 manned aircraft"—a comment aimed at tens of thousands of southern California aerospace workers worried about their jobs. In a speech near the Boeing plant in Seattle he called for building more Boeing B-52s. In Fort Worth, Texas, he praised the B-58 Hustler, manufactured at the Convair plant there.

Eisenhower also received stinging criticism from the Republican aspirants—his own Vice-President Richard Nixon and New York Governor Nelson Rockefeller. On July 23, 1960, those two candidates met in Rockefeller's New York apartment and made a deal known as the Fifth Avenue Compact. In return for Rockefeller conceding the nomination, Nixon agreed to a joint statement calling for significant increases in nuclear missiles. "There must be no price ceiling on America's security," they declared, in a thinly veiled criticism of Eisenhower.

Eisenhower was not a Nixon fan. Faced with a choice between Kennedy and Nixon, however, he finally decided to give Nixon some political help. At the end of his public career, the president who complained continually about narrow, self-interested defense politics showed that he too could play the game.

In late July, Eisenhower suddenly authorized an additional $500 million in defense spending. Previously, he had refused to spend the money appropriated for programs he thought unneeded. Now, he clearly tried to help Nixon by boosting the Republican "record" on defense spending. The windfall included $100 million for the B-70. Pressure from the presidential campaign had brought the bomber, which Eisenhower still believed to be a white elephant, back to life.

Once he decided to engage in defense politics himself, Eisenhower showed he knew how to pull out all the stops. With Nixon present in his office, the president made a telephone call to W. Alton (Pete) Jones, the chairman of the board of Cities Service Company. Jones was one of Eisenhower's closest friends, a bridge partner and hunting companion. To help Nixon, Eisenhower told Jones, "the government was accelerating some of its spending." (Eisenhower had just released the $500 million.) He pointedly suggested to Jones that "certain companies might do the same thing" to help the Nixon campaign.

As the campaign came down to the wire, the election was too close to call. California was a key to the election, and during their swings through the state both Nixon and Kennedy pledged to revive the B-70 bomber, a major source of defense jobs in the Los Angeles area.

Nixon needed a boost in California. On October 30, only nine days before the election, Eisenhower gave him one. In a transparently political maneuver, the Defense Department announced that $155 million in additional funds would go to a "substantially augmented development program" for the B-70.

Announcement of the administration's sudden revival of the B-70 stole Kennedy's thunder in Nixon's home state. Speaking two days later in San Diego, Kennedy described Eisenhower's last-minute release of funds for the B-70 as a cynical election ploy. "We could not get the administration to release the funds until this week," said Kennedy. "That is progress. And why do you think they did it this week? I wonder."

Nixon carried California on November 8, but Kennedy won the election by a whisper—only 18,575 more votes than Nixon.

The Air Force also won, by a larger margin. It now had a commitment to build at least four B-70 bombers and possibly as many as twelve. The four would provide prototypes for a "usable weapon system," with fully developed nuclear armaments and electronic equipment. At that point, the plane could quickly move into the next phase—full-scale production of a fleet. Eisenhower's final lame-duck budget reflected the Air Force's victory by fully reinstating the B-70 program.

Dwight David Eisenhower delivered his farewell address to the nation on January 17, 1961. The speech is a remarkable reflection on the theme of democratic governance of a nation in which the roles of industry, the military, science, education, and government itself are of necessity intertwined. In the speech's best-remembered lines he said: "In the councils of government, we must guard against the acquisition of unwarranted influence, whether sought or unsought, by the military-industrial complex. The potential for the disastrous rise of misplaced power exists and will persist.

"We must never let the weight of this combination endanger

our liberties or democratic processes. We should take nothing for granted. Only an alert or knowledgeable citizenry can compel the proper meshing of the huge industrial and military machinery of defense with our peaceful methods and goals, so that security and liberty may prosper together."

Less well known was his warning about the role of education and science: "The prospect of domination of the nation's scholars by federal employment, project allocations, and the power of money is ever present—and gravely to be regarded. Yet, in holding scientific research and discovery in respect, as we should, we must also be alert to the equal and opposite danger that public policy could itself become the captive of a scientific-technological elite."

In his memoirs *Waging Peace,* Eisenhower touched on the endemic conflict between the national good and local self-interest that all citizens had to face. "Each community in which a manufacturing plant or a military installation is located," he wrote, "profits from the money spent and the jobs created in the area. This fact, of course, constantly presses on the community's political representatives—congressmen, senators and others—to maintain the facility at maximum strength."

If Eisenhower saw the issues so clearly and with such conviction, why did he do so little about the dangers while in office? Eisenhower himself was part of the problem. He had supported a strategy of massive nuclear retaliation as the U.S. answer to the vast Soviet advantage in troop strength. That policy put a premium on accelerated development of nuclear weapons. When he finally changed his mind, the process was already out of control. Publicly—and more often privately—he did resist the demand for more nuclear weapons. What made Eisenhower such a bitter critic was his own deep knowledge of military politics. He had risen to power in the Army as a skillful bureaucratic politician. Despite his constant complaints of military insubordination, he did not stop it. Politically cautious, he would not risk a divisive, open fight with the military and its many allies.

Eisenhower realized the limitations of presidential power. He served as a minority president with a Democratic Congress. He chose to husband his power and his personal popularity carefully, understanding the political climate of an aroused, fearful American public. He successfully rebuffed some weapons that he felt were unneeded. But his own deeply rooted anticommunism fed his concerns about Soviet aggression and growing nuclear strength and dampened his efforts to curb the arms race.

Eisenhower's "great tragedy" was the "opportunity lost" for peace, wrote his biographer Stephen E. Ambrose. He allowed "the tyranny of technology" from the experts "to override his own common sense." But, Ambrose concludes, "In a limited and halting but nevertheless real way, Ike had opted for peace. . . . As a professional soldier of the old school, Eisenhower felt his first responsibility was the nation's security, which he realized could never be enhanced by an arms race in the nuclear age. This was Eisenhower's fundamental insight."

With his prophetic farewell, the awesome responsibility of deciding how much defense was enough now passed from the man who was then the oldest president in the nation's history to the one who was the youngest.

THE WHIZ KIDS
AND THE
BOMBER GENERALS

Standing on a windswept podium in front of the U.S. Capitol, the young president called for a bold new American defense and foreign policy: "We shall pay any price, bear any burden, meet any hardship, support any friend, oppose any foe to assure the survival and success of liberty." Taking John F. Kennedy at his word, Robert McNamara, the new secretary of defense, went directly from the inaugural ceremony to the Pentagon, where he began scrutinizing dozens of top-secret photographs.

During the next two weeks, Secretary McNamara and Deputy Secretary Roswell Gilpatric studied photos of the Soviet Union until their eyes glazed over. Taken by Discoverer, the first U.S. spy satellite, and earlier by U-2 spy planes, these pictures revealed amazingly clear details of Soviet military installations. By early February 1961, McNamara came to a startling conclusion. The "missile gap" that Kennedy had described so vividly during the presidential campaign *did* exist. But it was the Soviet Union, *not* the United States, that lagged behind. The Discoverer photos turned up just four Soviet SS-7 ICBMs, plus a few more under construction.

Several days later, McNamara disclosed his findings to Pentagon reporters. NO MISSILE GAP EXISTS, STUDY SHOWS, bannered the *Washington Post* on February 8. Republicans charged that Kennedy had misled the electorate during the campaign. A furious Kennedy summoned McNamara to the White House.

The president told McNamara he had embarrassed him deeply, making his campaign look dishonest, when Kennedy had in good faith believed in the missile gap. The secretary of defense offered his resignation, which Kennedy refused. McNamara agreed, however, to a deception. Henceforth, the administration would publicly deny what McNamara had just learned about relative U.S.-Soviet missile strength. In one brief incident, McNamara discovered the inseparable connection between American politics and national defense.

Continuing the fiction of the missile gap provided a vital rationale for Kennedy and McNamara as the self-confident young leaders of the New Frontier implemented a radical change in American defense policy. President Eisenhower had abandoned the drive for "nuclear superiority," and held down the size of conventional American forces, convinced that the United States could not be the world's policeman. Rejecting these cautious Eisenhower policies, Kennedy and McNamara set out to reassert American might with a massive buildup of both nuclear and conventional arms.

Seeking to guarantee nuclear superiority, Kennedy's first budget tripled production of Polaris submarines and the Air Force's Minuteman missiles. Although the Soviet Union had only a few missiles, clearly they would develop ICBMs as quickly as they could. Furthermore, Kennedy wanted a more flexible nuclear strategy. Instead of relying on Eisenhower's "massive nuclear retaliation," he sought weapons for a "counterforce" capability. If deterrence failed, the theory went, both sides might limit nuclear exchanges to counterforce attacks against each other's military forces. Kennedy, a decorated PT-boat commander in World War II, hoped the new strategy would provide a more credible deterrent to war, and less disastrous consequences if war came.

By building up conventional forces, particularly the Army's elite Special Forces (Green Berets), Kennedy sought the capability to meet communist challenges anywhere with a "flexible response," rather than by just threatening nuclear retaliation. Relying on superior weapons and modern techniques, the United States could fight the Cold War as it expanded to the former colonial countries of Asia and Africa. American counterinsurgency forces would defeat the communist-led "wars of national liberation" of which Premier Khrushchev boasted in 1961.

Despite Kennedy's defense buildup, conflict continued between the president and the Air Force over bombers and the size of the nuclear force. Following McNamara's advice, President Kennedy surprised and infuriated the Air Force by reneging on his campaign pledge to build the B-70 Valkyrie bomber. Instead, he reaffirmed Eisenhower's original 1959 order to fund the project only as an experiment with several prototype planes. Kennedy and McNamara agreed that the rapidly developing ICBMs obviated the need for a new bomber.

The battle over the B-70, pitting Kennedy and McNamara against the Air Force and its congressional supporters, brought into focus a fundamental dispute over American military policy and who should control it. The principal protagonists were Defense Secretary McNamara and General Curtis LeMay, who in May 1961 had been promoted to Air Force chief of staff.

Robert Strange McNamara, the Harvard Business School graduate who became president of the Ford Motor Company at the age of forty-four, quickly made himself the most powerful secretary of defense in history. With the full backing of President Kennedy, McNamara set out to coordinate, rationalize, and control national defense. A brilliant, self-confident intellectual, he redesigned both Pentagon decision-making and military strategy. Without hesitation, he chose the weapons—a prerogative which the uniformed military services had always considered their own.

McNamara imposed on the Pentagon a new, rigorous style of management. Though historian Arthur Schlesinger called him a "humane technocrat, for whom scientific management was not an end in itself, but a means to the rationality of democratic government," others saw McNamara as a badly flawed, bloodless machine whose rationality left no room for human judgments that could not be quantified.

For his civilian aides McNamara recruited a group of young

men who had worked at the Rand Corporation, a California research institute established by the Air Force in 1946. Academics by training, these men became known as the "whiz kids," a term with connotations of precocious intelligence tinged with adolescent arrogance. They included Alain Enthoven, an economist McNamara soon named to head a new Office of Systems Analysis; economist Charles Hitch, who became the Defense Department comptroller; and political scientist William Kaufmann, a consultant on strategic issues.

McNamara and his team applied to the Department of Defense the management technique of systems analysis. They used the most sophisticated tools of the physical and social sciences to analyze and solve military problems, even highly theoretical questions of nuclear strategy. They believed that systems analysis could provide answers to questions involving many complex variables: How much explosive carried by which weapons would destroy a certain number of targets most effectively? What proportion of our weapons could survive a surprise Soviet attack? How many would be needed to have enough left to respond with a crushing counterattack? Would this capability deter the Soviet Union from launching an attack in the first place? They also analyzed the cost-benefit ratio of military options to determine which weapons could best accomplish a designated mission at the lowest possible cost.

On the basis of systems analysis and cost-benefit ratios, the McNamara team led by Alain Enthoven decided that the B-70 simply was not cost-effective. There would be a much bigger bang for the buck from Minuteman and Polaris missiles. In addition, the missiles, in their hardened underground silos or hidden beneath the seas, would be less vulnerable to attack than bombers.

Air Force officers could not match the whiz kids at using their analytic techniques. When Enthoven testified before Congress, he overwhelmed the generals with charts and graphs showing that "the B-70 would add minimal extra firepower at huge cost." Still, the military rejected the notion that a computer-generated "truth" provided better answers than the judgment and experience of men who had actually fought a war.

"I am profoundly apprehensive of the pipe-smoking, tree-full-of-owls type of so-called professional defense intellectuals," said

General Thomas D. White, who had just retired as Air Force chief of staff. "I don't believe a lot of these often overconfident, sometimes arrogant young professors, mathematicians, and other theorists have sufficient worldliness or motivation to stand up to the kind of enemy we face."

General LeMay shared White's contempt for the whiz kids and for McNamara. He believed the civilians had usurped the proper role and expertise of the military. In LeMay's analogy, McNamara was a reckless amateur who ran the Defense Department like "a hospital administrator who tried to practice brain surgery." Exasperated by McNamara's iron grip on Air Force programs, LeMay would ask friends: "Would things be much worse if Khrushchev were secretary of defense?"

Kennedy had mixed emotions in appointing LeMay chief of staff. In case of war, he wanted tough military leaders like old Iron Ass. Yet he and McNamara knew that the independent, hardline general would be difficult. Always the political pragmatist, Kennedy and his advisers finally decided they "would have a major revolt on their hands" if they bypassed LeMay, who had powerful backing in Congress. Later, Kennedy was so irritated by LeMay's relentless advocacy that he "ended up in sort of a fit" after their meetings, reported Deputy Defense Secretary Gilpatric.

As a young Air Corps officer in World War II, McNamara had been in awe of LeMay. McNamara observed how LeMay inspired airmen to fly nearly suicidal bombing raids over Germany by flying the lead plane. Later in the Pacific, McNamara listened as LeMay conducted a 20th Air Force debriefing after the first low-altitude bombing attack on Tokyo.

"Who was the son-of-a-bitch who sent us in at seven thousand feet when the B-29s are supposed to be flying at twenty-five thousand?" asked a young pilot who had lost his wingman in the raid.

"I did," replied LeMay. "We lost fewer men and got better results that way."

McNamara admired LeMay's leadership, his tactical brilliance, and his crisp reports, which gave facts about targets hit and planes lost without a cloud of excuses. McNamara said he believed LeMay was "the greatest fighting commander to emerge from the war."

The gulf that separated LeMay and McNamara in 1961 dramatized the differences between the old warriors and the new defense intellectuals. McNamara, the administrative emblem of Kennedy's New Frontier, dazzled the city with his icy brilliance, his command of the new scientific tools of modern decision-making. The cigar-chomping LeMay attacked Washington's political jungle with the same blunt tactics that won triumphs in World War II.

LeMay fought McNamara's unwillingness to build yet more B-52 bombers. He resisted McNamara's effort to impose a common fighter plane, the TFX, on both the Air Force and Navy. Having only one plane might sound logical to a cost analyst, but both services believed that different missions required different capabilities in an airplane. LeMay fought McNamara for more ICBMs, because he still believed in seeking sufficient superiority to prevail, either with a crushing preventive strike or in retaliation. LeMay resented the fact that McNamara had increased the Army and Navy shares of the defense budget, while the Air Force's share declined. LeMay lost all these fights. And in the abortive 1961 Bay of Pigs invasion of Cuba, Kennedy infuriated LeMay by calling off air cover for the CIA-backed Cuban exiles, without even consulting the Air Force. Finally, LeMay fought to preserve the future of the bomber by pressing for the B-70.

By now even those committed to the bomber role wondered if the B-70 was the right plane for the times. Designed to fly at 70,000 feet, the huge plane could be spotted easily by enemy radar. Flying at Mach 3 (2,000 miles per hour) offered impressive possibilities of escape—but not from Soviet antiaircraft SAM missiles, which flew three times faster. For several years, B-52 pilots had been training to attack at low altitudes to escape Soviet radar detection, and the B-70 wasn't designed for low-level flight. Nevertheless, Air Force leaders felt that in the confusion of battle the B-70s still could penetrate Soviet airspace. And they simply could not give up on the B-70 with no other bomber in development.

From his own experience, LeMay believed deeply in the need for leadership at the scene of battle. As a defense practitioner, he understood the dicta of Carl von Clausewitz, the nineteenth-century German military genius who stressed the confusion of war. Clausewitz believed the general triumphed who best understood and coped with the uncertainty, "friction," and "fog of war." Even in the nuclear era, LeMay believed these ideas still applied. The human judgment of a bomber commander was needed in the era of push-button, computerized war.

The Air Force presented its classic arguments to a skeptical McNamara: With a man at the controls, bombers were more flexible than missiles, permitting bomber pilots to seek out targets of opportunity. Bombs were more accurate than the early generation of missiles; they carried a heavier explosive load and therefore were better able to wipe out hardened targets.

"With the manned systems, you can maneuver them, you can change their position, you can threaten with them," LeMay told a Senate committee. "You can launch them and recall them, and you have all the flexibility in the world necessary to do things that might well prevent the war from ever starting."

McNamara thought he had demolished all these points. In his view, the B-70 only duplicated the missile's role, without performing nearly as well. Having to send a fleet of bombers into the air in order not to lose them on the ground was a sign of weakness rather than an advantage, McNamara reasoned.

With its back to the wall, in mid-1961 the Air Force hastily devised a new mission for the plane. Working with North American Aviation, the Air Force transformed the B-70 into the RS-70 —RS for "reconnaissance strike." After the first round of a nuclear war, the plane would scan the damage and then destroy important targets that remained. A computerized radar would instantaneously photograph and direct missiles at targets. The idea was creative. The RS technology, however, had yet to be invented.

McNamara and Enthoven found the RS-70 an even easier target. In a memorandum to Kennedy, they methodically laid out their doubts about whether the "processing and display function in an RS-70 can be made operational by 1970, let alone 1967, on the basis of any known technology, or whether the human interpretation job required of the operation *can ever* be done."

McNamara quoted to Kennedy the doubts of Army General Maxwell Taylor: "Is it worth several billion dollars of national resources to be able to overfly Soviet targets with a few score

73

manned bombers looking for residual weapons . . . after each country has exchanged several thousand megatons of nuclear firepower on their respective target systems?"

Engineers who worked for North American Aviation realized that the RS-70 was a last-ditch concoction aimed at salvaging the bomber. Nevertheless, they whipped up designs and rushed them to the Pentagon as the Air Force prepared for a congressional battle that would decide the B-70's fate.

The B-70 episode completely poisoned what had been at best an uneasy relationship between McNamara and the Air Force. McNamara ordered LeMay not to defend the B-70 before Congress. When members of Congress protested, McNamara insisted he was not trying to muzzle the general, only to prevent him from presenting "misstatements of facts." In reality, McNamara was trying to enforce the administration's B-70 decision, while the Air Force worked with old friends in Congress to overturn it.

Kennedy's men may have seized the reins of power for a "new generation of leadership," but many in Washington refused to follow. Among the doubters were congressmen who had worked for years in partnership with the military services. When the showdown came, the Air Force had a powerful ally in Georgia Congressman Carl Vinson, the eighty-four-year-old chairman of the House Armed Services Committee.

Known as the Swamp Fox for his canny political instincts, and as Uncle Carl for his unassuming manner, Vinson had served in Congress for forty-eight years, longer than any other member. He had chaired one military committee or another since 1930. A small, wiry man with balding head, Vinson looked like a simple country lawyer who had come up the Democratic political ladder from rural Baldwin County, Georgia, through the time-honored route of prosecutor to state legislator to county judge to congressman.

His power in the House stemmed from his seniority. But to see Vinson only as a stereotypical southern politician was to underestimate him. The modern, "two-ocean" U.S. Navy came into existence in Vinson's congressional office. When President Truman established the Department of Defense, he offered to make Vinson its first secretary. "Aw, shucks, I'd just as soon run things from here," Vinson replied.

Vinson's knowledge of military matters was matched only by his command of political deal-making. "If one more military base or defense plant were built in Georgia," the expression went, "the state would sink under its own weight." The installations had been located there to please Vinson and Georgia Senator Richard Russell, chairman of the Senate Armed Services Committee.

Vinson shared the Air Force's concern about the future of the manned bomber. He also worried that congressional power was at stake. For two years, Congress had approved development of the B-70 and appropriated the money. Kennedy and McNamara simply refused to spend it. The congressmen also resented McNamara's attempts to cancel their favorite weapons systems and close bases in their districts by fiat. Of the committee's thirty-seven members, twenty-one had work on the B-70 bomber being performed by North American or its subcontractors in their districts.

Vinson decided to draw the line against further usurpation of congressional power. On March 1, 1962, the Armed Services Committee unanimously authorized $491 million to proceed with development and eventual production of the B-70. The committee went beyond simply "authorizing" the Defense Department to spend the money; it "ordered and directed" the executive branch to build the B-70.

Vinson had issued a constitutional challenge. "If this language constitutes a test as to whether Congress has the power to so mandate, let the test be made and let this important weapons system be the field of trial," the committee report said.

"We don't want to run the Department of Defense," said Vinson. "We just want to sit at the table and get across an idea once in a while."

McNamara was ready for a head-on confrontation, but Kennedy's legislative aides warned that he would lose on the House floor and see much of his legislative program wrecked in the process. On the eve of the crucial House vote, Kennedy and Vinson settled their differences in what became known as "the Rose Garden agreement." During their walk in the White House garden,

Vinson agreed to withdraw his constitutional challenge and Kennedy promised to restudy the bomber issue, thus effectively burying it. For two more years, Congress voted funds for the B-70 by overwhelming margins (the Senate vote in 1962 was 99 to 1), but Kennedy and McNamara again refused to spend it.

If Kennedy won by stopping the B-70, it proved a pyrrhic victory. He paid in other ways for thwarting Congress and the Air Force. It was one thing to use McNamara's vaunted systems analysis to theorize about weapons, but another to put theory into effect. Systems analysis was not much good at telling presidents how to work their way through the political thickets of the Pentagon and Congress.

Shelving the bomber meant making tradeoffs on other weapons. The trading began soon after John Kennedy took office. In 1961, the president approved a total of 950 Minuteman ICBM missiles, far more than Carl Kaysen and Jerome Wiesner, his arms-control and science advisers, recommended. They believed the discovery of an overwhelming U.S. missile superiority signaled a rare opportunity for serious arms-control negotiations with the Soviets. They proposed a force of 300 Minuteman missiles. McNamara thought the right number was between 600 and 800. SAC Commander Thomas Power wanted 10,000; LeMay argued for 2,950; Air Force Secretary Eugene Zuckert recommended 1,450. The arms-controllers wanted a minimum deterrent; the Air Force a war-fighting, first-strike capability.

The initial compromise was 950. Kennedy asked McNamara to explain the 300 total advocated by Kaysen and Wiesner. "Well, they're right," said McNamara. "Then why the 950 total?" asked the president. "Because that's the smallest total we can take up to the Hill without getting murdered," replied McNamara.

As McNamara later acknowledged: "The secretary must understand the president's political equations, and help him minimize the political cost" of bucking the military and Congress.

In 1961, Kennedy and McNamara also played politics with another weapon. Despite deep reservations, they approved development of the Skybolt, a long-range nuclear missile to be fired from B-52s. "I used the Skybolt to shoot down the B-70," quipped

Kennedy. He had promised the Air Force the Skybolt to ease the pain of losing the B-70. When Skybolt performed poorly in tests, Kennedy and McNamara then canceled that program in 1962. This time, McNamara appeased the Air Force by promising to raise the Minuteman force to 1,300.

This continuous political bartering of weapons dashed arms-control hopes in the Kennedy administration. According to Arthur Schlesinger, McNamara and Kennedy raised the ICBM total far beyond the levels they knew were adequate because they were afraid of "risking public conflict with the Joint Chiefs and vociferous B-70 lobby in Congress." After the Kennedy buildup, the Soviets trailed by a 4-to-1 margin in strategic missiles and hurried to catch up.

Towards the end, both Kennedy and McNamara—like Eisenhower before them—sensed the futility of seeking nuclear superiority, or a counterforce capability. The Cuban missile crisis of 1962 convinced Kennedy there were no nuclear options except mutual destruction. The United States and the Soviet Union came closer to the brink of war then than any time since World War II as the U.S. demanded that the Soviets withdraw nuclear missiles they were installing in Cuba. Kennedy and McNamara were now ready to settle for sufficiency, the ability to retaliate with "assured destruction." In 1963, Kennedy signed the limited test-ban treaty that Eisenhower had first sought in 1957. The Joint Chiefs of Staff gave their grudging support, at a price. On the day the Senate ratified the treaty, it also approved, 77 to 0, the largest peacetime defense budget in American history.

On November 22, 1963, President Kennedy started his day early in Forth Worth, Texas. He was already running hard for reelection. Texas was a trouble spot. Many voters in that conservative state believed Kennedy was soft on national defense, soft on communism. His speeches repeated the themes of the 1960 campaign. He stressed how Fort Worth had contributed to, and benefited from, his making America number one again in defense and space. Speaking at a chamber of commerce breakfast, Kennedy praised the TFX fighter, being built by General Dynamics in Forth Worth. He cited local defense products as having helped stave off the communists in Laos, Berlin, and Cuba. He noted that Texas ranked fifth in the country in defense-procurement dollars, and second in military personnel on active duty.

Playing defense politics to the hilt, the president planned to repeat the same litany in a luncheon speech at the Dallas Trade Mart. His prepared text described how the Kennedy administration had made us again the world's strongest military power—"the watchmen on the walls of world freedom."

Kennedy never delivered the speech. As the presidential motorcade traveled along a ten-mile route through downtown Dallas toward the Trade Mart, he was struck by two bullets fired by an assassin. The president was pronounced dead at 1 P.M. at Dallas's Parkland Hospital.

8

VIETNAM
AND THE TEST
OF AIR POWER

Soon after Lyndon Johnson became president, the bomber dispute took on a chilling new reality. While the theorists continued to debate how best to prevent or fight an atomic war, the president had to confront American involvement in a real war.

Under Kennedy, the still-confident whiz kids had supplied strategy, weapons, and manpower in growing amounts to the Republic of South Vietnam. By the end of 1963, fourteen thousand American military advisers were teaching the Vietnamese how to fight the Viet Cong in the south, using the modern techniques and weapons of "counterinsurgency." But the new president's defense advisers warned him in late December that South Vietnam was in danger of collapse. The Air Force proposed to turn the tide by striking the communist North Vietnam heartland with the strategic airpower of its B-52 bombers. And General Curtis LeMay, the Air Force chief of staff, sought presidential support for a new bomber.

Having finally abandoned the B-70 as a lost cause, LeMay now pressed for a new bomber—the advanced manned strategic aircraft, or AMSA. While the B-70 had been intended to penetrate the Soviet Union flying fast and high, the AMSA would attack fast and low, to escape detection by Soviet radar. As the new president met with defense advisers at his south Texas ranch, LeMay asked only for $55 million to get AMSA studies underway.

Defense Secretary Robert McNamara testily objected that this piddling sum would mushroom to $10 billion for a bomber force whose military purpose the Air Force could not explain. With the French and British producing a supersonic transport that could outrun U.S. bombers, retorted LeMay, the Air Force would become a laughingstock. President Johnson ended what LeMay described as a "pretty bloody" argument by postponing the discussion until a later time.

Lyndon Johnson's mind was on other problems. He was trying to reassure a nation still grieving for John Kennedy. He was obsessed with domestic concerns: the unfulfilled legislative program he had inherited from Kennedy, and his own vision of long-overdue civil-rights laws and social programs aimed at creating what he would call the Great Society.

In fact, neither expensive new bombers nor upping the ante in the still-small U.S. involvement in Vietnam figured in the president's agenda. In less than a year, Johnson would have to run for office in his own right. He planned to campaign as a "peace president" who would stay out of war in Southeast Asia and avoid nuclear confrontation with the Soviet Union.

His Republican opponent, Senator Barry Goldwater, was a hard-line conservative who called both for new strategic nuclear weapons and for increased American support for our embattled ally in South Vietnam. Johnson's 1964 campaign rhetoric depicted Goldwater as an irresponsible warmonger whom the nation could not trust with the nuclear trigger.

As he steered deftly through the nuclear and Vietnam issues, the president worried about General LeMay, whom he considered a political time bomb. LeMay's term as Air Force chief of staff would expire in May 1964. But Johnson knew that LeMay in retirement might become an outspoken Johnson critic and Goldwater ally, publicly advocating not only a new bomber but bombing communist North Vietnam. After LeMay refused his offer of another job, as an ambassador, Johnson told the general: "I don't know what's going on in the future, but I've got an election coming up, so I'm reappointing you." The reappointment would expire three months after the election. In the case of

LeMay, Johnson had decided as he had with FBI chief J. Edgar Hoover—that "I'd rather have him inside the tent pissing out, than outside pissing in."

When LeMay pressed again in August for an immediate commitment from the president on the AMSA bomber, Johnson again stalled, promising an answer in December—after the election. McGeorge Bundy, the White House national security adviser, reassured the president that neither LeMay nor Goldwater would cause "any serious political trouble" on the bomber issue before the election.

It was more difficult to put off Vietnam. Johnson's defense advisers warned that South Vietnam would soon topple without American intervention. Supported by Marine Corps and Navy commanders, in September 1964 LeMay recommended a classic strategic-bombing campaign against North Vietnam. It would knock out the military bases, transportation system, and industry that permitted North Vietnam to supply the Viet Cong in the South. "We should stop swatting flies and go for the manure pile," LeMay advised. Johnson was horrified. "Some are eager to enlarge the conflict," he told a campaign audience. "They call upon us to supply American boys to do the job that Asian boys should do."

On November 3, Johnson won a landslide victory, thanks in part to public perception of him as a peace candidate and Goldwater as an irresponsible advocate of nuclear weapons. By March 1965, however, President Johnson and his defense advisers agreed that the United States must really enter the Vietnam war. Americans were being killed in Viet Cong mortar attacks on airbases. The nation's prestige was at stake. No ranking official recommended withdrawal. But there was huge disagreement about how to conduct the war. A central argument concerned the use of massive strategic airpower against North Vietnam.

The debate became sensationalized by LeMay's statement in his 1965 autobiography that he would "bomb [North Vietnam] back into the stone age," if it didn't cease aggression. LeMay was crudely and unfairly caricatured as the mad bomber general. In fact, the entire Joint Chiefs of Staff by 1965 supported the Air Force recommendation for a swift strategic air campaign against ninety-four critical targets in North Vietnam, including airbases, industry, the port of Haiphong, the railroad supply line from China, and the irrigation system. If we entered the war, the Joint Chiefs felt we should use maximum force. Its purpose was to cut off Viet Cong aid at its source, to make war too costly for North Vietnam.

Instead, President Johnson and his civilian advisers, led by McNamara, decided on "gradualism" in a "limited war seeking limited objectives." It combined an infantry campaign in South Vietnam with carefully controlled and gradually escalating air attacks against the Viet Cong and North Vietnam. The bombing campaign, called Rolling Thunder, began in March 1965 and continued for four years. Its purpose was to reduce the flow of enemy supplies and to bring North Vietnam to the bargaining table. At first, bombers were limited to targets near the border between North and South Vietnam. Strikes were prohibited against most of the key strategic targets sought by the military. B-52 bombers were used in a tactical role, hitting troop units and jungle supply trails. The Strategic Air Command called it "hitting flies with a sledgehammer." The slow escalation exactly reversed everything the military believed in. It eliminated surprise and the application of decisive force. It signaled the enemy as to what was coming, permitting the North Vietnamese to move resources, build up defenses, minimize their losses, and increase American losses.

General William Momyer, who commanded the 7th Air Force in Vietnam, described the weakness of the air plan: "To wait until [the enemy] has disseminated his supplies among thousands of trucks, sampans, rafts, and bicycles, and then to send our multi-million-dollar aircraft after those individual vehicles—this is how to maximize our cost, not his."

Johnson and McNamara rejected a strategic air campaign for several reasons. Most critically, they feared that a crippling blow to North Vietnam would bring China into the war, and possibly the Soviet Union as well. Furthermore, McNamara did not believe that strategic air power could be decisive; the war would be won or lost on the ground in the south—and by the ability of South Vietnam to govern itself. Reacting to mounting political protests both at home and abroad, President Johnson repeatedly ordered bombing halts, hoping for a signal that North Vietnam would negotiate a settlement. It never came. Instead, the president noted later, the enemy used the bombing pauses to resupply its forces.

Concerned about the danger of a larger war and the antibombing protests at home, Johnson and his civilian aides picked the targets for attack. "I'm not a LeMay," he would tell visitors. "I won't let those Air Force generals bomb the smallest outhouse north of the 17th parallel without checking with me. The generals know only two words—spend and bomb."

In the nuclear age, Johnson had decided that war was too critical to be trusted to generals. From the perspective of the armed services, civilians had usurped the proper role of the military by trying to run the war themselves.

American bombers and fighters dropped far more bombs on Vietnam than the total dropped by the U.S. in World War II. The destruction was devastating, both to civilians and the enemy. In the ground war in South Vietnam, tactical air strikes were used whenever contact was made with the enemy. Yet they never stopped the ability of the North Vietnamese and the Viet Cong to fight. Except for two brief periods in 1972, strategic bombing was not employed against key targets such as the port of Haiphong. "In Japan we dropped 502,000 tons of bombs and won the war," LeMay told his biographer Thomas Coffey. "In Vietnam we dropped 6,162,000 tons and lost. The difference was [that] McNamara chose the targets in Vietnam and I chose the targets in Japan."

Whether strategic bombing could have been decisive or would instead have provoked a wider war are unanswerable questions. Some critics contend that strategic bombing could not succeed against a peasant society that did not depend on the infrastructure of modern industrial nations. Another assessment is that the communist supply lines could not have been severed, except by blowing up Soviet ships before they unloaded at Haiphong and by hitting Chinese rail shipments before they crossed the North Vietnam border. No American president would authorize such bombing raids. The military learned again, as it had in Korea, that American presidents in the nuclear era would not risk war with the Soviet Union or China.

With hindsight, it is fairly clear that the U.S. strategy of "a limited war with limited objectives" was bound to fail. It permitted North Vietnam to dictate the war's pace, and the Vietnamese had far more patience than the United States. As a proving ground for new U.S. weapons and counterinsurgency tactics, Vietnam proved a miserable failure. Given the weakness of South Vietnam and its leadership, it is probable that no American strategy, no matter how clever in theory, could have prevailed.

While the war raged in Vietnam, the Air Force continued its pursuit of a new stategic bomber. When General LeMay retired in February 1965, he told his Washington staff: "It takes a long time here to get things done; however, water wears away the stone." The Air Force followed his advice, trying to wear down or outlast McNamara, who dominated nuclear strategy in the Johnson administration as he had under President Kennedy.

In four years, McNamara's views had started to change. He had come to reject the doctrine of counterforce. American nuclear superiority was no longer so overwhelming. The Soviets in 1964 had enough second-strike capability to assure the destruction of at least 20 percent of the U.S. population and two-thirds of its industry. Even if we built new missiles and a new bomber, the USSR still could deliver unacceptable damage. The best the United States could hope for was "mutual assured destruction."

Those were the arguments McNamara used in December of 1964 in persuading Johnson to turn down the Air Force's request to develop the AMSA bomber and a new fighter interceptor, and the Army's proposal to install the Nike X antimissile system. He did, however, support one new weapon development: a missile based on a new technology called "multiple, independently targetable reentry vehicles" or MIRV. If successful, this innovation would permit a single missile to release its multiple warheads against a number of different targets.

McNamara saw MIRV as a way to hold down the total number of Minuteman missiles and to fight off the AMSA bomber. In his top-secret briefing paper to President Johnson for the December 1964 budget meeting, McNamara argued that for the same cost of AMSA, or less, the MIRV system could rain more than twice as many nuclear weapons on the Soviet Union. McNamara also saw MIRV as a hedge against Soviet development of an antiballistic missile defense system (ABM). The Soviets soon had their own MIRVed missiles. To nuclear war strategists, MIRV provided a bigger and more effective nuclear deterrent. Arms-controllers, however, saw MIRV as adding a destabilizing new dimension to the arms race, one far more ominous than a new bomber.

After LeMay's retirement, the Air Force, with a new generation of leaders, continued to press the bomber fight. The name of the game was now systems analysis, so the Air Force sent its brightest officers to graduate school to learn how to defend their most prized weapon in the same terms used by the civilian defense intellectuals. And the leadership style changed from blunt World War II warriors to men much better attuned to a corporate style of management, and to the endless bureaucratic and political infighting of Washington.

McNamara still mightily resisted a new strategic bomber. But worn down by five years of pressure from the Air Force, Congress, and industry, he decided in 1965 to offer the Air Force a new airplane. The FB-111 would be an enlarged bomber version of the F-111 fighter (the controversial TFX), which McNamara earlier had imposed on both the Air Force and the Navy. Figuring the FB-111 was better than nothing, General John P. McConnell, LeMay's successor, accepted what was at best a medium-range bomber. To reach most targets in the Soviet Union it would require at least several aerial refuelings, and could carry only a small load of nuclear weapons. The 210 FB-111s would replace 345 older B-52s and 80 B-58s, which would be retired from service.

At the December 1965 defense-budget discussion, McNamara presented President Johnson with a bargain. Transforming 210 F-111s into fighter-bombers would cost $1.5 billion, he said. Developing and building the 200 AMSA bombers sought by the Air Force would run between $9 and $11 billion. Johnson, increasingly preoccupied with the war in Vietnam and its diversion of resources from his Great Society programs, snapped up the deal.

By then, McNamara also acknowledged the need for a bomber as part of the strategic deterrent. As Soviet missile strength increased, he said, the United States should increase its own ability to guarantee "assured destruction" after taking a first strike. While still stressing that the many-headed MIRVs were our best protection, he now conceded that a force of 260 of the most modern Boeing B-52s plus the new General Dynamics FB-111s would be an extra guarantee of safety.

After seven years as secretary of defense, McNamara was replaced in early 1968 by Clark Clifford. He left the Pentagon disillusioned with how all his plans had gone awry. The limited-war strategy had failed in the Vietnam War, which he later described as "a great tragedy, both personally and for the nation." The arms race had gotten out of hand. "Our current nuclear superiority over the Soviet Union is both greater than we originally planned and in fact more than we require," he said in 1967. The cool rationalist decided that "a kind of mad momentum" drove development of ever-more-powerful nuclear weapons. He had contributed to the momentum, trading one weapon for another, using his vaunted systems analysis to get more bang for the buck. Yet to the end, he stubbornly opposed a new strategic bomber.

Because of the effect of the Vietnam War on his presidency, Lyndon Johnson announced on March 31, 1968, that he would not seek reelection. Neither modern weaponry, nor systems analysis, nor counterinsurgency tactics could defeat a determined foe fighting what was, by our standards, a primitive guerrilla war in the jungles and countryside.

Meanwhile, the almost-forgotten B-70 bomber finally took to the air. Both demonstration models flew for short periods at their designated Mach 3 speed. North American Aviation and the Air Force had accomplished a significant technical feat, and had acquired valuable new data about supersonic flight.

On June 8, 1966, at the request of the General Electric Company, the Air Force arranged a "photo opportunity" at Edwards Air Force Base in California for GE to take an advertising picture of a formation of the five Air Force planes powered by GE engines. Flying in a tight formation, the B-70 and an F-104 fighter touched wing tips. Both planes plunged to earth, killing Major Carl Cross, the B-70 copilot, and test pilot Joseph A. Walker. After years of controversy, the B-70 left the scene with a final disaster—the Air Force's collaboration in an industry publicity stunt.

The second and last B-70 bomber was flown to Wright Patterson field outside Dayton, Ohio, in January 1969, just as Richard M. Nixon became president. It went on display in front of the Air Force Systems Command's museum. Walking past the bomber every day were the Air Force officers who had been trying to design and build a new strategic bomber for fifteen years. They had been stopped by three successive presidents. Now they would try Richard Nixon.

General Curtis LeMay commanded the B-17 strategic bombers (above) that bombed Germany and the B-29s (below) that bombed Japan during World War II. Later LeMay built the Strategic Air Command into the world's most powerful nuclear force. (*Photos: USAF*)

Dutch Kindelberger and Lee Atwood (below), chairman and president of North American Aviation, built it into one of the nation's most important defense companies. Above, Kindelberger shows President Dwight Eisenhower a model of his company's F-100 fighter. (*Photos: Rockwell International*)

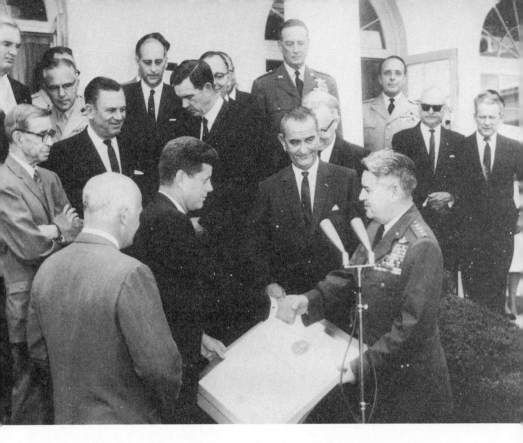

President John F. Kennedy congratulates LeMay as he is sworn in as Air Force chief of staff in 1961. Among the onlookers are Senator Stuart Symington (top left), Representative Carl Vinson (in front of him), Senator Howard Cannon (to his left), Representative George Mahon (looking down), General Thomas White (in front of pillar), General Lyman Lemnitzer (beside pillar), Vice-President Lyndon Johnson (between Kennedy and LeMay), and Air Force Secretary Eugene Zuckert (back to camera). Later LeMay bitterly fought Kennedy's decision not to build the B-70 bomber (below). (*Photos: John F. Kennedy Library, above, and USAF, below*)

Secretary of Defense Robert McNamara reports to President Johnson on progress in Vietnam. The B-52 below is shown bombing the Viet Cong in 1966. Johnson and McNamara refused the Air Force's request to build a new strategic bomber to replace the B-52. (*Photos: Lyndon B. Johnson Library, above, and USAF, below*)

President Richard Nixon approved development of the B-1; here he congratulates Air Force Chief of Staff John Ryan. Rockwell's Washington lobbyist Doc Watson (left) is shown with Senators Howard Cannon and Barry Goldwater, both ardent B-1 supporters. (*Photos: National Archives, above, and Ralph J. Watson, below*)

The advocates: Above, President Gerald Ford makes a 1976 campaign speech at Rockwell's California B-1 plant, promising to build the bomber and bring more jobs to the state. Below, Representatives Richard Ichord (left) and Robert Wilson (right) pose with John Winkel, Washington vice-president of Hughes Aircraft Co., a B-1 sub-contractor. After retiring from the House, Ichord and Wilson became lobbyists for Rockwell, Hughes, and other defense contractors. (*Photos: Gerald R. Ford Library, above, and Richard Ichord, below*)

The opponents: Above, Terry Provance, chief field organizer of the National Campaign Against the B-1 Bomber, speaking at a 1976 conference in Washington. Below, among the demonstrators at the Capitol are Michael Mann (front left), of the Campaign staff; Jeremy Stone (in the hat), of the Federation of American Scientists; and Sandy Gottlieb (right), of SANE. The opponents pressed presidental candidate Jimmy Carter to oppose building the B-1. (*Photos: Robert Brammer*)

President Carter speaks to the press at the White House, with Defense Secretary Harold Brown. After Carter canceled the B-1, Air Force Chief of Staff David Jones, below, loyally supported the commander-in-chief, refusing to lead the customary effort to overturn a negative decision on the bomber. (*Photos: Jimmy Carter Presidential Library, above, and USAF, below*)

Leaders of the congressional effort to save the B-1: Above, Senators John Tower and John Glenn; below left, Representative William Chappell; and Anthony Battista, of the House Armed Services Committee staff. (*Photos: Senate Historical Office, top left; others from the subjects*)

Air Force B-1 enthusiasts: Top left, Hans Mark, the Air Force secretary who rebelled against Carter's 1977 decision to cancel the bomber; below holding the model, General Kelly Burke, with his staff, who in 1981 won the fight to build the B-1; and top right, Air Force Chief of Staff Larry Welch, who in 1987 called it the best bomber in the world. (*Photos: USAF*)

The current players: while in the Air Force, Generals Kelly Burke, Thomas Stafford, and Guy Hecker played key roles in reviving the B-1. After retiring, they formed a consulting firm that represented Rockwell and other defense manufacturers; above, they visit the Paris Air Show. Below, President Ronald Reagan, who made the decision to build the B-1, campaigns in 1984 at the Rockwell B-1 plant, with board chairman Robert Anderson at his side. Representative Les Aspin, chairman of the House Armed Services Committee, in 1987 criticized the Air Force for producing an inadequate bomber. (*Photos: top, USAF; right, Representative Aspin; bottom, Rockwell International*)

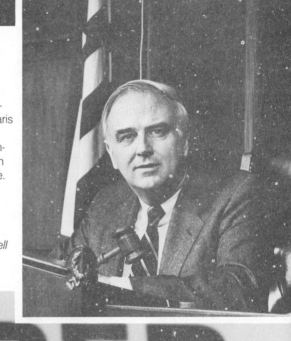

The planes: Top and right, early production models of the B-1 in flight; below, artist's rendering of the Stealth, the secret advanced-technology bomber being developed by the Northrop Corporation for the Air Force in the late 1980s. (*Photos: USAF*)

THREE

The Parable of the of the Born-Again Bomber

9

THE GREENING
OF
CALIFORNIA

President Richard Nixon set out in 1969 to achieve a series of difficult, and in some ways contradictory, goals. He sought to extract the United States from Vietnam without simply pulling out in disgrace. He worked to stay ahead in the strategic-arms race while at the same time trying to reach an arms-control agreement with the Soviet Union. Nixon wanted to reduce overall defense spending, but at the same time he had to deal with an economy wracked by the baffling concurrence of inflation and rising unemployment.

Under a policy of "Vietnamization," Nixon pulled American ground troops out of the war, but continued the air campaign—actually expanding it into Laos and Cambodia—in an effort to bring North Vietnam to a settlement. In addition, the president and Henry Kissinger, his national security adviser, sought to strengthen the U.S. position in the world through bold strokes of great-power diplomacy. They opened relations with the People's Republic of China, both to eliminate that nation as an adversary and to put pressure on the Soviet Union. They offered trade and détente with China and the Soviet Union in return for help in ending the Vietnam War. They began modernization of the U.S.

nuclear deterrent to reassert American power, and to provide bargaining chips to use in negotiating arms control with the Soviet Union.

Nixon's 1968 victory over Vice-President Hubert H. Humphrey had raised expectations in an ailing aerospace industry. "All of Mr. Nixon's statements on weapons and space are very positive," declared North American Aviation's Atwood, "I think perhaps he has a little more awareness of these things than some people we've seen in the White House."

The previous three presidents had all approved the nuclear-weapons and space programs whose contracts had built North American into a multibillion-dollar conglomerate. But North American and many other large aerospace companies faced financial crises in 1969. A drought in new strategic-weapons projects had been followed by defense cutbacks as the United States tried to disengage from Vietnam. General Dynamics, Boeing, Northrop, North American, Lockheed, Grumman—all needed work. One major contract could make the difference between hitting the top of the *Fortune* 500 or sliding close to bankruptcy. Because of a sluggish domestic economy, commercial aircraft sales had fallen sharply. In California alone, a hundred thousand aerospace workers were out of work.

North American was particularly hard hit. Production of its F-100 Super Sabre fighter had ended. Work on the Apollo space program neared completion. Efforts to sell the Sabreliner, a commercial aircraft, had gone nowhere. And the B-70 bomber project finally ended after ten years and $1.5 billion in government spending. The aircraft division had not won a new contract in eight years. It scratched along on research handouts from the Air Force for the proposed AMSA bomber.

In 1967, North American Aviation had merged with Rockwell Standard Corporation, a Pittsburgh-based manufacturer of auto parts and other machinery. Rockwell hoped to benefit from North American's high-technology skills and defense contracts. North American sought to reduce its dependency on defense. At first, the new company was called North American Rockwell; in 1973, the name became Rockwell International. Lee Atwood served as president under chairman Willard Rockwell, Jr. One of the newly merged company's first acts had been to raise thousands of dollars from its executives for Nixon's 1968 election campaign fund.

"There was an expectation that we would get something if Nixon won," recalled Gary Hillary, a Washington representative for North American Rockwell at that time.

The defense manufacturers were encouraged by Nixon's campaign pledge to overcome a "security gap," which he ascribed to the Johnson administration's failure to develop new strategic weapons. They also cheered Nixon's promise to root out the Pentagon whiz kids, McNamara's civilian aides, who had killed many weapons projects the military and industry wanted.

If the Nixon administration approved the military's requests, three major prizes beckoned: the long-sought new strategic bomber for the Air Force; a new Air Force fighter plane; and a new nuclear-powered submarine. The costs of developing, building, and maintaining those three weapon systems could reach $200 billion, a bonanza for thousands of defense contractors. Winning one of the prime contracts could keep a giant firm prosperous for fifteen years. Virtually every state in the country would benefit, with jobs for several hundred thousand workers.

Nixon gave the defense industrialists and military leaders further reason for confidence when he appointed Melvin R. Laird as secretary of defense and David Packard as deputy secretary. A Republican congressman from Wisconsin, Laird at forty-seven was one of the shrewdest politicians in Washington. As ranking Republican on the House Defense Appropriations Subcommittee, he knew the Defense Department inside out. Unlike McNamara, Secretary Laird appreciated the politics of the military-industrial process. A big, hearty man who loved the give-and-take of deal-making, Laird had fully participated in the game by which congressmen jockeyed and traded influence to win defense contracts and bases for their states and districts—and campaign contributions for themselves. Laird's large balding head soon appeared in political cartoons in the shape of a bomb or missile.

Laird's key goal was to get the U.S. out of Vietnam and to redirect the money to modernizing strategic defense. He offered the military a tantalizing deal to overcome hawkish resistance to a Vietnam withdrawal: "Live within your budgets, support me on Vietnam, and you can do what you want with your money." He returned to the military the power over weapons selection that McNamara had taken away. Virtually negotiating a treaty with the military, Laird restored the supremacy of the Joint Chiefs of

Staff in the picking of weapons. Power flowed away from Mc-Namara's Office of Systems Analysis with its civilian experts. Laird called his plan "defined decentralization."

As his deputy secretary, Laird chose industrialist David Packard. A self-made tycoon, Packard had started out as a young man tinkering in his California garage and had gone on to co-found the Hewlett-Packard Company, a phenomenally successful pioneer in computer technology.

Laird quickly divided responsibilities with Packard. Laird would deal with Congress and the Vietnam War. The tall, self-confident Packard would administer the Defense Department. He would restore harmony among the civilian leadership, the military, and industry. In running defense procurement, Packard would seek new efficiency by requiring weapons to prove themselves in research and development before they moved into production.

Packard had barely settled into his office when Air Force Chief of Staff John Ryan and Air Force Secretary Robert Seamans presented their top priority—the strategic bomber. To signify a fresh start, the Air Force now called it the B-1. In the tradition of impressive names, such as the B-17 Flying Fortress, the B-1 would be known as the Excalibur, for King Arthur's invincible sword. When someone pointed out that Excalibur was the brand name of a popular condom, the Air Force quietly dropped the name and never came up with a substitute.

The battle for the advanced manned strategic aircraft (AMSA), now officially the B-1, had gone on so long that in the Air Force the acronym was said to stand for "America's Most Studied Aircraft," or, according to critics of the plane, "Almost Solid Avionics"—in other words, crammed with electronics gear of dubious value.

John Ryan was one of a long line of SAC generals who rose to head the Air Force. He stressed to Packard the bomber's vital role in strategic defense. A "mixed force," which included bombers as well as missiles, would complicate Soviet defenses and increase American safety. With the still-remarkable B-52 fleet aging (some of the older models were fighting in Vietnam), Ryan insisted a new, more capable bomber was needed. Packard agreed.

In approving General Ryan's proposal, David Packard broke the stalemate on the strategic bomber. "How much do you need the first year?" asked Packard.

"Two hundred million dollars," replied Ryan.

"If Congress won't buy it for you, I will," joked multimillionaire Packard.

The project that won Packard's approval in 1969 was basically the same plane first requested by General Curtis LeMay in 1963. It would fly at high altitude at Mach 2.2 (about 1,500 miles per hour) and then make its attack on the Soviet Union while flying at near supersonic speed, dropping to tree-top level to avoid Soviet radar. Its wings would sweep back for supersonic speed and low-level attack, but would swing forward for takeoffs, landings, and long-distance cruising. An escape capsule would permit the entire crew to eject in a craft that could land on water or land. The B-1 would be smaller and sleeker than the B-52, yet would fly much faster, carrying nearly twice as many nuclear weapons.

Within the defense community (including quiet dissenters in the Air Force), a number of experts still questioned the need for a new bomber—particularly the costly high-performance penetrating bomber the Air Force wanted. Ivan Selin, the acting assistant secretary of defense for systems analysis, tried to convince Packard that the B-1 was too complicated and too costly for its intended nuclear mission. If a new bomber was indeed needed, Selin said, it need not be a complex supersonic plane. In fact, the same mission might be accomplished much more cheaply and effectively by a large plane standing outside the Soviet Union and firing long-range cruise missiles—tiny, pilotless drones that carried nuclear warheads. He urged that the proposed B-1 at least be simplified by reducing its speed requirements.

Packard dismissed Selin's objections and gave the Air Force its way. He agreed with Laird that decentralized decision-making worked best. It had been a key to success in his innovative company. Surely the military knew best what was needed in a bomber. Seven years was long enough to debate the AMSA concept. "We're trying to give these professional military people and service secretaries a larger say," Packard explained. "It's difficult for anyone to carry out a decision that has been imposed from above."

. . .

The Air Force lost no time. It chose three defense firms to compete for the prized contract: North American Rockwell of California and Pennsylvania, Boeing of Seattle, Washington, and General Dynamics of St. Louis, Missouri. The survival of North American Rockwell's aircraft division hung on the B-1 contract decision.

In the early days of the Nixon administration, Lee Atwood had set out to win the contract for the Air Force's new F-15 fighter. Historically, North American had built the nation's best fighters, and company officials felt certain they would win the contract. To Atwood's bitter disappointment, the F-15 contract went instead to McDonnell Douglas Corporation of St. Louis. The announcement, which came two days before Christmas in 1969, meant dismissal slips during the holiday season for thousands of North American Rockwell workers.

Board chairman Rockwell wanted to quit the B-1 competition. Rockwell and his Pittsburgh executives had had a bad first taste of defense contracting, having spent $25 million on the F-15 competition. If the nation's most respected fighter builder couldn't win the F-15 contract, Rockwell questioned, how could it possibly compete for the B-1 against Boeing, the nation's premier builder of bombers and large commercial airplanes?

But Robert Anderson, who became president when Atwood retired in January 1970, persuaded Rockwell to stay in the B-1 competition. "We can't quit," contended Anderson. "It would mean the end of the aviation division." A skeleton force agreed to work on the B-1 project at half pay. In late January 1970, North American Rockwell shipped its bid proposal to the Air Force in a 75-volume document containing 9,772 pages.

Hundreds of Air Force officers made technical evaluations of the proposals submitted by the three competitors. The final decision, however, would hinge as much on political and economic pressures as it would on merits of the proposals. To plead its case, Rockwell enlisted politicians and business and labor leaders, who testified to the economic needs of a state with 100,000 aerospace workers, including 30,000 professional engineers, out of work. In California, the company distributed thousands of flyers asking: "Where did we fail? We produced the greatest aircraft ever. We helped put a man on the moon. We competed for every last nickel." California Senator George Murphy and Governor Ronald Reagan, Republicans facing tough reelection fights in 1970, interceded for Rockwell at the Pentagon and White House.

The most effective North American Rockwell lobbyist may have been an obscure Los Angeles congressman, Glennard Lipscomb, an unpretentious former accountant whose constituency was filled with Rockwell workers. When Melvin Laird became secretary of defense, Lipscomb moved up to Laird's place as ranking Republican on the subcommittee that determined Defense Department appropriations. He and Laird remained close friends. Along with Richard Nixon, they belonged to the Chowder and Marching Society, which served as both social club and political network for conservative Republican congressmen. While the Nixon administration considered the competing proposals, Lipscomb phoned or met with Laird fifteen times. He unabashedly pled sheer economic need: North American Rockwell represented an important part of the nation's defense industrial base. Without the contract, its aircraft division would fail.

Laird and Packard were sympathetic. Rockwell had entered the B-1 competition in the first place only because of the encouragement of David Packard. In the midst of the F-15 fight, Packard told Atwood that North American Rockwell should submit a bid for the B-1.

Before the B-1 contract was awarded, North American Rockwell's Anderson went to Packard to present his company's case. During their conversation, Packard discussed the health of the aerospace industry. He noted that Boeing "was in good shape" with the B-747 transport, McDonnell Douglas now had the F-15, and General Dynamics would build the Trident. Anderson was encouraged by the conversation to think that Rockwell's turn would come next—to build the bomber.

In Packard's view, any of the three top contenders would be able to build the B-1. "You could just throw darts at a board and pick the winner," he said later. Packard was concerned not only about building a good bomber but about the perilous financial condition of several major aerospace firms. He thought it was important to maintain the nation's defense-industrial base.

The government continued its unstated policy of spreading contracts around to maintain the economic health of all the major defense contractors. Multiple objectives were served: keeping aerospace workers employed, politicians happy, and the defense-industrial base intact.

President Nixon and his key White House aides concurred in the Rockwell choice. Equally important in their consideration was appreciation that North American Rockwell had paid its political dues in the 1968 campaign. In the view of one high-ranking Nixon administration official, politics was decisive. "That Rockwell got the nod was no accident," he recalled later. "Rockwell had the inside track due to political contributions."

Senator Murphy announced the prize contract award on June 5, 1970. At his side stood a jubilant Ralph J. (Doc) Watson, North American Rockwell's Washington lobbyist. Murphy described the $1.35 billion contract in terms of its economic impact: it would produce 43,000 jobs in California alone, as well as work for 7,000 subcontractors throughout the country. If the government later decided to produce the Air Force's requested force of 240 bombers, the contract would exceed $10 billion, making it the largest weapons procurement program in history. The next day's *Los Angeles Times* ran a banner head: 43,000 NEW JOBS. A relieved Willard Rockwell told *Fortune* magazine, "We knew as a company we had just one more chance."

In Washington state, however, the news brought bitter disappointment. Boeing immediately laid off workers, and Republican Representative Thomas Pelly demanded a congressional inquiry into the means by which North American Rockwell had won the contract. The Air Force responded that it had the lowest bid and highest rating in the contract review.

Others in Congress challenged the bomber itself. Their criticism signaled a new attitude about defense programs. In the past, men like Carl Vinson and Richard Russell ruled like monarchs over the defense committees they chaired. Most congressmen quietly went along. Unless they served on the defense committees, most legislators were cut off from the information needed even to question a weapons system. That data was controlled by the tight inner circle of military officers, congressional defense committees, and defense experts from the executive branch, industry, and the academic think tanks who together made the decisions.

Dissension over the Vietnam War, though, promoted change in congressional handling of defense policy. Decisions handed down from the White House, the Pentagon, and the congressional defense establishment no longer were sacrosanct. Questions about the war, and protests against it, led to questions about the value of strategic defense programs whose costs ran into the billions.

The first major challenge from the floor of Congress came in 1970, over development of an antiballistic missile (ABM). To the surprise of the traditional military-industrial decision-makers, the Senate almost defeated the proposed ABM, the Safeguard. The vote was 51 to 50, with Vice-President Spiro T. Agnew casting the tie-breaking vote. A bipartisan group of legislators who opposed the Vietnam War and the ABM then formed a group called Members of Congress for Peace through Law (MCPL). They found their own military experts and assigned teams to monitor new weapons programs.

In 1971 MCPL chose Representative John Seiberling, a Democrat from Akron, Ohio, and Senator George McGovern, a South Dakota Democrat, to prepare a report on the B-1 bomber. McGovern had flown a B-24 bomber in World War II. He advocated a complete American withdrawal from Vietnam and redirection of defense spending to social programs at home. Planning to run for president in 1972, George McGovern staked out his ground as a peace candidate. Heir to an Akron tire fortune, Seiberling had pledged during his 1970 campaign to work not only for American disengagement from Vietnam, but also for the diversion of weapons money to fight poverty and rebuild America's decaying cities.

McGovern and Seiberling concluded in their study for MCPL that the B-52 still could fill the strategic-deterrent bomber role. For its eventual replacement, they favored a less costly standoff bomber capable of firing long-range cruise missiles.

The Air Force reacted quickly to the challenge, inviting Seiberling to a top-secret briefing at SAC headquarters outside Omaha. He was accompanied by his administrative assistant Don Mansfield, a retired bomber pilot who had quit the Air Force because he opposed the Vietnam War. Mansfield doubted the B-1's ability to penetrate the Soviet Union in the midst of a nuclear war.

After Air Force briefing officers described how the B-1 would

fly a typical mission, Seiberling asked searching questions about
the plane's performance. The answers did not reassure him. The
B-1's Mach 2.2 supersonic speed requirement, for example, greatly
increased the cost of the plane, but could virtually never be used
because it would consume too much fuel. Finally, the briefer fell
back on the service's appeal of last resort. "If nothing else," the
general said, "this plane will force the Soviets to spend billions of
dollars to defend against it."

Seiberling laughed. "That reminds me," he said, "of the story
of the farmer who described to a friend how he bought pigs in the
spring for $4 and sold them in the fall for $4. 'You can't make any
money that way,' said the farmer's friend. 'That's what I found
out,' said the farmer." Seiberling's point: How could the United
States make any net gain if we wasted billions of dollars that
otherwise could be more usefully invested, just to get the Soviets
to do the same thing?

Meanwhile, Robert Anderson, the new president of North
American Rockwell, requested an urgent meeting with McGovern
at which he implored the senator to support the B-1 program as
"a compassionate Democrat." If the bomber were scrapped, he
said, thousands of workers would be forced into the growing ranks
of the unemployed.

McGovern responded with the ideas of his liberal anti-war
candidacy. "Wouldn't you rather build public transportation systems than bombers?" he asked.

"Sure," replied a smiling Anderson. "Can you get me a contract?"

McGovern knew that he could not. As a practical matter, any
defense cuts after Vietnam would go to reducing the deficit.

And the defense firms themselves showed little enthusiasm
for switching to risky new ventures in the commercial marketplace. Asked in 1969 about the conditions under which North
American Rockwell would build high-speed ground transportation systems, aerospace group president John R. Moore responded:
"If the government provided the risk capital, and if the vehicle
contained enough technology or patentable elements so that we
could close out other producers, and if we could market it, then it
would be viable." The hypothetical situation described by Moore
existed only in the Defense Department's sole-source weapons
contracts.

. . .

The small ripples of congressional opposition presented little threat to the B-1 bomber program. What worried President Nixon, however, were warnings from within his own administration that the plane might become a political disaster.

In-house opposition to the B-1 came from several quarters, including the office of Richard Stubbing, a young budget examiner in the White House's Office of Management and Budget (OMB). A graduate of Notre Dame with an advanced degree from the Harvard Business School, Stubbing served in 1970 as OMB budget examiner for Air Force programs.

Stubbing observed an intriguing pattern in defense-contract awards: companies that failed in commercial aerospace ventures subsequently reaped rewards from the government. After Lockheed failed with its L-1011 passenger jet, it won the contract for the Air Force's giant C-5 transport plane. General Dynamics failed with its Convair 440, and was then given the F-111 fighter contract. Douglas faced disaster with its DC-10 airliner but was saved by a government contract to produce the same plane as the KC-10 refueling tanker. And now, North American Rockwell, a failure with its commercial Sabreliner, had won the B-1 contract. In all these defense contracts, the principal loser was Boeing. Because Boeing was successful in building commercial jets, the government didn't feel it needed the support of government airplane contracts.

Stubbing became the point man in a 1970 effort within the Nixon administration to stop the B-1 bomber in its relatively inexpensive infancy. He coordinated the paper flow as the OMB, the Office of Systems Analysis in the Pentagon, the National Security Council (NSC) staff, and the White House Office of Science and Technology joined forces to oppose the bomber. The agencies unanimously recommended that Nixon cancel the B-1 development project. The civilian analysts predicted that the plane would cost twice the Air Force's estimate, and that its performance had been overstated by 50 percent. At a minimum, they recommended redesigning the B-1 to eliminate its most expensive, least useful features. Walter Slocombe, an NSC staff member, called the paper he wrote for the White House's Defense Program Review Committee "The B-1 Bomber—Nixon's TFX"—a reference to the political and technical problems that plagued the Kennedy administration with the TFX/F-111 program. Slocombe warned that the B-1 had a "fiasco potential of tremendous proportions" in terms of development problems and costs.

Top White House officials informed Nixon that the Air Force estimate of $8 to $10 billion for 240 B-1s was ridiculously low. In a memorandum, White House aide Peter Flanigan noted that North American Rockwell itself said the bombers would cost $20 to $25 billion, while John Foster, the Defense Department director of research and engineering, estimated the ultimate cost at $37 to $40 billion.

After listening to his skeptical advisors, including OMB Director George Shultz and White House science adviser Edward David, President Nixon seriously considered stopping the B-1 program. In late 1970, he requested that the Pentagon make a new analysis, reconsidering the bomber program. To the Air Force's dismay, it looked as though Nixon was about to adopt the negative view of the three previous presidents.

When he learned that Nixon was backing off from the B-1, Deputy Defense Secretary Packard became livid. For a year he had resisted opposition to the bomber within the administration. (One critic he sent packing was James Schlesinger—an OMB assistant director who would later become secretary of defense.) Opposition from the president was a far more serious matter.

At Laird's urging, Packard met with Nixon. He bluntly told the president he would resign if the plane was canceled. Realizing the Pentagon's determination, and seeing a nasty confrontation in the making, Nixon called off the bomber review. He told Laird he could keep the B-1 development program rolling. After all, research and development were relatively inexpensive. The decision about actual production could still be deferred.

As White House concerns shifted in 1971, Nixon and his top aides soon began looking at the B-1 from an entirely different perspective. From being considered in 1970 as a costly, questionable military weapon, the B-1 suddenly became transformed by the spring of 1971 into a necessary economic asset and potent political weapon. It figured in two secret political operations integral to Nixon's 1972 reelection strategy. One aimed to create more defense-industry jobs; the other, to raise vast sums of campaign money.

John Ehrlichman, President Nixon's chief domestic adviser, believed a Republican victory in the southern and southwestern Sun Belt states was essential to Nixon's reelection. And the key to sweeping the Sun Belt was restoring economic vitality in that region. All the prospective Democratic candidates were lambasting Nixon for the nation's high rate of unemployment. Ehrlichman looked at unemployment numbers, keyed them to battleground states, and saw that an increase in aerospace employment would create jobs most quickly in those states.

Out of Ehrlichman's strategy, the White House in 1971 conceived a plan known to some administration officials as "Keep California Green." Nixon expected California, with its forty-five electoral votes, to be critical in 1972. Unemployment was the main issue that could hurt the president, and unemployment in California had reached a thirteen-year high of 7.5 percent. Nationwide, 1,253,000 defense industry workers, including 207,000 in the aircraft industry, had lost their jobs since the peak Vietnam spending year of 1969. The Nixon administration's own budget-cutting efforts, aimed at fighting inflation, had compounded the problem with a two-year, $9 billion reduction in the Pentagon budget.

In the irrational world of defense politics, the White House now would cut defense spending in some areas to deal with inflation, and at the same time boost defense spending in others to meet another goal—the president's reelection.

"Keep California Green" laid out a plan to attack unemployment by pouring more money into defense contracts within the state. (As it applied to other parts of the country, the plan was known as the Industrial State Unemployment Project.) The plan was coordinated out of the White House by Peter Flanigan, a former Wall Street investment banker who served as Nixon's political emissary to the business community. Defense contractors were on his list. In April 1971, John Rose, a young attorney working for Flanigan, drew up "an action plan" with an ambitious goal: to create 100,000 new defense jobs in California by Labor Day 1972.

Nixon administration officials, among them Assistant OMB

Director William Howard Taft IV, combed every inch of the defense budget for programs where new jobs could be added, especially defense contracts that could be padded without requiring new authorization from Congress. Particularly attractive was any program that could employ the high-paid defense workers who were most likely to vote Republican. In the bureaucratic jargon of one White House memorandum, the aim was "development of governmental and private sector programs of high-skill employment (e.g., aerospace plus electronics engineers)." The emphasis was on "short-term high-employment programs." In September 1971, the campaign strategists considered closing nine East Coast military bases and moving the personnel to California.

In his eagerness to create California aerospace jobs, White House aide Rose pushed projects which even his superiors thought were too expensive. In a memorandum, Rose argued for an early start building seven B-747 command-post aircraft. Even though it would cost $128 million in 1972 to create only 800 California jobs, Rose contended to Flanigan and OMB Deputy Director Caspar Weinberger that the jobs would provide the president with important political credit in California.

Indeed, the White House did create thousands of short-term jobs, by injecting new funds into dozens of research-and-development projects. Some ended after the 1972 election, but in the meantime virtually every major defense contractor in California, including North American Rockwell, benefited in some way. The company's main reward from "Keep California Green" was iron-clad protection against further attacks on the B-1 bomber. The bomber project became untouchable.

Other administrations had manipulated defense spending in presidential election years—Eisenhower's last-minute revival of the B-70 in 1960, for example—but none matched the sophistication and thoroughness of "Keep California Green."

Ernest Fitzgerald, a civilian Air Force cost analyst later fired by Nixon for his whistle-blowing on defense waste, knew what was happening. Just as "Keep California Green" got under way in the spring of 1971, Fitzgerald pronounced the B-1 "a bigger boondoggle" than the C-5A (an Air Force transport notorious for cost overruns, technical defects, and politics aimed at helping the ailing Lockheed). The B-1 contract was awarded, said Fitzgerald bluntly, "to make jobs for southern California."

As the 1972 election approached, Nixon nervously watched the California unemployment statistics and asked for progress reports on "Keep California Green" from his top aides, Robert Haldeman and John Ehrlichman, and from administration officials including George Shultz.

Responding to Nixon's worry over a report that defense-equipment orders had dropped off, Shultz wrote the president a confidential memorandum on March 28, 1972, reassuring him that "defense activity has . . . now begun to increase," and that "our programs to stimulate the defense area are starting to have an impact." Less than two weeks later, Weinberger reassured Haldeman that California "employment is up 96,000 over comparable figures in March of last year." California seemed to be turning green according to plan.

Another old political practice achieved its ultimate refinement in the 1972 election. With a boldness and zeal unmatched in previous campaigns, the Nixon reelection team, headed by John Mitchell and Maurice Stans (who had resigned their posts as attorney general and commerce secretary), set out to raise a $60 million campaign war chest. Methodically working their way through the *Fortune* 500 list, Mitchell, the general campaign chairman, and Stans, the finance chairman, requested millions of dollars in secret campaign contributions from America's largest corporations. They focused particular attention on the chief executive officers of defense contractors and other companies dependent on the federal government for direct business or favorable regulatory decisions. Stans and Mitchell were not bashful about citing specific upcoming federal decisions, nor were the company executives reluctant to talk about their interests in various federal contracts.

When Stans and Mitchell solicited Willard Rockwell, Jr., for a major contribution in 1971, his company was not only fighting to keep the new B-1 program alive, but was competing for another prize, the contract to build the space shuttle for NASA. Rockwell understood that the Nixon emissaries expected his corporation to contribute a minimum quota to the campaign. He set out expeditiously to raise it. Rockwell contributed $135,000 through its Voice in Politics Club, in which its executives were asked to contribute up to 1.5 percent of their income to "the candidate of your choice." The candidate of everyone's choice was Richard M. Nixon. Following directions from Nixon headquarters, Rockwell helped the Nixon campaign disguise its political war chest and evade legal limits on campaign gifts. Dozens of checks were written to such innocuous-sounding Nixon fronts as Citizens for Improved Government and Citizens for a Better America.

Secrecy also protected corporations that met their quotas by using corporate funds illegally. The secret contributions would be prohibited after April 7, 1972, when a strict new campaign-disclosure law went into effect. Racing to beat the deadline, North American Rockwell vice-president James Daniell hurried on April 6 to the Nixon campaign headquarters at 1701 Pennsylvania Avenue, across from the White House. There, Daniell delivered his last big batch of checks to campaign treasurer Hugh Sloan. When Daniell later sent Sloan other checks, he enclosed a note saying they were in "partial payment of our pledge."

Richard Nixon knew exactly how much he had received from the country's major corporations. The only record of $20 million in secret gifts was kept in the desk drawer of Rose Mary Woods, his personal secretary. Reviewing his benefactors, the president would find listed more than $3 million in secret contributions from defense contractors, including Rockwell's $135,000 in gifts, $98,300 of which was recorded simply as from "Employees of North American Rockwell."

Investigations of the Watergate special prosecutor later revealed that many corporations had made illegal contributions, some of which were used in the Watergate burglary coverup. But the prosecutor found no evidence that North American Rockwell's campaign gift from about six hundred company executives had been collected illegally.

Nixon kept up with the status of the major defense contracts. At a chance restaurant meeting with North American Rockwell lobbyist John Rane, the president offered an encouraging "Hang in there on that bomber." Speaking with Willard Rockwell at a gathering of business executives invited to Camp David, he volunteered, "I'm sorry I can't do more business with you on the B-1." Rockwell was puzzled. He did not know that the White House at that moment was reconsidering its B-1 decision. Rockwell thought the president had done just fine.

But in May of 1972, the North American Rockwell chairman learned that the space-shuttle contract might be slipping out of his grasp to the Grumman Corporation, with its Long Island plants. In terms of electoral votes, New York also was a crucial state, and Grumman a not-insignificant player in Republican defense politics. Willard Rockwell and Robert Anderson met with Flanigan to discuss the contract award. Rockwell told one Nixon aide that his company had made the low bid and deserved the contract. "If politics is going to be played on this thing," Rockwell said, "I have a few tickets around and will ask for some help."

North American Rockwell won the contract. When his White House contact then asked Willard Rockwell to share part of the contract with Grumman, he graciously complied. Grumman got to build the shuttle wings, a lucrative second-place prize worth several hundred million dollars. In the now-familiar manner, another huge defense contract was carved up with careful attention to politics and the economic health of various aerospace companies.

While his aides built his secret campaign war chest and manipulated the defense contracts, Richard Nixon achieved a far loftier triumph, the signing on May 26, 1972, of the first strategic arms limitation agreement (SALT I) and antiballistic missile (ABM) treaty with the Soviet Union. The agreements prohibited both nations from deploying anything but token antiballistic missile forces and placed a limit on offensive nuclear weapons for five years. It also kicked off a new round of politics over the B-1 bomber.

Once the SALT agreement was signed, a group of senators led by J. William Fulbright, chairman of the Senate Foreign Relations Committee, questioned spending billions on new strategic weapon systems at the very moment the country had agreed to limit nuclear weapons. At that point, Defense Secretary Laird bluntly announced the quid pro quo of arms control. Unless Congress approved strategic modernization with the B-1 and Trident, said Laird, neither he nor the Joint Chiefs of Staff would support the SALT agreement. Laird said that not to build those weapons would be "to raise the white flag of surrender."

As in the Kennedy administration, an arms-control agreement came at a price. One nuclear threat would be limited, but only at the cost of expanding the arms race in other areas. Nixon refused to bargain on any of the new weapons, including the multiple-warhead MIRV missile. Congress not only approved the B-1 and Trident programs; it eagerly added $797 million in requested additional defense spending, aimed at boosting employment. The president was not the only politician facing reelection.

In 1971 and 1972 the politics of defense produced something for everyone. Those who favored arms control were grateful for an agreement that at least halted antiballistic missiles. The Air Force had its new bomber going. The beleaguered aerospace companies and their workers found renewed prosperity. The United States maintained its lead in the nuclear arms race. While news reports focused on the arms-control agreement, the Nixon administration quietly began installing the multiple-warhead MIRV missile. Richard Nixon won reelection, trouncing Senator George McGovern, sweeping every state but Massachusetts and the District of Columbia.

Finally, American participation in the Vietnam War ended in January 1973, after the Air Force belatedly got a brief chance at the strategic bombing it had recommended nine years earlier. From December 18 through 29, 1972, B-52s pounded the port of Haiphong and targets around Hanoi in an operation called Linebacker II. Air Force partisans proclaimed that the so-called Christmas raids "won the war," proving the value of strategic air power. Others noted that the United States lost fifteen B-52s in the first four days of the raids, and that the United States gained no concessions in the treaty signed three weeks later in Paris.

News of possible White House involvement in a break-in at the headquarters of the Democratic National Committee in the Watergate office building in June 1972 had caused a few newspaper headlines, but for the moment the president seemed fully in command.

10

THE
GOLDPLATED
BOMBER

Good times returned to Antelope Valley. With the B-1 bomber in full development, men and women hurried down from small towns in the majestic high country to work in the production hangars looming over the Mojave desert. Southern California's long aerospace drought ended in 1970 as Rockwell hired workers at the huge Palmdale plant, forty miles northeast of Los Angeles.

At the Palmdale factory and at Rockwell's design headquarters near the Los Angeles Airport, fourteen thousand workers tackled an immense challenge: to transform an Air Force vision into reality. The Air Force did not want just another airplane; the B-1 must be extraordinary: it must fly farther and faster than any other bomber, carry an unprecedented forty tons of nuclear weapons, take off quickly from modest-sized runways, perform difficult maneuvers, and protect its crew with unusual safety features. Most important, this bomber had to penetrate the heart of the Soviet Union, overcoming the most sophisticated defenses.

This ideal bomber would be a flying temple to enshrine the Air Force ethos: the dominance of strategic air power. Air Force leaders had been fighting to build such a bomber for more than a decade. Their B-1 would silence those who believed that the bomber was an anachronism in the age of missiles.

Developing a major new weapons system in the nuclear age is no small feat. By definition, a new weapon must advance the state of the art and be able to counter a specific enemy threat. The problem, of course, is that Soviet military technology is also constantly evolving, so strategists and designers must try to read the future. But the gestation period of something as complex as a new strategic bomber can easily be ten years or more. If the strategists guess wrong, today's brilliant technological breakthrough will be obsolete even before the first production model takes to the air.

Difficulties of all kinds—holdups, setbacks, cost miscalculations—are expected in the development of any new weapon. But the B-1 may have been in trouble from the start because so much was asked of it. The specifications laid down by the Air Force were extremely ambitious—meant to answer every possible need and desire. Critics, appalled by the range of the desires, labeled it the "goldplated bomber." North American Rockwell faced tremendous, perhaps impossible, challenges to meet the plane's performance standards, technical requirements, cost estimates, and schedule.

Even in the early stages of development, warning signals were raised from Air Force officers monitoring progress at the Rockwell factory. These officers worked for the Air Force Systems Command, whose aeronautical division at Wright Patterson Field in Dayton, Ohio, supervised development and production of new aircraft. With the project under way for barely a year, plant monitors warned their Dayton headquarters of a project in disarray. The B-1 was not meeting its performance goals, was behind schedule, and was running over cost. Rockwell was defensive and evasive about the problems.

The Air Force field office reported one instance in which a Rockwell employee, a retired Air Force colonel, threatened a young captain monitoring the project, implying that he could hurt the captain's career advancement if he didn't cease his criticisms. This retired colonel was one of hundreds of officers who had gone through the "revolving door," many of them working in industry on the same projects they had served as officers.

Plant representatives soon learned that their critical reports to Dayton headquarters were not appreciated. In fact, Major General Douglas Nelson, the B-1 program director, gave the press and Congress glowing pictures of a program on schedule and below cost. The Air Force monitors at Palmdale wondered if he was describing the same plane on which they reported so many problems.

Then the Dayton command ordered officers at the plant to correct deficiencies in their reporting system. They should stop relaying bad news about the B-1 in their official reports, which might fall into the hands of the B-1's congressional critics or budget monitors in Washington. They were instructed to find other means of reporting problems, such as private letters.

Colonel Earl A. Hoag, the chief plant representative at Rockwell, agreed to tighten the distribution list of the monthly B-1 status reports. He even agreed to tone down the "tenor and substance of the report." But he couldn't resist asking headquarters, "What deficiency are we endeavoring to overcome?" He thought the "deficiencies" were with Rockwell and the airplane, not with the reporting system.

The Air Force plant reps felt that their reports should be thorough and, if necessary, negative. As one of them later wrote, "those in the highest levels of government" could not make wise decisions about the B-1's future unless "they were building on a basis of truth." These officers failed to appreciate that in defense politics, "truth" is sometimes avoided to ward off critics intent on scuttling a program.

The Air Force decided to deal with the critical reports by eliminating the messenger bearing bad news. The "messenger" was Lieutenant Colonel Thomas H. Hobbs, manager of the B-1's Cost Schedule Control System, who edited the monthly status reports sent from the factory to headquarters.

A West Point graduate with a master's degree in aeronautical engineering, Hobbs was a decorated hero of Korea and Vietnam. In 1972, suddenly and without explanation, he was removed from his monitoring job at Rockwell and assigned to an empty office with nothing to do. His "outstanding" officer efficiency rating report was downgraded by the Dayton command, and he was denied the promotion to full colonel recommended by his commanding officer. Eleven months later, Hobbs retired from the Air Force rather than accept transfer to a job with a helicopter unit in Missouri, a job assignment far below his rank and outside his experience.

Tom Hobbs had served the Air Force and his country through a career of unusual breadth and achievement. After the Korean conflict, he specialized in the management of the most sensitive nuclear-missile development programs. He volunteered for flight duty in Vietnam, where he won the Distinguished Flying Cross and ten Air Medals. He also volunteered for hazardous test-flight work. With the same meticulous sense of duty, he had reported deficiencies in the B-1 development program.

The Air Force's treatment of this talented leader sent a clear message to junior officers: pointing out defects in the B-1 program could be hazardous to one's career. In the upper echelons of the Air Force, the political expediency necessary to get a strategic bomber overrode the requirement for tough management of the project. Conscientious colonels at Palmdale and even generals in the Pentagon had to learn the lesson and get on board.

According to its contract, Rockwell received a profit fee based on the quality of its work. Lieutenant General Otto Glosser, Air Force deputy chief of staff for research, development, and acquisition, headed the fee-award committee that judged Rockwell's performance. After making a plant visit to Palmdale, where he got a first-hand look at the many deficiencies that remained uncorrected, Glosser recommended payment of less than 40 percent of the maximum fee.

Back in Washington, an assistant secretary of the Air Force rebuked the general. "What the hell are you trying to do, kill the program?" he asked. "How do you think this is going to look to Congress?" The assistant secretary had a realistic concern. Fervent opponents of the B-1 in Congress lay in wait for bad news to use against the bomber. Glosser was overruled; Rockwell received 95 percent of its allowable fee for work completed.

The Air Force approached the B-1 as if it had learned little from the failure of its two earlier efforts to develop a replacement for the B-52 Superfortress. The debacles of both the B-58 Hustler and B-70 Valkyrie indicated the limits of an exaggerated emphasis on technological innovation. Each achieved dazzling supersonic speed, but fell victim to technical failures, high costs, and inability to perform their strategic mission well.

Despite two costly experiences, the Air Force leaders were undeterred. Strategic Air Command generals dominated the Air Force. Most were pilots by background, with little knowledge of aeronautical engineering; they were awed by technology, having experienced the magical feats that man and machine can accomplish together in the sky. SAC bomber pilots, taunted as "trash haulers" by the non-SAC fighter pilots flaunting their flashy supersonic planes, wanted to reach higher and faster into the wild blue yonder. And the Air Force as a whole felt driven to demolish all the criticisms that bombers were outmoded in the age of cheaper, faster intercontinental missiles. If a new plane showed only a small improvement over the B-52, critics would say it wasn't worth the cost. Carl Covington, a Defense Department official involved for years with the bomber's development, summed it up: "The Air Force wanted a bomber that would do everything." And everything is what it called for.

The B-1 bomber's demanding requirements had been basically established in a six-month 1963 study by Colonel David C. Jones and Lieutenant Colonel James Allen. Neither of these bright Pentagon aides had any experience designing airplanes. They didn't approach their assignment from a technical or engineering viewpoint. As pilots, they thought more about how they wanted the plane to fly than about what might be the best way to accomplish the bomber mission. They had a mandate from Curtis LeMay, then Air Force chief of staff, who carried on his crusade to get a "manned missile" that could silence bomber critics like Robert McNamara.

The 1963 Jones-Allen study started the long, complex process by which the Air Force builds a new weapon. The two officers drew up the initial requirements (mockingly called "desirements" by critics of the system) of what the plane should do. Once the different air commands approved the requirements, industry was asked to submit preliminary design proposals. After many rounds of feasibility studies, the industry would bid on a research-and-development contract to build and test a few prototype planes. If the plane proved worthy, production would be approved. From 1970 to 1976, Rockwell and the Air Force struggled on the research and development, trying to turn 1963 desires into reality.

Industry executives and engineers did nothing to discourage the Air Force in its ambitious requirements. Industry wanted the contracts and the Air Force wanted the plane. Given enough time and money, many aeronautical engineers believed that virtually anything could be done in the space age.

In an illustrious career, Harrison Storms, Rockwell's chief engineer, had introduced dramatic improvements to the fabled P-51 Mustang, had designed the Apollo capsule that went to the moon, had helped figure out how the B-70 could fly at Mach 3, and now worked on the B-1 design. Storms and his colleagues relished working at the edge of the technological frontier. Costs and delays were minor matters for the politicians to worry about. Not one aerospace company is known to have suggested at the outset that any of the B-1's requirements would create serious problems. Once the contract was landed, the problems could be handled, they hoped.

Rockwell's contract award in 1970 was based on a bid of $1.35 billion for research and development, including construction of five experimental planes. General Electric received another $406 million to develop the engines. But these figures were only crude estimates. No one at Rockwell or in the Air Force could accurately predict how much it would cost or how long it would take to develop a plane with features that had yet to be invented, much less built and tested.

Development costs were only the beginning. Actually building the proposed fleet of 240 B-1s would cost much more—even the first Air Force estimates in 1970 put the cost at nearly $9 billion. Billions more would be required to maintain and operate them. Even in an era of astronomical defense budgets, a strategic bomber could swallow up a large chunk of the funds allocated to new weapons.

By 1973 the Systems Command no longer could keep a lid on the technical and cost problems in Palmdale. The General Accounting Office reported that the plane was behind schedule and lacked any reasonable cost controls or estimates. Critical performance standards had been reduced, including range and takeoff distance. After three years of development, the estimated cost per bomber had risen from $27 million to $50 million. The Air Force was finally shaken enough by criticism from Congress and the Defense Department to bring in new people to direct the program. They demanded that Rockwell do the same.

Rockwell chose as its new B-1 program manager Bastian (Buzz) Hello, an aeronautical engineer who had directed the company's Apollo launch operations at Cape Canaveral. A native of Philadelphia and graduate of the University of Maryland, the soft-spoken Hello was a talented technician as well as a skilled manager. Working on the Apollo project, he inspired workers to solve tough problems. All his abilities would be needed at Palmdale.

Hello soon discovered why Rockwell was having so much difficulty producing the first experimental B-1. The sleek four-engine plane looked simple—more like a graceful fighter than a lumbering B-52. But looks were deceptive. The plane was expected to perform feats requiring complex—sometimes incompatible—systems. The B-1 was supposed to fly high at Mach 2.2—and attack almost at treetop level, just below Mach 1. The low-level attacks, presumably skimming underneath Soviet radar, would need a sophisticated terrain-following radar-navigation system. The plane would be loaded with other intricate new defensive and offensive avionics—electronic equipment designed to help it avoid enemy attackers and search out its targets. It was supposed to have a range of 6,000 miles, allowing it to penetrate the far reaches of the Soviet Union and then escape quickly to a safe haven. It was equipped with an intricate escape capsule, rather than traditional ejection seats. The B-1 had to be able to carry a heavy load of nuclear bombs and short-range missiles. Finally, in order to escape an enemy missile attack at home, this 190-ton behemoth also was expected to lift off the ground using less than 6,000 feet of runway.

All these requirements created inherent contradictions. Every aircraft design involves tradeoffs among requirements for speed, range, and payload weight. High speeds take more fuel and detract from range, particularly at low altitudes. The heavier the load, the larger the plane and the engines must be. The bigger the engines, the more fuel they consume. Planes were best designed to fly well at either high or low altitudes, not both.

The Air Force decided that the B-1's requirements could be met

THE PARABLE OF THE BORN-AGAIN BOMBER

only by a plane with variable-sweep wings—wings that could be locked in various positions. For takeoffs, the wings would be fully extended forward for maximum lift. They could then be swept back for smooth, fast low-level flight, and extended again for high-altitude cruising. If a goose can do it, why not a B-1?

No one had ever designed a swing wing for a huge bomber (although they were already in use on the F-111 fighter). It involved building huge hinges, on a scale never before attempted. If the plane was to take off from most Air Force runways, it would need an afterburner for the extra thrust to lift it off the ground. This meant giving the engine a great deal more power than was needed at cruising speed. A variable air inlet—an expensive and complicated device—had to be improvised to control air flow in supersonic flight.

The problems with the swing wings might have been foreseen and avoided from the outset. As far back as 1966, Air Force Colonel James Boyd, one of the developers of the fixed-wing F-15 fighter, had argued that the variable-sweep wing was a flawed idea. What it added to the plane's flexibility, he maintained, was more than lost in added weight and complexity, not to mention expense. General McConnell, the Air Force chief of staff, told Boyd to explain his theory to the Air Force team working on the specifications for the B-1. They ignored his advice.

Other dissenting voices also were ignored. Air Force Lieutenant Generals Glenn Kent and Otto Glosser and Brigadier General Jasper Welch had all argued for stripping the plane of its goldplating. The supersonic requirement made little sense to them. So much fuel would be consumed at high speed that the B-1 could make only a brief supersonic sprint—which might help the crew escape a momentary danger, but could not take them far. Without the supersonic requirement, the B-1 would not need complex swing wings. Overall costs could thus be cut by 25 to 40 percent. Other gains would be reduced weight, greater range, and a shorter development schedule. Glosser had won only one point: the bomber was no longer required to fly at supersonic speed at tree-top level.

Glosser, who headed the fee-award committee, had earned a degree from Cornell in aeronautical engineering and a graduate degree from Ohio State in electronic physics. He had managed the

Atlas and Minuteman missile programs. But the top Air Force leaders, with experience mostly as pilots, didn't think he knew as much as they did about airplanes. In his own mind, Glosser finally realized that the B-1 represented a graphic example of what happens when powerful people become obsessed with an idea such as the ultimate supersonic bomber. They will ignore all scientific evidence that doesn't fit their idea, and they will persuade other people to go along with them—or force them to.

Glenn Kent, who tried to warn in 1960 about the high-altitude vulnerability of the B-70, was the Air Force's prize maverick. He started out as a high-school basketball coach in Colorado, joined the Air Corps in World War II, and served as a weather officer. Afterwards, with graduate degrees from Harvard and the University of California, Kent became the Air Force's most provocative intellectual. He stood his ground against the Kennedy-Johnson whiz kids, using their own analytical systems. And he dared to disagree with anyone, including Curtis LeMay. When accused of "never backing the Air Force position," the slim, feisty Kent replied, "I always back the Air Force position, once I decide what it is."

To save money, simplify the plane, and save valuable time, Kent tried to convince the B-1 designers to use a navigation system already developed for the A-7 attack plane. In response, Systems Command bureaucrats changed the specifications for the B-1's guidance system so the A-7's system couldn't meet it.

The Air Force tolerated only a very few men like Kent and Glosser, recognizing their brainpower, but it did not welcome their suggestions about simplifying the B-1. They were among the rare officers who would stand up to peer pressure to fight for a more practical bomber.

Kent believed that the basic flaw in Air Force weapons design came from a misplaced notion at the outset. The Air Force started out setting down rigid and glamorous requirements, especially for high speed, then stubbornly refused to reconsider them. Decide the mission first, said Kent, then flexibly design aircraft specifications to meet it. Instead of competing with the ICBM mission, Kent thought the bomber could perform other useful tasks, including an attack on Soviet troops massed for attack. Flying twice the speed of sound wasn't needed for that mission, nor was it needed for an insurance-policy role in the strategic nuclear deterrent. But the original desirements stood, virtually unmodified.

With time, and at great cost to the government, Rockwell finally resolved many of the technical challenges. But the B-1's escape capsule posed a special problem. It encompassed not only the crew quarters but nearly a quarter of the fuselage. The evolution of this requirement epitomized the goldplating phenomenon in the Air Force.

Back in 1963, when Allen and Jones laid down the first AMSA specifications for General LeMay, they decided it should have a "shirtsleeves" environment. In contrast to the cramped B-52, they wanted the B-1 to give its crews room to move, as well as the ability to fly without oxygen masks. Neither Jones nor Allen dreamed where their "requirement" would lead.

As hundreds of Systems Command engineers worked on the B-1, the requirement for a shirtsleeves environment somehow mushroomed into the complex escape capsule. "A lieutenant at Systems Command can put a tailhook on a plane that a general can't take off," said General James Ferguson, who learned as the Systems Command leader how bureaucracy prevents flexibility and change.

While the escape capsule represented the high value placed on protecting the crew, its added weight, complexity, and cost almost overwhelmed the bomber. For the crew to escape from the plane, the capsule was supposed to be blasted away from the craft, then dropped by parachute to a safe landing—on Arctic tundra, jungle floor, or ocean waves—where it would serve as a habitat for the crew for several days. Intricate rockets and engines were needed to permit the escape capsule to work in virtually any situation—even with the mother plane flying at a 45-degree angle 300 feet above the ground.

As costs soared and Rockwell fell further behind in its development schedule, company executives tried to get the Air Force to modify some of the most problematical requirements. Rockwell president Robert Anderson urged the Air Force to eliminate the escape capsule, lower the speed required and simplify other items. Before joining Rockwell in 1968, Anderson had worked up through the ranks to become a division manager at the Chrysler Corporation. Anderson had graduated first in his class at the Chrysler School of Engineering, and he appreciated the technical side of building complex machines.

He tried to persuade the Air Force to replace the controlled-atmosphere capsule with ejection seats used in most military aircraft. "Why can't bomber pilots wear pressure suits like fighter pilots do?" he asked. The answer: "Because bomber pilots have to fly in the plane much longer." The Air Force refused to make the change.

General Welch later recalled the frustrations he, Kent, and Glosser experienced in trying to "beat down the B-1 design requirements into something more buildable, affordable, and practical." It was tough going. "People didn't want to see the requirements whittled down," said Welch. "Nothing was ever settled. Anyone who lost came back to fight again."

In Welch's view, the "escape capsule was a disaster"; it was built anyway because "the capsule's supporters in the engineering and scientific community of the Air Force Systems Command, NASA, and industry had totally lost touch with reality, yet were uncontrollable in pursuing their messianic visions."

When Deputy Secretary Packard approved the B-1 design back in 1969, senior Air Force generals celebrated with a late-afternoon drink in the private dining room of Air Force Secretary Robert Seamans. They persuaded General Glosser to attend.

"You guys have got your way," he said. "You've won. But the requirements you've put in there for supersonic speed and the escape capsule are going to ruin the plane. I'm here to tell you it's a hollow victory. You're not going to build any more B-1s than you did B-70s."

In 1974, the entire government nearly slid to a halt as federal investigators and the news media exposed how the break-in at Democratic National Committee headquarters at the Watergate, and the subsequent coverup, reached all the way to the Oval Office of the president of the United States. As the Watergate scandal closed in on him, Richard Nixon resigned in disgrace on August 9 and was replaced by his vice-president, Gerald Ford.

A new secretary of defense, James Schlesinger, who had been a nuclear strategist at the Rand Corporation, headed a new Pentagon team. General David C. Jones, who as a colonel had been instrumental in planning the B-1, now became Air Force chief of staff.

A big man with a thatch of white hair, Schlesinger was a tough-minded pragmatist who was not going to tolerate a B-1 program with runaway costs. According to General Accounting Office estimates, the total program cost had risen from $11 billion in 1970 to almost $19 billion by mid-1974. The actual extent of the cost overruns remained a secret closely guarded by a few top Air Force officers and Rockwell executives; overruns were a serious liability now when the nation was suffering its largest peacetime budget deficit to date, and the president was trying to cut government spending by $5 billion.

As its problems rose, the B-1 had its first moment of glory. On October 26, 1974, Rockwell workers and Air Force officers cheered, as the first gleaming white prototype test plane rolled out of the Palmdale production hangar. When antiwar protestors tried to disrupt the ceremony by lying down in front of the B-1, Schlesinger shouted, "Keep the plane rolling."

In the midst of the enthusiasm, most listeners overlooked the cautionary note in Schlesinger's speech. "Major technical risks" would have to be resolved, Schlesinger said, and the nation must be "fully assured that the added capabilities are commensurate with the cost" before production of a B-1 force would be approved.

David Jones well understood Schlesinger's gingerly approach to the B-1. Jones was a bright, self-educated South Dakota farmboy who never even graduated from college, much less from one of the service academies that traditionally produced the nation's military leaders. He was the first Air Force chief of staff who did not come from the "bomber mafia" of the SAC commanders. Having served in many different Air Force commands, he learned to appreciate their different perspectives. As an aide to Curtis LeMay in the 1950s and 1960s, he had learned about the complexities of national-defense politics. LeMay had assigned him to the Air Force's rebellious effort to save the B-70, then given him the job of working up requirements for what became the B-1.

Soon after Jones became chief of staff in mid-1974, Secretary

Schlesinger warned him that his support for the B-1 was not un-conditional. When its costs topped $100 million per plane, Schle-singer said the plane would be too expensive and congressional opposition too difficult to fight. As a war strategist, bombers ap-pealed to Schlesinger because they appeared to cause the Soviets great worry, leading them to spend billions on bomber defenses. But he was determined not to sacrifice other military needs—fighters, close air support, and transportation for the infantry—merely to satisfy the Air Force's zeal for a new bomber.

Jones took Schlesinger's warning to heart; he also believed in the importance of meeting other airpower needs. Soon after the rollout ceremony, Jones flew to Palmdale to inspect the B-1. Standing beside the plane next to Rockwell official Buzz Hello, Jones said, "I'll support this plane right up to the point that it will fragment the Air Force. Then I will turn against it." Hello was stunned to hear anything less than unconditional support from an Air Force chief of staff.

In December 1974, Jones summoned ten of the twelve four-star Air Force generals to an extraordinary secret Pentagon meet-ing. Its code-name was Corona Quest. Jones called the meeting because he questioned whether the B-1 bomber was worth a cost that might eat up the budget and force sacrifice of other Air Force needs. If the project went forward, Jones felt the Air Force would have to be united, with everyone accepting the consequences.

Furthermore, General Richard Ellis, the Air Force vice chief of staff, a strong advocate of the B-1, believed that the bomber would be canceled by Schlesinger unless the Air Force brought cost and development problems under control.

Prior to the meeting, Jones had assigned his staff to prepare a study on how the B-1 program would affect the Air Force budget. They were to project the probable size of future Air Force budgets, the amount of money that would be consumed by the B-1, and the amount left to develop and build other Air Force weapons.

Guards stood watch at each end of the fourth-floor Pentagon corridor that held the quarters of the Air Force chief of staff, as staff officers worked for forty-eight hours on the budget and cost projections. The night before Corona Quest convened, junior bud-get officers completed their study. The results were devastating. Even the most optimistic projections showed that the B-1 would eat up the eagle's share of the Air Force procurement funds for the next ten years. Its costs now exceeded $100 million per plane—a total of more than $24 billion for a 240-bomber force. This was the magic number at which Schlesinger threatened to stop supporting the plane. Projects already in production—the A-10 attack plane, the F-15 and F-16 fighters—would have to be cut.

Major General Kenneth Chapman of the Office of Research and Development flipped through the pages, chart after chart, and exploded: "We'd have to cancel practically every program in the Air Force. This analysis has got to be screwed up. Congress will give us more money than this."

"This is the biggest problem the Air Force is facing," said Lieutenant General William (Broadway Bill) Evans, the deputy chief of staff for research and development. "We have to give the chief [Jones] the truth. But these numbers are a disaster."

But the next day, other officers representing the Systems Command, which would build the B-1, and the Strategic Air Command, which would fly it, told the Corona Quest gathering a much more optimistic story. They claimed that the B-1's costs had been overestimated and future Air Force budgets underestimated. By the time the meeting had ended, the numbers had been modified so they were much less menacing within the Air Force, as well as to budget watchers in Congress.

For the next three years, some Air Force officers claim, two sets of books were kept on estimated B-1 production costs—one for public consumption and one so the highest Air Force leaders could keep track of what was really happening. (The Air Force denied double bookkeeping, and no one produced evidence proving it.)

One general who witnessed the manipulation of the budget figures at the Corona Quest meeting told a young captain who had worked on the original estimates: "Son, if I'd seen what you just did when I was a captain, I would have gotten out of the Air Force a long time ago."

Whatever his own feelings about the B-1, General Jones did not invite to the Corona Quest the general most likely to oppose continuation of the B-1. Conspicuous by his absence was General John Vogt, the Air Force commander at NATO. Vogt believed that an overemphasis on strategic airpower shortchanged the conventional forces that would have to fight a land war in Europe.

Jones finally made his position clear. The bomber would not go forward unless all the Air Force commanders united in unequivocal support. They did. The bomber remained the core of Air Force identity and could not be abandoned. With the Air Force generals standing together, it would be difficult for Schlesinger to cancel the B-1. High-priority fighter planes were kept going as well. But the cost of the planes meant sacrificing funds for training and maintenance, and for the low-priority Air Force concern for troop transport and close air support.

The crisis of Corona Quest finally pried the Air Force away from some of the B-1 goldplating that was threatening the program. The Rube Goldberg escape capsule was replaced by traditional ejection seats. The supersonic speed capability was reduced from Mach 2.2 (1,500 miles per hour) to Mach 1.6 (1,000 miles per hour). Even then, the Air Force leaders understood that fuel and range restraints dictated the plane would actually be flown at subsonic speed. Cost savings were effected, but the aerodynamic design of the B-1 had already been established. The entire fuselage had been designed originally to accommodate the huge escape capsule.

Meanwhile, Rockwell's Buzz Hello was shocked to learn that the Air Force had suddenly decided to request $1 billion from Congress for additional items omitted in previous cost estimates. Hello knew congressional critics with sharp pencils would soon be on the attack. Hello called Major General Abner Martin, the new B-1 program director at Systems Command. "You've just topped the magic number," warned Hello. "Don't you remember what Senator Goldwater said? At $100 million he was getting off. You guys are in the process of blowing it."

The Air Force had always understated the cost of the B-1 to Congress. Skillful playing of defense politics required that the embarrassing real costs of weapon systems not be revealed at the wrong time. The only safe time was when the government was so deeply committed to a project that it couldn't realistically be canceled. With the production decision still ahead and Schlesinger wavering, the B-1 could be dropped just as the B-70 had been. A relatively minor reduction by Congress in the B-1's 1974 appropriation had thrown Rockwell's precarious development schedule even farther off track. Further delays would spark new criticism and place the production decision in even greater jeopardy.

Buzz Hello had earned his reputation in the factory as a practical man who proclaimed that difficult technical problems were overcome by "brute force and awkwardness" rather than by genius. He knew the Air Force had put impractical, difficult features in the plane, but he saw his engineer's job as one of solving them. He rallied his troops to attack each new problem in building the plane. He believed hard work by ordinary people is what got things done. But now Hello saw that brute force and hard work was needed outside the factory as well.

If Rockwell's B-1 bomber were not to end up beside the B-70 outside the museum at Wright-Patterson Field, Hello decided he'd have to start learning his way around the halls of Congress.

11

WHO'S
ON
WHO?

While the U.S. Congress debated the 1975 Defense Authorization Act, a tight-knit group of Air Force officers and Rockwell officials secretly worked together at the Pentagon, vigorously plotting the battle tactics of defense politics. They planned, coordinated, and for three years executed a sophisticated lobbying strategy aimed at winning continued approval of the B-1 bomber from an increasingly reluctant Congress. In the trade, they called it "Who's on Who."

It was a kind of matchmaking, pairing each member of Congress with the individuals or groups most likely to persuade that legislator to vote for continued funding of the bomber. The contact might be made by the chief Rockwell lobbyist in Washington, Ralph J. (Doc) Watson; by an Air Force officer such as Colonel Grant Miller, who worked full-time on the B-1's safe passage through Congress; by the president of the United Automobile Workers—or even by the president of the United States.

Conversations at the Pentagon meetings followed a predictable pattern:

"Who's on Baker?" Miller would ask. Howard Baker, a Republican senator from Tennessee, though not yet his party's Senate leader, needed lobbying.

"Kelly's got Baker," Watson would reply. Jack Kelly, a retired Air Force colonel, was the Washington lobbyist for Avco Corporation, which had a subcontract potentially worth $1 billion to build the B-1's wings at its Nashville plant. Avco officials were lobbying the entire Tennessee congressional delegation, whose members understood the importance the B-1 held for their state's economy.

The Air Force and Rockwell had launched an ambitious and meticulously orchestrated lobbying operation. The team meeting in the conference room of the Air Force Office of Legislative Liaison on the fourth floor of the Pentagon consisted of able men and women for whom defense politics was a way of life.

Doc Watson headed the Rockwell group. A World War II fighter-pilot ace who joined Rockwell after retiring from the Air Force as a colonel, Watson was a Capitol Hill fixture. A small, jaunty man with an ear for a good story, he befriended congressmen and kept them ready to hear Rockwell's case for its defense projects. John Rane, a Rockwell aeronautical engineer, helped Watson keep members of Congress up to date on the technical status of Rockwell projects. They proudly called their team the "Doc and Johnny show."

Genevieve (Ginger) Allen, a young Mississippian who had joined Watson as a secretary, soon proved a bright and shrewd addition to the lobbying team. Watson felt that her beauty enhanced luncheon and dinner meetings with congressmen.

Whenever a critical congressional vote was on the agenda, Buzz Hello flew in from California to attend the Pentagon strategy sessions and direct Rockwell's lobbying activities. Hello impressed the members with his low-key manner and total command of the technical and production details of the B-1. If he needed more clout, he could ask Rockwell President Anderson or Board Chairman Rockwell to call members of Congress, the president, or the secretary of defense.

The Air Force side of the lobbying coalition was directed by Lieutenant General Marion Boswell, the assistant vice chief of staff. He made certain that the considerable resources of the Air Force, particularly its legislative-liaison office, were brought to bear on the problem. A 150-member staff answered queries from members of Congress, kept a file on their voting records and statements, supplied them with transportation for "official trips," kept them informed of projects in their districts—and of course, worked assiduously to gain their votes for Air Force programs. Major General Ralph Maglione ran the legislative-liaison office, but General Boswell took the lead on the B-1.

Colonel Grant Miller, an attorney who spoke with an Oklahoma twang, led the Air Force's B-1 drive on Capitol Hill. He targeted key votes and directed day-to-day strategy. At the Pentagon, Miller operated out of a special office across the hall from General David Jones, the Air Force chief of staff. With an easygoing, folksy manner, he befriended not only the B-1's congressional advocates but its leading opponents as well. That way, he kept well informed, and he kept his political lines open.

The Pentagon lobbying meetings were sometimes attended by John Gray, a staff representative of the Air Force Association, a powerful nationwide organization of active and retired Air Force personnel and other defense supporters. As a nonprofit educational group, the association was technically prohibited from lobbying. But through its local chapters, it could encourage its 250,000 members to support the B-1 bomber.

As lobbying assignments were made at the Pentagon meetings, the participants made careful notations on tally sheets spread out on the conference table. These scorecards also showed how each of the 100 senators and 435 representatives had voted on the B-1 in the past and how he or she was expected to vote in 1975. Special attention was focused on "swing votes"—uncommitted members whose votes might be swayed by the right argument or by the right person. The key was to pinpoint who could be most persuasive with each member of Congress, then to solicit and guide that person's help. The "who's on who" assignments were recorded in code, lest the tally sheets fall into unfriendly hands. What emerged from the strategy meetings was an intricate, delicately woven—and highly questionable—lobbying network.

Lobbying coalitions have long been an integral part of the Washington political system. Organizations with common interests regularly pool their resources to strengthen their political clout. What was unusual about the B-1 strategy meetings at the

Pentagon was not only their sophistication and organization, but the participants themselves. Military officers are forbidden by law from lobbying Congress, not to mention doing so in coordination with the defense industry.

The Air Force worked with the defense contractors with cavalier disregard for Title 18 of the U.S. Code, the statute that specifically prohibits officials of the executive branch of government from lobbying the Congress. Title 18 is often ignored by members of the executive branch, which is worrisome in itself. But when military officers ignore it, the offense is compounded: The military is required to obey civilian authority and stay out of politics. The political trades of pork-barrel politics are the more unseemly —indeed, dangerous—when the stakes involve the nation's defense.

The Air Force's B-1 lobbying effort was neither the first nor the last joint exercise by the military and industry to advance their mutual interests. In theory, the large legislative-liaison staffs maintained by each of the armed services, as well as by other departments of government, are supposed to supply information to members of Congress only at their request. In practice, these officers are intermediaries in the constant pursuit of influence and trading of support that form a regular political duet played by the executive and Congress.

The Air Force–Rockwell coalition developed into a formal apparatus in direct reaction—and direct proportion—to the growing congressional threat to the program. On August 3, 1973, the Senate Armed Services Committee cut $100 million from the B-1 funds requested by the Air Force, expressly to indicate "the committee's dissatisfaction and serious concern regarding the management of this program." Ironically, the funding cut exacerbated all the program's management problems, including meeting deadlines. The Air Force and industry regarded the congressional slap as the worst kind of "micromanagement." Without warning, a ten-year, multibillion-dollar weapon program could be thrown off track by policies changed in the annual congressional authorization and appropriation process.

Congressional opposition grew more vocal and better organized in 1974. In the Senate, George McGovern won 31 votes for an amendment that would have cut the B-1's development appropriation by 50 percent. A House amendment to kill the plane outright, though, was defeated 309 to 94. Although those were wide margins of defeat for the opponents, the Air Force–Rockwell coalition perceived them as ominous challenges to the safe old monolithic establishment that had conducted defense business in Congress up until then.

After the Vietnam War and the disgrace of Watergate, Congress more strongly asserted its will on defense issues against the presidency and the executive branch. Antiwar sentiment and antimilitary bias swelled into powerful currents in the country during the middle 1970s. These views were shared—or at least recognized—by some members of Congress, emboldening them to challenge defense programs such as the B-1.

Institutional change also had overtaken some old congressional procedures. No longer could a powerful, autocratic committee chairman automatically impose his will on a military-procurement contract. Reformers in the Democratic party had punctured the iron-clad seniority system and managed to oust several committee chairmen, including Democratic Representative F. Edward Hebert from Louisiana, chairman of the House Armed Services Committee.

These reforms made it harder for the defense industry to gain approval for its programs. Once the power of committee chairmen was curbed, anyone—defense contractor or military service—pursuing a multibillion-dollar program such as the B-1 needed the support of many more members of Congress. As power in Congress fragmented, many of the members scrambled to get a share of defense contracts and bases for their states and districts, just as they had traditionally sought publicly financed dams and highways. Needless to say, the national interest was no better served in this mad scramble for military assets than it had been when one autocrat called the shots.

Dutch Kindelberger and Lee Atwood foresaw this decentralization of congressional power back in the 1960s, after North American Aviation's B-70 bomber was defeated. Shrewd businessmen as well as aviation visionaries, they realized that broad congressional support would be needed to sustain huge defense programs over the necessarily long periods of development and production. Building a broad base of support entailed spreading the subcontracts around the country to make sure that enough constituencies had a direct stake in a given weapon system. By the 1960s, North American had established a division for advanced systems planning. This division tried to predict economic, political, and social trends in order to judge if various defense projects were viable. Deciding how and where to subcontract the work was a politically crucial part of planning a vast project like the B-1.

Both Rockwell and the Air Force sought to broaden support by showing political sensitivity in awarding subcontracts on the B-1. For example, Rockwell contracted with the LTV Corporation of Fort Worth to build parts of the fuselage, even though they could easily have been made in Rockwell's own factories. But a hefty subcontract would sway the large Texas congressional delegation, whose members included John Tower, an influential Republican on the Senate Armed Services Committee, and Democratic House Majority Leader Jim Wright of Fort Worth.

The Air Force itself chose Seattle's Boeing Company to develop the offensive avionics for the B-1. Boeing had lost the prime B-1 contract to Rockwell, and the Air Force wanted to mollify the two influential senators from Washington state—also known as "the senators from Boeing": Scoop Jackson, a power on the Armed Services Committee, and Warren Magnuson, chairman of the Senate Appropriations Committee.

By the time the initial subcontracts were awarded, more than five thousand corporations in forty-eight states had at least a small piece of the B-1. So did most of the nation's 435 congressional districts. Most of those contracts involved only one or two hundred jobs, but for many local economies those jobs were very important. And local leaders let their congressmen know it.

Although politics guided some subcontracting decisions, a project of the magnitude and complexity of the B-1 demanded a diversity of highly specialized skills. In many cases, Rockwell faced a "make or buy" decision—whether to make the part in-house or buy it from a subcontractor. Costs, skills, production schedules—as well as politics—entered into these decisions. "It paid not to be greedy," explained a Rockwell executive. "We made money on the subcontracts too." The result was a wide geographic distribution of jobs, a broad basis for skillful lobbying.

But there was a price to pay. Parceling out the subcontracts for maximum political impact did not make for efficient production. Spreading the work around always complicated the logistics of building a weapon, and sometimes it compromised the quality.

Preparing for the 1975 congressional fight, Rockwell and Air Force lobbyists armed themselves with meticulous lists of every B-1 subcontract location, cross-referenced by state, town, and congressional district. The studies, prepared both by Rockwell and by the Air Force comptroller's office, showed how many dollars of B-1 money flowed into a congressional district each month. This information allowed the lobbyists to show members of Congress, down to the last dollar, how their constituents benefited from the B-1. The data became even more potent as subcontractors, mayors, and union leaders were enlisted to lobby their members of Congress.

One of Grant Miller's first actions in 1975 was to do some research at the U.S. Department of Labor to find out which labor unions worked on the various B-1 contracts, and how many union jobs were at stake. He soon knew exactly how many members of two major labor unions—the United Automobile Workers and the International Association of Machinists—worked in each B-1 plant.

At Miller's suggestion, Air Force Chief of Staff Jones met with the unions' presidents, Leonard Woodcock of the autoworkers and Floyd (Red) Smith of the machinists. General Jones carefully stressed the need for the B-1 to modernize the U.S. strategic deterrent. But the union chiefs clearly understood the job implications as well—both ordered their unions to join forces with the Air Force–Rockwell lobbying coalition. Union support was vital, especially in influencing the liberal congressional Democrats most likely to oppose the bomber. Woodcock also ordered the UAW to quit a liberal coalition opposing the B-1—with the auto industry in trouble, aerospace jobs became all the more important.

．　．　．

The Air Force made lobbying assignments for government officials, generals, members of the Air Force Association, and cooperative members of Congress. Rockwell organized the other contractors who worked on the B-1. Company lobbyists in Washington held breakfast meetings at the Army-Navy Club on Farragut Square with representatives of such major B-1 subcontractors as Boeing, General Electric, Avco, Eaton AIL, Sunstrand, LTV, Westinghouse, Goodyear Aerospace, and IBM, along with lobbyists from the United Auto Workers and the Machinists. At these sessions the participants decided which company would contact which congressmen. General Electric, with its huge engine plant in Ohio, focused on that state's delegation. LTV concentrated on the Texans. The AiResearch division of Garrett Corporation, which made the central air-data computer, focused on Arizona congressmen. AIL, which would make the plane's defensive avionics, lobbied the New York congressional delegation. Sunstrand Corporation of Rockford, which made the rudder control systems, concentrated on Illinois congressmen. The Harris Corporation, which made the electrical wiring system, contacted Florida congressmen. Sanders Electronics lobbied New Hampshire members. In addition, Rockwell brought to Washington its 167 local plant managers from around the nation to lobby their elected representatives.

The Air Force even assigned a high-ranking general to work full-time promoting the B-1. In 1974, Major General James Allen supervised a nationwide effort to build support for the bomber. He directed a speaker's bureau, which booked B-1 proponents to speak in states or districts represented by congressmen hostile to the B-1. Air Force officers would appear at a meeting of a local Chamber of Commerce or Air Force Association chapter to explain the B-1's importance to national security—and to the local economy. Sometimes the speaker also pointed out when the local congressman or senator had not been supportive. Senators Patrick Leahy, a Vermont Democrat, and Thomas McIntyre, a New Hampshire Democrat who headed the key Armed Services Research and Development Subcommittee, both felt the sting as the Air Force politicked for the bomber at the grass roots. At a meeting of the New Hampshire chapter of the Air Force Association, an officer spoke both about the virtues of the B-1 and about Senator McIntyre's equivocal support for it.

As the B-1 appropriations approached a vote in June 1975, Rockwell and the Air Force worried about a rebellion among Senate Democrats. Democratic Senators Alan Cranston and John Tunney of California took the lead in advocating production of the B-1, which would provide thousands of jobs in their state. But the Air Force did not consider them effective advocates, as both usually voted like doctrinaire antidefense liberals. If the Democratic majority in the Senate was to be convinced that the bomber deserved support on its merits, more credible leadership was needed.

The lobbying coalition took aim at two influential Democratic senators: John Glenn of Ohio, whose defense pronouncements carried the weight of his experience and celebrity as a Marine pilot and astronaut, and Sam Nunn of Georgia, a member of the Senate Armed Services Committee with a growing reputation as a military expert. Neither senator had committed himself to support the B-1. If they turned against the project, others were likely to follow.

To influence Glenn, the Air Force and Rockwell first called on all the obvious assets. Glenn was lobbied hard by the United Automobile Workers, and by executives and union officials from General Electric, which was manufacturing the B-1's engines at Evendale, outside Cincinnati. GE was the largest employer in Ohio, and the UAW was among Glenn's key political supporters. Rockwell further enticed him by assigning B-1 work to a long-idle plant in Columbus. Despite these overtures, however, Glenn would not commit himself.

The vital key to convincing Glenn came from a legislative aide, who told Air Force and Rockwell lobbyists that Glenn did not think the B-1 bomber was needed as part of the strategic nuclear deterrent—but that he did believe strongly in the need for a new bomber to fight in a conventional war.

This information threw the Air Force into a dilemma. Some officers privately agreed with Glenn, but the SAC-dominated leadership scorned the notion that their $100 million superbomber would be part of the conventional fighting force—that would be like hitching a thoroughbred to a milk wagon. For the Air Force, the strategic nuclear mission was everything. It had no plans even to install racks for conventional bombs in the B-1.

Nevertheless, the Air Force decided to pay lip service to

Glenn's ideas. General Russell E. Dougherty, the SAC commander in 1975, sent his deputy, General Kelly Burke, to assure Glenn of SAC's "strong interest" in conventional bombing. Glenn wanted more than interest. He asked for a written commitment that the B-1 would be equipped to carry conventional bombs. On the eve of the Senate vote, Air Force aides hand-carried a letter to Glenn from Defense Secretary Schlesinger promising that the B-1s eventually would be outfitted for conventional nonnuclear bombing. After reading Schlesinger's letter aloud on the Senate floor, Glenn finally cast his vote for the B-1. As one Air Force general later said, "There was no damn way we were going to risk losing a $100 million strategic asset in some conventional shootout. But if the senator wanted us to say we'd do that, we were ready to oblige him."

Georgia Senator Nunn presented a more puzzling problem. Although a strong military supporter, he remained noncommittal on the B-1. The Air Force could appeal to Nunn's parochial interest for weapons built by Lockheed or Martin Marietta; those aerospace giants were major employers in Georgia. But little B-1 work was being done in the state.

The lobbying coalition tried to influence Nunn by contacting him through Dr. Daniel Callahan, a Georgia friend. Callahan practiced medicine in Warner Robins, Georgia, home of Robins Air Force Base. As president of the mid-Georgia chapter of the Air Force Association, Callahan encouraged his four thousand members with the motto "Every day in middle Georgia is Air Force Appreciation Day." When Callahan urged Nunn to support the B-1, the senator knew that the doctor spoke for a formidable advocacy group—one concerned not only about the Air Force but about the health of its area's major economic resource, the giant base that provided twenty thousand jobs and a $450 million annual payroll.

For whatever reasons, Senator Nunn finally cast his vote for the B-1.

The floor debates on the B-1 in 1975 focused on military and strategic considerations. Was an expensive new penetrating bomber needed as part of the nuclear deterrent? Could the job still be done by the aging fleet of B-52s? Was a standoff plane firing long-range cruise missiles the answer? The discussion was all very reasonable and responsible and serious.

But in the lobbying behind the scenes, the issue was jobs. The Air Force and Rockwell tried to turn a principal B-1 liability—its stupendous cost—into a national economic asset. If the B-1 was indeed a flying pork barrel, as its opponents claimed, pork in the sky could do absolute wonders for the economy. Rockwell and its subcontractors bombarded Capitol Hill with statistics showing that the B-1 provided an economic bonanza for the entire nation —not just the districts where the plane was being built. Rockwell's carefully biased analysis sought to demonstrate that a $15 billion investment in the B-1 would add $41.4 billion to the gross national product and produce 69,300 aerospace jobs and 122,700 jobs in supporting services. These 192,000 jobs would produce $28.6 billion in personal income after taxes, and the taxes collected on the $28.6 billion by federal and state governments would amount to a $13 billion windfall. The amazing bottom line was that for a mere $2 billion net "investment for national security," the nation could have the added protection of the Peacekeeper. ("Peacekeeper" was Rockwell's euphemistic name for the B-1 at the time of the promotion campaign. A few years later President Reagan recycled the name to promote the MX missile.)

Rockwell lobbyists trotted out their B-1 employment-and-spending figures for each state and congressional district. To counter Congressman John Seiberling from Akron, Ohio, one of the most knowledgeable and articulate B-1 opponents in the House, Rockwell's John Rane sent a brochure to Akron business and civic groups. Building the B-1 would create $60 million worth of new business in Ohio's 14th Congressional district, the brochure stated: this new business would generate $133 million in disposable income after taxes. "In other words," the Rockwell pitch concluded, "you don't have to 'cut metal' on the B-1 in order to benefit from it."

That the health of the American economy somehow depended in part on large defense expenditures had been taken for granted by many politicians ever since World War II. But in the mid-1970s some congressmen began to contest the doctrine that inflating the defense budget was a good way to stimulate the economy. To prove their case, congressmen like Seiberling and their economic advisers took Rockwell's data and stood them on their head.

Seiberling did his own economic study, which concluded that while his Ohio constituents paid $84 million in taxes for the B-1, they received only $70 million of benefits in return. An infusion of defense dollars in Akron was not the answer, he maintained. The solution was to spend those dollars instead to create jobs that produced goods the society could really use. Seiberling argued that defense spending ties up scarce capital without in fact producing many jobs. "There are fewer jobs per billion dollars in defense, and except for California and Texas, most states suffer unemployment as a result of defense spending," he said.

The Public Interest Research Group at the University of Michigan challenged the benefits to the economy of defense spending. In a study called *The Empty Pork Barrel*, the Michigan analysis showed that spending for weapons procurement, a capital-intensive enterprise, produced 55,000 jobs for each $1 billion spent. However, public-sector spending on a mix of construction, public works, services, and manufacturing produced 65,000 jobs per $1 billion expended. In this kind of analysis, each additional $1 billion in defense spending meant a net loss of 10,000 jobs.

Nevertheless, the liberal case for conversion to a peacetime economy remained hypothetical, thanks to the efforts of Rockwell and its hired and volunteer lobbyists. As Gerry Whipple, the UAW's tough-talking western regional vice-president, put it, "California has been built on food, defense, and oil. You can't expect us to convert into industries for garbage disposal or cheap houses. There are some super-liberal congressmen with their heads in the clouds who dream of building houses instead of bombers. But workers can't have pride building low-cost housing, when the low-income families just use them for putting garbage in the hall. The people making the B-1 bomber think they're working for the good of the community, and people have pride in it." Neither Congress nor the country would in fact divert billions from the B-1 to build mass-transit systems, fund health-care programs, or improve public schools.

Rockwell supplemented its Washington lobbying with a secret grass-roots campaign code-named Operation Common

Sense. James Daniell, a marketing vice-president in Rockwell's Pittsburgh office, directed a comprehensive promotional scheme. A onetime football star at Ohio State and World War II hero, Daniell was a dynamic booster who saw little difference between marketing a bomber and promoting a consumer product. His program included a massive letter-writing campaign by workers at Rockwell's 167 plants; solicitation of support from national organizations such as the Veterans of Foreign Wars and the American Legion; and production of films and advertisements as well as prepared articles, columns, and editorials that willing editors could print in newspapers and magazines.

Daniell came to Washington to chair the monthly meetings of Operation Common Sense in the conference room of Rockwell's Washington offices on Pennsylvania Avenue. Participants, including Rockwell's Washington lobbyists, worked on such disparate projects as soliciting the support of the National Council of Jewish Women and countering the promotional efforts of Rockwell's aerospace rivals advocating standoff bombers and cruise missiles. The committee financed a thinly veiled B-1 promotional film, *The Threat: What One Can Do*, and paid a $39,350 consulting fee to *Washington Alert*, a newsletter edited by news personality Martha Rountree, who wrote glowingly of the B-1's virtues.

Daniell's efforts went beyond Common Sense. As a fishing and hunting companion of board chairman Willard Rockwell, he persuaded Rockwell to extend the lavish hospitality the company routinely provided for its favored commercial customers to include members of Congress, high-ranking military officers, and administration officials. Daniell and lobbyist Doc Watson coordinated the hospitality at four company retreats: a fishing complex at North Bimini Island in the Bahamas for winter weekends; a hunting plantation called Pinebloom near Albany, Georgia; a leased hunting lodge with twenty-four duck blinds on Wye Island in the Chesapeake Bay near Washington; and Nemacolin, Willard Rockwell's own hideaway resort, complete with trout fishing, near Farmington, Pennsylvania. Many congressmen accepted invitations to these idyllic spots; so did top Pentagon officials such as Admiral Thomas Moorer, chairman of the Joint Chiefs of Staff, and Malcolm Currie, who as the Pentagon's director of defense research and engineering held authority over B-1 development.

Doc Watson and John Rane also kept busy in Washington. In

one three-month period in 1974 they entertained or called on 155 members of Congress. When House Minority Leader Gerald Ford (soon to be president) needed rush transportation for a speech in Michigan and back to Washington the same night, Doc Watson commandeered a Rockwell plane for him.

Like hundreds of other corporations, Rockwell took advantage of a 1974 campaign-financing law intended to promote reform. Daniell and Watson carefully distributed donations from Rockwell's Good Government Political Action Committee to members of the key military congressional committees and others in a position to help Rockwell projects. The new law made it legal for corporations to run political-action committees (PACs) with money volunteered by employees. In short order, Rockwell was contributing more than $100,000 in an election year to candidates who could best help the corporation's defense business.

Rockwell's promotional, entertainment, and campaign-contribution schemes were still gaining steam in 1975, when some of the strategies began to backfire. Rockwell's "grass-roots" letter-writing campaign, for example, turned out to be a little too well organized and orchestrated. Representative Les Aspin, a Wisconsin Democrat, was besieged with three hundred pro–B-1 letters from workers. They were written on five different colors of stationery but nearly identical in content. Aspin's staff finally traced the letter-writing campaign to an Admiral television plant in Harvard, Illinois, just across the border from his congressional district. Admiral had no part at all in the B-1; it just happened to be a subsidiary of Rockwell. One Admiral letter-writer handed the B-1 opponents a golden postscript: "I've been asked to do this," the Admiral worker wrote to Congressman Aspin. "Vote any way you want."

Rockwell's hard-nosed congressional lobbying, based almost exclusively on jobs, seemed heavy-handed—even to the Air Force. General Boswell admonished his associates that the B-1 had to be sold primarily on its defense merits. The assumption that a few jobs back home could change their minds on an important national-defense issue offended some congressmen. For example, Representative Thomas Downey, a Long Island Democrat elected in the anti-Vietnam, anti-Watergate class of 1974, resented the lobbying by a dozen Long Island firms with a piece of the B-1 action: "They figured if they built the windshield blades in your district, you were for it." Downey still pragmatically supported most of the largest defense contracts helping his constituents, but not the B-1.

In the end, the 1975 effort to kill the B-1 in the Senate, led by Senator McGovern and Senator William Proxmire of Wisconsin, failed by a vote of 57 to 32. A similar effort in the House failed too, although a motion by Representative Les Aspin to eliminate preproduction funding for the bomber collected a surprising 164 votes.

General Boswell told Air Force lobbyists to get rid of the records of their well-coordinated campaign of "who's on who" with an emphasis on B-1–created jobs. In addition to general questions of propriety, Air Force leaders suspected that Senator William Proxmire, the scourge of the military, soon would expose the whole lobbying plan.

Within a few months, Proxmire had a field day as a muckraker. At a Senate hearing, he cross-examined Rockwell president Anderson about the company's secret campaign contributions to Richard Nixon in 1972; about the Operation Common Sense grass-roots lobbying blitz; about free winter vacations taken by Pentagon officials on Bimini in 1974; and about the Chesapeake Bay hunting weekends enjoyed by the Pentagon sportsmen, when Rockwell not only provided accommodations, but took care of cleaning and dressing the geese.

Proxmire disclosed that the Pentagon's Defense Contract Audit Agency had disallowed $183,435 in Rockwell lobbying expenses and another $143,947 in entertainment expenses for the years 1974 and 1975. A later audit showed $653,000 in disallowed lobbying expense, including $115,895 for Operation Common Sense and a "Keep the B-1 Sold" public-relations campaign, plus $83,645 in "military relations costs" for sending speakers around the country. Rockwell had charged all these promotional expenses to the taxpayer as part of the costs incurred in building the B-1.

After being grilled by Proxmire and subjected to embarrassing newspaper headlines, Anderson testily asked Doc Watson, "Are you still proud of your duck blinds [on Wye Island]?"

"Well," replied Watson, ever the Washington pragmatist, "we got the B-1 and the space-shuttle contracts, and we've made a lot of friends."

That was the way things worked, and were accepted as working, in the Washington military-industrial-political defense network. The fellowship of weekend duck hunting was a form of friendship. Doc Watson and Massachusetts Representative Silvio Conte, ranking Republican member on the House Defense Appropriations Subcommittee, for example, were friends with strong common bonds. Conte helped Rockwell and often enjoyed the company's hospitality, including one Wye Island excursion in which he shot a prize buck deer. But there came a time when Conte told Watson that constituent pressure would no longer permit him to vote for the B-1. Despite strong disapproval from his superiors in Pittsburgh, Watson kept Conte on the Rockwell hospitality roster.

In Watson's view, the people at the corporate headquarters did not really understand Washington. A hunting trip or a campaign contribution was not a chip to be exchanged automatically for a contract or a favorable vote. Members of the club helped each other when they could, as others do in many fields of special-interest politics. They saw themselves as patriots, in general alliance against politicians they regarded as dangerous or misguided —the McGoverns, Seiberlings, Proxmires, and Aspins who they thought underestimated the Soviet threat and would disarm the country.

Despite congressional votes to keep the B-1 development going, Buzz Hello realized that the politics of the B-1 were about to spin out of control. Because Congress had cut back part of the B-1's development funds, the decision whether or not to produce the plane had been delayed until 1976. Hello tried to get the Air Force to reappeal to Congress for the funds, but the attempt was put off. Hello was appalled: "Don't you realize what you're doing?" he asked. "You're going to be facing a production decision right in the middle of a presidential election year."

12

JIMMY CARTER
AND THE
ANTI−B-1 COALITION

One steamy afternoon in August of 1975, a group of about forty Democrats showed up at the air-conditioned Ramada Inn in Waterloo, Iowa, curious to meet a little-known southern politician who wanted to become president. As he greeted the Iowans in one of the motel banquet rooms, Jimmy Carter radiated the warmth and assurance of a man who felt at home.

Carter was there working on the first act of a scenario that he hoped would take him from a peanut farm in Georgia to the White House. Early in the new year, Iowa Democrats would hold caucuses to select some of the forty state delegates to the 1976 Democratic National Convention. Iowa's convention votes were not significant in number, but the national news media would be out in force to cover the first delegate selections of the 1976 presidential campaign. A dark-horse Iowa victor, bathed in media glory, would instantly be seen as a serious contender. Jimmy Carter intended to be that victor.

For more than a year the former governor of Georgia had been working the grass roots of Iowa, sleeping on sofas in the living rooms of strangers, discussing grain prices with the familiarity of a fellow farmer, sipping coffee and munching doughnuts in small-town cafes across the state, appearing at dozens of receptions, and trudging through acre upon acre of Iowa cornfields.

Iowans liked Carter. They saw him as one of their own—plainspoken and unpretentious, a man in touch with their deeply ingrained moral and religious values. Carter was a lay preacher. He called for "a government as good as its people." He mistrusted the power brokers in Washington. He seemed well informed about the issues Iowans considered important. Although he said little about what he planned to do as president, he was making friends and convincing people to trust his values and his judgments.

In Waterloo, Carter spoke briefly, then asked the audience not only for questions, but for their opinions and advice.

"If you become president," asked Bob Brammer, a young man from nearby Cedar Falls, "would you build the B-1 bomber?"

Carter replied that there was "a gross waste of money in the Pentagon" and the B-1 was an exceedingly expensive weapon system. He assured Brammer that as president he would certainly take a very hard look at the need for such a bomber before he would ever consider approving its production. He added, "All nations should reduce atomic weapons to zero."

In 1975, Carter knew virtually nothing about the military merits of the B-1 bomber. He understood that it was controversial, and he could not avoid noticing how often at these small gatherings some intense young man or woman would press him to take a position on the issue.

What Jimmy Carter did not know was that Brammer and the others who questioned him about the B-1 were not appearing in his audiences by accident. They too were participants in a grass-roots campaign, organized, in their case, by the American Friends Service Committee (AFSC) and other peace groups. Their agenda was as ambitious as Jimmy Carter's: to turn America away from the arms race and direct the nation's energy toward building a just and peaceful society. Just as Carter used the Iowa precinct caucuses to gain national attention for his candidacy, the peace activists used them and the B-1 question to rally troops to their cause.

Based on the centuries-old Quaker commitment to pacifism

and social action, the Friends Service Committee was the most venerable and widely known American peace-activist organization. For years it had concentrated on ending U.S. involvement in the Vietnam War. Despite the U.S. troop pullout from Vietnam in 1973, AFSC leaders saw no decline in the arms race, no shift in national priorities. Unless the defense establishment were checked, they believed, America would soon be involved in other Vietnams. Developing new projects to challenge the defense buildup was the joint responsibility of the AFSC "peace staff" and a study group called NARMIC—National Action Research on the Military-Industrial Complex.

The campaign against the B-1 was the 1973 brainchild of Peter Barrer, a member of the peace staff in AFSC's New England office in Cambridge, Massachusetts. With his engineering degree from Cornell, Barrer went to work for Shell Oil, exploring for petroleum in the Gulf of Mexico. Disillusioned by oil-company pollution of the gulf, by the Vietnam War, and by racial discrimination, Barrer decided that protest marches were not enough: the nation's institutions had to be radically changed. In 1971 he dropped out of a Harvard graduate program to work for the AFSC.

In Barrer's view, the ideal target for an antimilitary campaign would be a weapon system produced by a large national corporation which also manufactured consumer goods on a large scale—for such a company was vulnerable to a consumer boycott. That the B-1 bomber became the target first of AFSC, and then of a national coalition, was an accident of geography. Lynn, Massachusetts, not far from Cambridge, was the site of one of General Electric's large plants. Barrer discovered that GE made more than toasters and television sets; it also held a multibillion-dollar contract to manufacture the jet engines for a new bomber called the B-1. GE was Barrer's perfect candidate.

Barrer envisioned a campaign with several objectives: to block the B-1's production, to educate consumers about GE's role in the military-industrial complex, to recapture the spirit of the antiwar movement, and to advance the idea of peace conversion. At an October 1973 meeting in Germantown, Ohio, leaders of the AFSC agreed that the B-1 bomber should become the central issue of a nationwide campaign. In addition to GE, other aerospace behemoths would be targeted—Rockwell and Boeing.

The plan soon gathered support from another national peace group, Clergy and Laity Concerned (CALC), which had been a major force in the Vietnam protest movement. CALC had recently waged a similar campaign against the Honeywell Corporation, which manufactured antipersonnel weapons used in Vietnam. Between them, AFSC and CALC had fifty chapters spread across the United States. They had employed or worked with hundreds of the most experienced Vietnam protest organizers. Together, the two groups believed they had the resources to make the bomber a major issue with the many thousands of Americans who had participated in the antiwar movement but who no longer had a cause to spur them to action. Their joint project was billed as the Stop the B-1 Bomber/National Peace Conversion Campaign.

In 1974, the AFSC hired Terry Provance, a twenty-six-year-old peace worker, to organize the campaign that would turn this theory into practice. As a student at Mt. Lebanon High School in suburban Pittsburgh, Provance had written to President Johnson protesting the Vietnam war. As a philosophy student at Purdue and seminary student at the University of Pittsburgh from 1969 to 1972, he had organized other students in anti-Vietnam protests, and in 1973 he had joined a group delivering medical supplies to Hanoi.

Provance took on the B-1 job because he saw that the energy of the peace movement would soon be dissipated unless a new and convincing cause was found to rally veteran protesters. In 1974 he crisscrossed the country to organize 75 local groups against the B-1. By the end of 1975, there were groups in 180 cities. Demonstrations against the B-1 were held at annual meetings of Rockwell, GE, and Boeing, as well as at Air Force bases and Internal Revenue Service offices. The campaign used all the old techniques of the Vietnam days—printing and distributing literature, sponsoring meetings, and organizing demonstrations—to get across the message that the B-1 was unneeded, wasteful, and dangerous. Rockwell's annual meeting in February 1976 at the Beverly Wilshire Hotel in Los Angeles was exactly the kind of opportunity that the anti–B-1 people knew how to exploit. Outside the hotel, protestors carried a huge balloon that showed the bomber inflated to the size of a white elephant. It wore a sign,

"Buy a White Elephant, Live on Peanuts." At the meeting inside, dissident stockholders took the floor to attack the B-1, asking if they too could vacation at the company resort camps where Rockwell regularly entertained congressmen and Pentagon officials.

Meanwhile, Provance and the AFSC leaders worked with other organizations to establish a national coalition. At a meeting in Washington, D.C., in June 1975, an umbrella group was formed by such diverse organizations as the conservative National Taxpayers Union, the Women's Strike for Peace, the Federation of American Scientists, the International Longshoremen's Association, Environmental Action, and Common Cause, each with its own agenda. Peace and antinuclear groups saw the campaign as naturally furthering their causes, but others had narrower reasons for joining the umbrella organization: the Taxpayers Union believed the B-1 was a colossal waste of money; the Federation of Scientists saw the bomber as an ineffective and superfluous weapon system; Environmental Action believed that a supersonic bomber would damage the environment (not to mention the population therein); and Common Cause, which sought to reform government, naturally gravitated to an issue that involved the practice of the defense industry making campaign contributions.

By January 1976, as Jimmy Carter left Iowa in triumph, what had begun as mainly a grass-roots campaign against the B-1 had snowballed into a national effort aimed at nothing less than defeating the B-1 in Congress and pressuring the 1976 Democratic presidential-primary candidates into commitments to oppose the bomber.

A month before he confronted Jimmy Carter in Waterloo, Bob Brammer had hitchhiked to Rock Cleft, Colorado, where the AFSC's annual Peace Conversion Conference met at a Quaker retreat center. The AFSC decided to form a new organization called the National Campaign Against the B-1 Bomber. Brammer was hired to coordinate the Washington efforts of the campaign. While he ran the Washington operation, Terry Provance continued to organize and mobilize grass-roots groups throughout the country.

Brammer was a 1971 graduate of Earlham College, a small

liberal-arts college in Indiana founded by Quakers. He had worked for a while as a social worker in Washington, D.C., and in the unsuccessful congressional campaign of an Iowa Democratic candidate opposed to the Vietnam War.

Brammer arrived in Washington with little political experience and few resources. His salary was $100 a week. Pat Tobin, the Washington representative for the Longshoremen's and Warehousemen's Association, supplied him with a case of canned tuna and an ancient one-speed Schwinn bicycle for transportation. Roger Tressolini of the National Taxpayers Union provided office and living space in an abandoned rowhouse at 625 East Capitol Street. Once he stepped outside the decaying house, Brammer had a magnificent view of the Capitol dome gleaming seven blocks away. He cleared the rubble from the second and third floors and launched the National Campaign Against the B-1 Bomber.

Brammer got some assistance when the coalition hired Steve Pearlman, a college friend who had graduated from Columbia Law School in 1973. Michael Mann, a twenty-two-year-old peace activist fresh out of Hampshire College in Massachusetts, soon joined the effort, his salary paid by Environmental Action. Mann eventually masterminded a legal maneuver that kept the Air Force tied up in federal court on the grounds that the B-1 program failed to comply with regulations requiring an environmental-impact study.

Their first anti–B-1 campaign goal for 1976 was to confront the Democratic candidates on the campaign trail the way Brammer had dogged Carter in Iowa. Armed with the candidates' campaign schedules, Brammer and Provance dispatched fellow workers to ask them about the B-1. Senator Birch Bayh of Indiana, former Senator Fred Harris of Oklahoma, and Representative Morris Udall of Arizona readily agreed to oppose the B-1. Even Scoop Jackson, the defense hard-liner from Washington, began for the first time to express some reservations about the effectiveness of the bomber. But as Jimmy Carter quickly rose to the top of the Democratic pack, nailing down a commitment from the Georgian became critical to the B-1 opponents. And Carter was as evasive on the B-1 as he was on many other issues. The coalition sent out grass-roots operatives to keep up the pressure on Carter. Taking advantage of his accessibility at small gatherings, they were determined to keep on his trail, if necessary up to the convention itself.

. . .

The second phase of the campaign involved linking up Terry Provance's grass-roots network, the national coalition of organizations, and those members of Congress who had actively opposed the B-1 bomber. The idea was to create a lobbying network that reached all the way from local communities to the halls of Congress.

Brammer and Pearlman set out to build working relationships with those who had been leading the congressional fight against the B-1. They included Senator Proxmire and his aide Ron Tammen; Senator McGovern and his aide John Holum; Senator John Culver of Iowa and his aide Charles Stevenson; Representative Seiberling and his aide Don Mansfield; and Representative Jonathan Bingham of New York and his aide Gordon Kerr.

The congressional aides were pivotal. As usual, crucial planning of strategy, writing of position papers, counting of heads, and the lobbying would be done in anonymity by the congressional staffs. Within a matter of weeks, Brammer and Pearlman were working in tandem with Tammen, Holum, Stevenson, Mansfield, Kerr, and a dozen other congressional aides who shared their zeal for stopping the B-1. They received help from Members of Congress for Peace Through Law, a bipartisan group devoted to arms control, and its staffer Barry Schneider. They worked with and learned from officers of the national organizations who had joined the cause: David Cohen and Mike Cole of Common Cause, John McCormick of the Environmental Policy Center, Jeremy Stone of the Federation of American Scientists, Roger Tressolini of the National Taxpayers Union, and many others.

On the face of it, a contest between the National Campaign Against the B-1 and the Air Force–Rockwell lobbying coalition seemed ludicrous. Brammer and Pearlman and their long-haired, blue-jeaned activists were taking on a defense establishment that controlled jobs, dispensed campaign contributions, had the power of life and death over military bases, and maintained long-standing alliances with the most influential wielders of power on the Congressional committees that controlled the military pursestrings. A closer look, however, would have shown that the activists had managed to put together a potentially effective if loosely knit coalition of most of Washington's liberal interest groups and a growing band of congressmen looking for a political

145

issue with which to oppose runaway defense spending and the arms race.

This diverse group managed to assemble a surprisingly sophisticated lobbying apparatus. In many ways it was a mirror image of the one directed by Rockwell and the Pentagon. The National Campaign Against the B-1 also compiled a detailed analysis of the voting record and interests of each member of Congress and made lobbying assignments from a Washington headquarters. From his Capitol Hill office, Bob Brammer sent a constant stream of bulletins to Terry Provance's local organizations. Field volunteers were alerted when an important vote was approaching in the House or Senate. They knew which congressmen needed to be bombarded with mail, telephone calls, and personal contacts by individuals who could influence them.

In the case of Representative Gus Yatron of Reading, Pennsylvania, for example, the campaign orchestrated an approach in his home town. Yatron was lobbied by a member of the League of Women Voters and a local official of the Textile Workers Union. The congressman voted against the B-1.

While Rockwell and Air Force strategists gathered at the Pentagon to plan which congressmen to lobby, the anti–B-1 coalition met in Proxmire's or Seiberling's office to do the same. At night, Brammer and Pearlman used the congressmen's long-distance WATS lines to contact their nationwide network of organizers. When a key vote was scheduled in Congress, the congressional aides and coalition workers activated a telephone-bank operation to keep pressure on their legislative supporters to answer roll calls and vote against the B-1—repeatedly.

Like any piece of legislation, the B-1 program had to go through many votes. First it had to be authorized in the armed-services committees of both the House and Senate; then it had to be approved by the appropriations committees of both houses.

In 1976 the B-1 program was approaching a decisive milestone. The Air Force and the Ford administration requested $1.9 billion not only to conclude research and development on the B-1 but to start actual production of 244 bombers. Once production began, there would be no turning back.

Early that year, Ohio's John Seiberling made a crucial tactical decision. The B-1's opponents would seek to delay the bomber, rather than attempt to defeat it outright. They would argue that 1976 was not an appropriate time for Congress to approve B-1 production. Because additional testing would not be conducted until late in the year, Seiberling argued, the production decision should be held over until 1977 so that the next president—whoever he might be—could base his decision on complete information. Seiberling knew there were not enough votes to defeat the B-1 in Congress. His call for delay was a thinly veiled appeal to Democrats who had good reason to let a Democratic president make the decision the following year. A number of congressmen would not take the political risk of voting against production but might be persuaded that it was acceptable, perhaps even good, to vote for delay.

Seiberling's tactic was Buzz Hello's worst nightmare come true. It was what he had predicted in 1974 when a funding cutback delayed the production decision until a presidential election year. He knew that in 1961 a newly elected president, John Kennedy, had killed the B-70 bomber; it could happen again. Rockwell and the Air Force redoubled their lobbying efforts to make sure Congress approved B-1 production in the 1976 session.

The first test came in the House of Representatives on April 8, 1976, when Seiberling's amendment to delay the production decision on the B-1 until 1977 was defeated 210 to 177. This was but the opening shot; many votes were yet to come, in both houses of Congress.

The next stage would be in the Senate, where the legislative strategy against the B-1 was directed by Ron Tammen, assistant to Senator Proxmire. Tammen, a native of Oregon, had worked in the 1964 presidential campaign of the conservative Republican Barry Goldwater. Tammen received his doctorate in Soviet studies from the University of Michigan and joined the CIA in 1966 as a specialist in Soviet and Chinese missile technology. In his work as a CIA analyst he saw that the military services magnified the Soviet threat to justify their own demands for new weaponry. By 1970 he was working for the congressional Arms Control and Foreign Policy Caucus (which evolved into Members of Congress for Peace Through Law), and then he became Proxmire's legislative assistant. Tammen brought to the B-1 fight a political operative's facility for counting votes, as well as the expertise of a trained weapons analyst.

Leading the fight on the floor was a new member of the Senate, a former Harvard fullback and Marine officer from Iowa named John Culver. No one in the Senate less fit the image of a peacenik; on the Armed Services Committee, he supported most programs for military readiness. Culver was respected for his sharp intelligence, and with his booming voice and sometimes overbearing demeanor, he was hard to ignore. He had been drawn into the B-1 battle partly because of a personal affront by the Rockwell Corporation.

During his five terms as a congressman from Cedar Rapids, Culver had helped Collins Radio Company, the largest employer in his district and in Iowa. His father had worked for the company. As a diligent congressman, Culver put in a good word for Collins when it was trying to obtain Pentagon contracts. In 1974, Rockwell purchased Collins Radio. To Culver's amazement, the president of Collins then criticized the senator in a radio broadcast for comments that merely raised questions about the B-1 bomber. What hurt most was that Collins had attacked without even the courtesy of discussing the issue with him, especially since he served on the Senate Armed Services Committee. "At that point," Culver recalls, "I decided to take a special interest in the B-1."

No one would intimidate John Culver. At one point the UAW invited him to an early-morning lobbying session held over eggs and coffee at the Quality Inn near the Capitol. A model of the B-1 graced the conference room where the union's big guns gathered, from President Leonard Woodcock down to all the regional and local UAW political operatives who had supported Culver's victorious Senate campaign. Before the UAW officials could speak or even eat a bite of breakfast, Culver warned them off: "I know why you are here," he said. "I know what you want me to do. Let me tell you something. This is my union. This is the union of Walter Reuther [the legendary UAW founder]. Is this union trying to tell me that it would rather have this bomber than Walter Reuther's national health-care plan?"

No one lobbied Culver at the Quality Inn that morning. In fact, Iowa's UAW members, who made agricultural implements, weren't concerned about the B-1; it was the UAW's aerospace workers who had thousands of jobs at stake. The Iowans rather admired Culver's position on the B-1 and his tough candor.

It was no coincidence that the leaders of the anti–B-1 effort in the Senate—McGovern, Proxmire, and Culver—all came from states with virtually no defense industry or military facilities. The absence of a significant defense complex in their own constituencies allowed them an extra margin of freedom on defense issues.

A tough, pragmatic politician, Culver could be just as intimidating to the anti–B-1 activists. About the same time as the UAW meeting, an Iowa peace activist suggested that Culver take on the issue. "You've got a lot of nerve asking me to stick my neck out on the B-1," thundered Culver. "I've got to get along with Barry Goldwater. Go out and build a political base in Iowa against the B-1, and then maybe I'll take it on."

As the Senate vote approached, the anti–B-1 coalition recruited three influential senators—Scoop Jackson of Washington, Sam Nunn of Georgia, and Robert Byrd of West Virginia.

Jackson and Nunn were both knowledgeable, respected defense experts. In military terms, Jackson had always stressed the value of missiles over bombers. Because they did not see overriding military arguments for the B-1, Jackson and Nunn had partisan reason to support the Democratic Senate majority, which favored delay. And as a 1976 presidential contender, Jackson was well aware that many liberal Democrats had adopted the anti–B-1 cause. Jackson and Nunn both also had parochial political reasons to justify support for a bomber firing long-range cruise missiles rather than for the B-1. The Boeing Company of Seattle aspired to supply the plane, whether by transforming its B-52s or its 747s, or by building a new plane; it also had the contract to build the first new air-launched cruise missiles, or ALCMs. In Nunn's case, the Lockheed Company of Georgia thought its C-5As should be converted to carry cruise missiles, and Martin Marietta was competing to produce the missiles. Whatever their motives, Jackson and Nunn now defected from support of the B-1 to vote with Culver against immediate production of the bomber.

Robert Byrd, the Senate's Democratic whip, had been the object of a nationwide lobbying campaign by the anti–B-1 coalition. Byrd was due to succeed retiring Mike Mansfield of Montana as the majority leader, and this was the right moment for him to support a cause advocated by liberal Senate Democrats, who found his record too conservative for comfort.

As he fought to line up the votes that would only delay the B-1, John Culver discovered how hard it was even to get other senators to focus on the issue. The first problem was explaining how to defend the vote politically. The second was convincing a member of Congress that costs are relevant, when astronomical defense budgets make all costs seem unreal. The third was overcoming a member's special political interest in a project. Fourth was that the main allies in weapons fights usually were peace groups, like Brammer's, whose arguments carried little weight in Congress. Last was persuading an overburdened member of Congress to take the time to tackle and understand what were often complex technical arguments.

Just before the Senate vote, the anti–B-1 coalition produced its own group of experts, including former Defense Secretary Clark Clifford, former Kennedy aide McGeorge Bundy, and General Maxwell Taylor, a retired chairman of the Joint Chiefs of Staff. Jeremy Stone of the Federation of American Scientists rounded up scientific experts who provided authoritative testimony that the B-1 either was unneeded, ineffective, or both.

The Senate voted on May 20. The Culver amendment to delay the B-1 production decision until February of 1977 was approved 44 to 37.

In one respect, the vote represented only a minor procedural victory in a long and continuing fight. But in another, it was a milestone, marking one of the few occasions in which the U.S. Senate had handed the military establishment a defeat on a major weapon. And because of the Senate vote, the issue spilled over into the political battles for the Republican and Democratic presidential nominations.

In the Republican contest, former California Governor Ronald Reagan, challenging President Ford from the right, made his chief point of attack the charge that Ford was weak on national defense. Under withering fire by Reagan, Ford abandoned the missile-reduction plans under discussion in the Strategic Arms Limitations Talks (SALT) with the Soviets; he called for a large increase in defense spending; and in mid-1976, six months before tests on the system were due to be completed, he committed himself to build the B-1 bomber. For maximum political benefit, Ford pointedly made his B-1 endorsement while campaigning in Cincinnati, where GE would build the B-1's engines.

Jimmy Carter also faced a new problem in his quest for the Democratic nomination. In March he lost the Massachusetts primary to Scoop Jackson. He won the Pennsylvania primary in late April, but his pollster Patrick Caddell worried about data showing up in Carter's public-opinion ratings. Voters increasingly characterized Carter as "fuzzy on issues, not specific, wishy-washy, changes stands." A CBS news poll showed that 43 percent of those polled thought Carter vacillated on issues. In early May, Carter's image problem was exacerbated when speechwriter Robert Shrum quit the Carter campaign. With a blaze of publicity, Shrum charged that Carter, the candidate who claimed to have a monopoly on honesty, was not candid on the issues. According to Shrum, Carter spoke out in public for a $5 to $7 billion decrease in defense expenditures, but privately believed that defense expenditures might have to be increased.

Confronted by *New York Times* reporter Charles Mohr with the alleged discrepancy, Carter icily replied: "I'm not a liar. I don't make a statement in private contrary to what I make in public."

During the spring campaign, Carter's "issues" problem raised doubts among the liberal, antiwar Democrats whose votes he needed in upcoming northern-state primaries against Morris Udall, the well-liked liberal Arizona congressman.

Stuart Eizenstat, the bright young Atlanta lawyer who served as Carter's chief issues adviser, decided that something had to be done to win over liberals who suspected Carter was less a true Democrat than a closet Republican. Liberals also worried that Carter, a Naval Academy graduate and former naval officer, held hard-line views on defense contrary to their own concerns for peace.

Just as Eizenstat was wrestling with his boss's image problem, President Ford came out with his unqualified support for the B-1, and the Democratic-controlled Senate voted to delay the bomber. Eizenstat recognized that the B-1 had become a highly visible symbolic issue, which offered a tailor-made opportunity for Carter. The candidate from Georgia could not only show how he differed from Ford on defense, but demonstrate decisiveness on an issue important to liberal Democrats. Eizenstat decided that Carter needed to take a firm stand. On the day of Culver's Senate victory, Eizenstat pointedly told the *Wall Street Journal*, "The next President is against [the B-1], if he is the next President."

Then Eizenstat, with Carter's approval, drew up a series of white papers spelling out in detail the candidate's position on issues. The papers were circulated to members of the Democratic platform-drafting committee, which included key liberals such as former Senator Joseph Clark, a Carter backer in Pennsylvania, who were pushing hard for an anti–B-1 plank. Carter's white paper said: "Exotic weapons which serve no real function do not contribute to the defense of this country. The B-1 is an example of a system which should not be funded and would be wasteful of taxpayers' dollars."

At the National Campaign Against the B-1, surprised and ecstatic campaign operatives quickly went to work to get the Eizenstat-Carter language adopted by the Democratic platform committee. Because the man who now seemed certain to be the Democratic nominee had come out against the B-1, the official party platform would do the same. Jimmy Carter had been maneuvered into taking a clear stand. The anti–B-1 coalition had achieved its first objective.

The citizens' campaign against the B-1 was framed for the faithful as nothing less than a crusade against the entire defense establishment. If the bomber were defeated, anti–B-1 campaigners hoped that the billions of dollars saved might be channeled into peace conversion—into homes, or hospitals, or mass transit.

Few members of Congress, however, shared the radical aims of the campaign organizers. Exposing and challenging the power of the military-industrial complex was not very high on the agenda of even the most liberal among them. Some agreed that the arms race must be slowed. Others opposed the B-1 because it was wasteful or ineffective. Many went along with the opposition merely because the B-1 issue had developed a life of its own. It had become a winnable issue; therefore winning became the overriding objective. There was not much careful thought about whether the B-1 was even the right weapon to kill off in order to challenge the arms race. It was the weapon at hand.

Citizen activists also failed to realize the political realities of Washington defense politics. Defeating the B-1 entailed a price—the trading-off of one weapon for another. Eisenhower and Kennedy had learned that when they attempted to kill the B-70, the B-1's predecessor. The B-1 debate in Congress followed an almost ironclad law of the politics of defense: Very few congressmen will vote against any weapon system without being able to defend their vote by saying they supported another more effective weapon.

Representative Thomas Downey, the young New York Democrat who was one of the brightest of the newly elected congressmen opposing the B-1, described the dilemma: "It's impossible in Congress for the opponents of the B-1 to say, 'Don't build the B-1, build a hospital,' because then the people making the decisions stop listening to you, stop taking you seriously. The antidote is always another weapon system that meets the same mission requirement."

The congressional B-1 debate in 1976 essentially pitted one weapon system against another. The real question was which weapon—the B-1 or the cruise missile—would be built. If the B-1 were defeated, it would be due in part to Congress's belief that the cruise missile was a better weapon. The cruise missile, a tiny unmanned craft, could fly at very low altitude in order to avoid radar as it made its way to Soviet targets.

The case against the B-1 was boosted when the Brookings Institution—a staid, cautiously liberal Washington think tank—published a booklet praising the cruise missile. The authors, former Air Force Colonels Archie Wood and Alton Quanbeck, contended that, compared to the B-1, the cruise was a much more effective and less expensive means of maintaining the bomber portion of the nuclear strategic deterrent. They also maintained that later-model B-52s built between 1960 and 1962 would be able to penetrate the Soviet Union until the 1990s. Furthermore, they said, either these B-52s or widebodied transports could stand off from the Soviet Union and effectively fire cruise missiles with great accuracy at targets more than 1,500 miles away. And cruise missiles were cheap. Hundreds of them could be produced for the price of a single B-1 bomber.

The Air Force and its congressional supporters, among them Senator Goldwater, responded that since the B-52s were wearing out, it was much more cost-effective to build the B-1 than to update the B-52s; that the cruise missile was still unproven; and that the proposed widebodied cruise carrier would be an easy mark for long-range Soviet fighter interceptors.

General Russell Dougherty, the SAC commander, explained the need for the B-1: "There is no weapons delivery system that is more important, more critical, or offers more deterrent utility within the total mix of our strategic forces than the B-1. A penetrating bomber can always be adapted to utilize and exploit any advantages of a standoff missile, while . . . being able to extract high levels of damage against deep targets, including those requiring a high order of accuracy and yield to achieve reasonable damage levels."

Such military debates were irrelevant to most peace activists. They opposed both weapon systems. When Brammer, Pearlman, and Provance established their congressional alliances at the outset of the campaign, they were warned by Seiberling aide Don Mansfield that the price of killing the B-1 would be to support the cruise as an alternative. Provance in particular disliked the tactics that followed, but the peace activists could not bring themselves to force a showdown that might shatter their partnership with Congress. They had worked hard and hungered for a victory. There would be none if they broke with their congressional allies and attacked the cruise-missile alternative. Brammer and Pearlman had become political pragmatists. In Washington, they argued the merits of the cruise missile over the B-1. In dozens of communications with the campaign's citizen supporters around the country, however, they stressed idealistic peace goals and neglected to mention that defeating the B-1 would hasten the advent of another fearsome weapon system.

Other organizations in the anti–B-1 coalition also were less than candid with their grass-roots membership. When Common Cause first joined the campaign, it strenuously publicized the issue among its members. But when a number of members protested that the organization had no business getting involved in a defense issue, Common Cause did not give up its Washington lobbying against the B-1. It simply stopped informing its members about the activity.

Neither Iowan Culver's victorious Senate vote in May 1976 nor Georgian Carter's statement of opposition to the B-1 in the Democratic platform ended the battle. Within ten days, Carter was listening to advisers other than Eizenstat and cautiously backing off from his unequivocal stand against building the B-1. His military advisers explained that there were not only good arguments for the B-1, but widespread and influential support for the bomber.

Culver's amendment was dropped in a House-Senate conference committee on the defense-authorization bill, and Seiberling lost again, 207 to 186, on an amendment to strip the B-1 production money from the House defense-appropriation bill. The anti–B-1 coalition, however, was gaining votes. The House margin of defeat had narrowed by nine votes.

The anti–B-1 coalition had one more chance in the Senate Appropriations Committee. Ron Tammen and the coalition staff thought they had accurate intelligence on how every member of the committee would vote on the B-1 production-decision delay. They expected a 16–13 win. The vote on July 21 went as expected until the name of Senator Warren Magnuson of Washington was called. To Proxmire's complete surprise, Magnuson, who had agreed earlier to support the delay, voted for the B-1. The vote against the B-1 appeared to have lost on a 14–14 tie. Proxmire managed to stall a final tally while Tammen raced around the Capitol to find the missing Robert Byrd. Byrd was located and cast a winning fifteenth vote. The anti–B-1 coalition finally would prevail in its modest effort to delay the plane's production.

The circumstances of the Magnuson vote disturbed some of his colleagues on the Appropriations Committee. The old man was frail and sometimes unsteady. Just before the vote he had received a call from an Air Force general. Magnuson was shaken by the general's message, the gist of which was that if the B-1 lost, the Boeing Company might well lose some important defense contracts.

In a final compromise reached in August between the House and the Senate, Congress approved production of the B-1 bomber, but agreed that only limited funds would be released, so that the next president could review the decision the following February.

The Rockwell–Air Force lobbying coalition was stunned by the defeat. In August, Rockwell president Anderson asked his company's 119,000 workers to write to Congress in support of the plane, a call that was ill-timed, since Congress had concluded its action. "We're going to lose this thing if they [Rockwell] push too hard," complained a worried Air Force general. In the spring, after Carter issued his statement against the B-1, Anderson had gone to the Carter campaign headquarters in Atlanta to argue for the B-1. Stuart Eizenstat told him, "The Democratic platform's against it and the candidate is against it."

Meanwhile, President Ford was closing the gap by which he trailed Carter. The political wind was shifting on defense issues. If Carter had seemed too conservative for antiwar liberals in the Democratic primaries, he was now perceived by many in the electorate at large as too soft on defense.

On October 7, Ford visited the Rockwell plant outside Los Angeles, posed for photographers in the cockpit of a B-1 bomber, and blasted Carter and his vice-presidential candidate, Walter Mondale, for advocating policies that would dangerously weaken America's defense against Soviet aggression. Playing on Teddy Roosevelt's maxim about speaking softly and carrying a big stick, Ford charged his opponents with wanting to "speak loudly and carry a flyswatter." He castigated Mondale for having voted three times against the B-1 in the Senate. Ford said a prerequisite for peace was the willingness of the United States to let our enemies know we are willing to defend the peace. "They may or may not understand that in English," he said, "but this B-1 is a message that they will clearly understand."

Ford wound up his speech with the economic pitch that presidential candidates, from Kennedy on, seemed to repeat every four years in California: the B-1 stood for jobs. The $5 to $7 billion in defense cuts proposed by Carter "would put you and thousands and thousands of others out of work." The Democrats' solution, said the president, would be "to put you back to work in dead-end public-service jobs."

Ford had requested the Rockwell appearance and "photo opportunity" in the B-1 from Bob Anderson, who had befriended Michigan's Ford years before when Anderson worked at Chrysler. Ford repeatedly had assured Anderson he would build the B-1. At this point, Anderson fervently hoped Ford would win the election.

Meanwhile, Jimmy Carter's defense advisers warned him to backpedal on his opposition to the B-1. His lead over Ford was shrinking rapidly and he now needed promilitary conservative support. The Carter campaign invited a group of defense contractors, including Rockwell's Anderson, to Atlanta, where they were given assurances that Carter was not antidefense. By mid-October Carter was taking the line that B-1 research and development should continue. He would make up his mind after the election about building the plane.

In late October, as Carter prepared for his last campaign swing, which would include a stop in Tulsa, he consulted with David Boren, Oklahoma's young Democratic governor. Boren had been the first governor to endorse Carter.

"What should I say in Oklahoma?" Carter asked Boren.

"Say you're for the B-1 bomber," replied Boren. He told Carter that a major Rockwell plant building parts of the B-1 was located right at the airport where Carter planned to speak.

Following Boren's advice, Carter carefully managed to convey to the Oklahomans that he was open-minded about building the B-1 and didn't oppose it.

On November 2, Carter scored a narrow victory over Gerald Ford and went home to Plains, Georgia, to recuperate from the campaign. But he could not escape the B-1 campaigners. Two days before Christmas, the National Campaign Against the B-1 was parked outside his front door. Led by Terry Provance, fifty peace activists maintained a day-long vigil. The president-elect's mother, Miz Lillian, served them coffee and told them, "Jimmy is really glad that you're here."

Finally, Carter came out and shook each one's hand. "I know why you are here," he said. He knew that they would not let him forget his May pledge not to build the B-1.

13

THE POLITICS
OF
A NUCLEAR ENGINEER

President Jimmy Carter took office on January 20, 1977, pledging dramatic changes in American defense and foreign policy. He would seek peace, arms control, and the advancement of human rights, rather than a further defense buildup confrontation with the Soviet Union: "We will move this year a step closer towards our ultimate goal—the elimination of all nuclear weapons from this earth. We urge all other people to join us, for success can mean life instead of death."

Carter's first acts signaled the seriousness of his idealism. On his second day in office, he tried to close a bitter chapter in American history by granting amnesty to Vietnam draft evaders. He proposed to the Soviet Union deep cuts in strategic arms. He appointed to key positions people dedicated to arms control, including Cyrus Vance as secretary of state. The president cut foreign aid to nations that violated the human rights of their citizens. At the same time, he made an effort to normalize relations with Fidel Castro's Cuba.

In his first meeting with the Joint Chiefs of Staff, the president shocked the generals and admirals by asking what would be required to reduce the U.S. strategic deterrent from nearly ten thou-

158

sand missile warheads to a "minimum deterrent" of several hundred.

On January 31, Carter further stunned his advisers on defense, foreign policy, and the budget at a marathon White House meeting on the defense budget. During the campaign he had promised to cut defense spending by $5 to $7 billion. Irritated by a brief Defense Department memorandum suggesting that only $3 billion could be cut from the next year's budget, Carter summoned Secretary of Defense Harold Brown, Secretary of State Vance, National Security Adviser Zbigniew Brzezinski, Bert Lance, director of the Office of Management and Budget, and General George Brown, chairman of the Joint Chiefs of Staff. For seven hours, the president delved into the most minute details of forty-three different defense programs. When the meeting ended near midnight, the weary new officials realized that former Naval engineer Carter, unlike his recent predecessors, meant to immerse himself in the most technical details of national defense.

But the first item—the B-1 bomber—was dealt with quickly. No other item on the defense budget offered a bigger opportunity for savings. The president ordered Defense Secretary Brown to reexamine the need for the bomber, and deferred action until the spring.

Never had the Air Force's relentless quest been closer to realization. If Carter abandoned his campaign rhetoric and affirmed former President Ford's decision to build the bomber, the production lines at Rockwell International would be ready to roll. But the anti–B-1 forces felt victory within their grasp. All parties busily pursued their own strategies to influence Carter's decision.

The National Campaign Against the B-1 Bomber renewed its effort. Two days after Carter's inauguration, Terry Provance and Bob Brammer staged anti–B-1 demonstrations in 145 cities, including Washington, D.C., where marchers gathered on the Ellipse directly behind the White House. The campaign's political strategy was to hold Carter to the moral high ground he had staked with the campaign pledge "I will never tell you a lie."

"If Carter builds the B-1, it will be a breach of faith," said Nancy Ramsey of the Women's International League for Peace.

The White House was bombarded with telephone calls, letters, demonstrations, and organized appeals, including a petition to the president from twenty-nine mayors. Representatives of local anti–B-1 groups and antiwar organizations lobbied the White House directly through Midge Costanza, the president's special assistant for public liaison.

At the Pentagon, the pro–B-1 forces tuned up. Rockwell lobbyists Doc Watson, John Rane, and Ginger Allen met in February with their counterparts in the Air Force legislative-liaison office to draw up a plan of action. The Rockwell team thought the meeting signaled the kickoff of their annual joint effort to advance the B-1 through Congress. "We've come for our marching orders," announced Johnny Rane cheerily to his military partners.

But the Air Force men broke the news: they would not be marching. The Air Force did not plan to lobby Congress this time around. If Carter decided to go ahead with the B-1, there would be no need to lobby. If he decided to kill the plane, the Air Force would not buck him. Those "orders came from the top"—meaning Air Force Chief of Staff David Jones.

Doc Watson, Rockwell's veteran lobbyist, was indignant. The Air Force and the aerospace industry had always pushed together for the bomber in Congress, even when Presidents Eisenhower, Kennedy, and Johnson had opposed it. Noting that citizens had a constitutional right to petition their government, Watson announced that Rockwell would continue independently to lobby Congress for the B-1.

Pressure also came from Congress, where the key military committees started advancing the B-1 program, without waiting for Carter to make up his mind. If he tried to kill the bomber, he would face stiff opposition.

Within Carter's administration, both his secretary of defense, Harold Brown, and his Air Force chief of staff, General David Jones, wanted to build the B-1 bomber.

As a young physicist with a brilliant academic record, Harold Brown had been a protégé of Edward Teller, father of the hydrogen bomb, at the Lawrence Radiation Laboratory in California. At thirty-three, Brown became the Defense Department's director of research and engineering in the Kennedy administration. He then served as President Johnson's secretary of the Air Force. Brown was one of the few whiz kids to advocate the AMSA, which became the B-1 bomber. In 1977, after seven years as president of the California Institute of Technology, Brown became the first scientist to head the Pentagon.

Carter's appointment of Brown initially pleased people with quite disparate views on defense issues. The military respected him as an eminent weapons expert and nuclear strategist. Arms-controllers welcomed him, based on his past proposals urging an agreement with the Soviet Union. Despite his administrative experience, Brown retained the personality of a shy academic. He preferred to express his ideas in writing, and didn't relish the give-and-take of Washington politics. He had supported the B-1 during the 1976 congressional debate, writing to Senator Proxmire that the Defense Department "has the best of the argument." Dr. Brown believed in manned bombers, both as insurance if another part of the nuclear triad failed, and for the added pressure they put on the Soviets. But he didn't buy the argument that the bomber had any value as a "psychological weapon" to show force. The former whiz kid still used cost-effectiveness as a key measurement in judging weapons.

Brown knew he had to walk a political tightrope. To run the Pentagon effectively, he needed the cooperation of the Air Force generals who ardently wanted the plane. But to establish his influence with the president at the outset, he could not buck him on a major issue. General Jones shared Brown's caution. In calling the 1974 Corona Quest meeting of top Air Force generals, he had shown that he was willing to abandon the B-1 if it caused dissension and hurt other vital Air Force programs.

Because of the political delicacy of their positions, General Jones and Secretary Brown took a judicious approach to the new bomber study Jimmy Carter had ordered them to conduct. A 1974 Joint Strategic Bomber Study (JSBS) had so loaded the case for the B-1 that Pentagon critics referred to it as Joint Strategic "BS." The study for Carter would carefully examine all points of view.

Brown appointed E. C. (Pete) Aldridge, the assistant defense secretary for program analysis, to chair the Modernization of the Strategic Bomber Force Study. This study measured the B-1 against the B-52 and against standoff bombers firing long-range cruise missiles. Brown asked the group to evaluate two critical questions: First was the future ability of bombers like the B-52 or B-1 to penetrate the ever-improving Soviet defenses, including "look-down, shoot-down" radar, which might permit Soviet fighters to find and defeat low-flying bombers. Second, the penetrating bomber's capability would be weighed against the ability of the tiny, low-flying cruise missiles to penetrate these Soviet defenses. The group studied three options for modernizing the bomber force: a pure penetrating force of B-1s; a mixed force of penetrating B-1s and B-52s armed with cruise missiles; and a force of B52s alone, some used as penetrators, some as cruise-missile carriers.

As soon as Secretary Brown's study group came up with preliminary findings in April 1977, Air Force partisans slipped the top-secret results to Rockwell officials. Gary Hillary, who headed Rockwell's aircraft division office in Washington, immediately called Pete Aldridge to express his dismay. The report definitely did not make a strong, unequivocal case for the B-1.

"Jesus Christ, Pete," said Hillary, "why do you have it like this [so neutral]?"

"We bent over backwards to make it look like we're not pushing the B-1," replied Aldridge.

Hillary then took his complaint to General Jones. "It doesn't come out that neutral," replied Jones. "I think there is a 60–40 chance Carter will go for the B-1."

Hillary sent the preliminary report to Bob Anderson, who saw that the Air Force position on the B-1 was gradually changing from total support to increasing equivocation. It seemed to Anderson that Secretary Brown and President Carter would keep asking for additional options until they got one they wanted—anything but the B-1. At the outset, Anderson had been confident Carter would see the utility of the B-1. He also knew that Brown had previously supported the bomber. As a trustee of Cal Tech, Anderson had become friends with Brown, then its president. Before Brown was sworn in as defense secretary, Anderson had telephoned him to offer a briefing on the B-1. Brown declined, saying he had "stayed up to speed" on the bomber.

Anderson's confidence received a jolt in the spring when he

met with Air Force Chief of Staff Jones. "What would you think of fifty B-1s?" asked the general. When Anderson responded that "it would be very expensive to build that few planes," Jones chilled him with his next question: "What would you think of zero B-1s?"

Other B-1 supporters thought the report was biased against the bomber, framed in such a way as to give Carter the freedom to choose any of the options. Cost comparisons were made for only a ten-year period—much more advantageous to the 349 aging B-52s than a twenty-year comparison would have been.

Carter again showed his interest in technical detail. As the sixth president in sixteen years to consider a new bomber, Carter placed a heavy burden of proof on the B-1 by asking Secretary Brown to determine "whether the B-1's ECM"—electronic countermeasures to help penetrate the Soviet Union—"will cut the mustard over the next twenty to thirty years." One Pentagon official said the means did not exist even to study the issue. The answer required a crystal ball.

The new study's analysis offered no clear choice in bomber forces. For the next ten years, it concluded, either the B-52 or B-1 could penetrate equally effectively. After that time, however, the B-52 would be less effective. But there were still questions about how long the B-1 would be an effective penetrator. The study recommended that to hedge against uncertainties—in new Soviet defense developments and in the still-experimental U.S. cruise technology—a "mixed force" would be best: a smaller force of about 120 to 150 penetrating B-1s should be supplemented by a modernized B-52 force armed with cruise missiles.

For years the Air Force had fought development of the cruise missile, which it perceived as a deadly competitor to the penetrating bomber it wanted so badly. The Air Force leadership did everything in its power to block the development of any such missile, including canceling production of an armed short-range cruise missile, the subsonic cruise armed decoy (SCAD), and its unarmed cousin, SCUD. The Air Force itself had developed SCAD and SCUD to help bombers penetrate Soviet defenses, but it canceled its own new weapons in the early 1970s, fearing that their deployment would support the case for a longer-range cruise missile. Air Force leaders preferred to hazard Soviet antibomber defenses rather than increase the domestic political threat to the B-1 bomber.

Development of the cruise missile went ahead only because Defense Secretary Laird and his deputy secretary, William Clements, had ordered it in 1972. They placed a Navy captain in charge of the program to assure that the Air Force could not sabotage it.

If an airplane could stand off 2,500 miles from its Soviet targets and fire cruise missiles, advocates for this system argued, why go to the expense of building a bomber whose key feature was its ability (which was questionable) to penetrate deep into Soviet territory? The question was valid, and just as it had finally given in to the ICBM, the Air Force now began to accept the inevitability of cruise missiles, in part because the other services began to adopt them.

Dr. Ivan Selin, Dr. Herbert York, and Paul Ignatius, former Pentagon officials who served as the new study group's senior consultants, told Secretary Brown that he could make a case for whichever option he wanted—the B-1s because they would be cheaper to operate than B-52s, or the B-52s because their ability to deploy cruise missiles gave an offensive punch equal to that of the B-1. What was most important, Selin stressed, was to develop the cruise missile and the new electronic offensive and defensive technology. It didn't really matter which airplane was chosen.

At the White House, Carter routed the study for analysis to Bert Lance at the Office of Management and Budget, and to the National Security Council (NSC), where Deputy Director David Aaron assigned it for immediate review to Victor Utgoff. A physicist who had made his reputation as a strategic-weapons expert at the Institute for Naval Analysis, Utgoff prepared a standard, impartial NSC analysis, outlining the various options in the Defense Department report.

Aaron was not pleased. "This is hopeless," he said, at a Saturday meeting with Utgoff. "One of the reasons we hired you was to do a good job on this." Aaron wanted Utgoff to produce a new review by the next day.

Utgoff surmised that his boss wanted a report that stressed the advantages of the cruise missile. After going over the material again, he decided he could make a strong case that B-52s armed with long-range cruise missiles would be adequate, and far more cost-effective than building B-1s.

Utgoff met Aaron at the White House on Sunday and made his oral presentation for the cruise-missile solution, using the data in the Brown study to reinforce the same arguments cruise advocates had been advancing for years.

"This is useful," Aaron responded.

When Congress voted to delay production of the bomber in 1976, it required the president to act by June 30, 1977. As the deadline grew closer, lobbyists pressed the White House from all directions.

Even Utgoff, the quintessential apolitical technocrat, was approached. First he was visited by a company executive and a labor union official from the Cleveland Pneumatics Company, which would make the B-1's landing gear. The two made it into the White House after Democratic members of Congress from Ohio wrote the president asking that they be given a hearing. Physicist Utgoff listened politely as the company executive and union official explained how many jobs were at stake, with consequences for the economic health of Cleveland.

Next came Michael Mann from the National Campaign Against the B-1, who argued that the cruise was more effective than the B-1.

"If we don't build the B-1," Utgoff asked Mann, "won't you be back here next year arguing that we also shouldn't build the cruise?"

"We'll see," he replied. The activists were intent now on winning the B-1 fight. They would worry about the cruise missile and the rest of the disarmament problem later.

Big labor unions with B-1 jobs at stake leaned heavily on the administration, particularly on Vice-President Mondale. When White House aide Bob Beckel reported, "The unions are divided on the B-1 issue," President Carter responded, "This isn't a labor issue; it's a defense issue."

Within the Carter administration, Rockwell found few firm friends. Normally, the defense industry deals with the deputy secretary of defense, who runs weapons procurement. As deputy secretary, Carter had appointed Charles Duncan, a campaign supporter and former president of the Coca-Cola Company. Rockwell President Anderson knew, however, that a soft-drink executive wasn't going to influence a weapons decision made by eminent scientist Harold Brown.

Carter himself was under siege by congressional factions on both sides of the issue. He agreed to receive a delegation representing each side.

On June 7, Senator Barry Goldwater led the pro–B-1 delegation to the White House to argue for the mixed force of B-1s and cruise-armed B-52s recommended in the Brown study. Stating this case to the president were George Mahon, the Texas Democrat who chaired the House Appropriations Committee; John C. Stennis, the Mississippi Democrat who chaired the Senate Armed Services Committee; Ernest Hollings, a Democrat from South Carolina; and Alan Cranston, the liberal California Democrat who opposed many nuclear weapons, but not the California-built B-1.

Cranston, a strong supporter of arms control, contended that the B-1 would not destabilize the arms race, as it was not suitable for a lightning-fast surprise first strike. Stennis argued that canceling the B-1 unilaterally, without seeking any Soviet concessions, would hurt the U.S. bargaining position in the SALT talks. Mahon also thought canceling the plane would be perceived by the Russians as a sign of weakness. He reminded the president that $3 billion of taxpayer money was already invested in the bomber, and that building it would dispel the belief that the president was antidefense.

Goldwater was dubious about missiles as the alternative to the bomber. "We've never test-fired an ICBM [over the polar route] with or without a warhead," he said. "We know about bombers. They can be launched and kept in the air for twenty-eight hours. Don't make the red button the only alternative."

President Carter told the senators that if he thought the B-1 was the best weapon, he wouldn't let $12 billion in extra costs stand in the way. But if the B-52 with cruise missiles was equally effective and cost half as much, that would make a difference. The president also noted that at the preliminary SALT talks, the Soviets did not seem to be concerned about the B-1, although they were worried about the cruise missile.

On June 10, President Carter met with some of Congress's leading B-1 opponents, including Senators George McGovern of South Dakota, Edward Kennedy of Massachusetts, Jacob Javits of New York, Clifford Case of New Jersey, and John Culver of Iowa, who served as the group's spokesman.

Culver argued that the B-1 at best would make a marginal contribution, while consuming a huge amount of the defense budget that could be better spent on a variety of other vital military needs, including strengthening conventional forces and resupplying NATO. Armed with cruise missiles, B-52s would be a much less expensive deterrent.

Culver also contended that the B-1 was not a barometer of the national will, and of no use even as a SALT bargaining chip, because the Soviets weren't worried about it. The Democrats reminded Carter that the B-1 had been an election issue, and that he had made clear his position against it. A recent public-opinion poll supported killing the B-1. Finally, they told Carter, domestic problems cried out for resources, and "human-misery needs should be emphasized."

A week later Carter had one of his several discussions on the B-1 issue with Defense Secretary Brown. Brown called for "keeping the B-1 bomber option open" by slowly starting production, perhaps after pausing for a year. He said there was some risk, though only a small one, that the B-52s would lose their ability to penetrate before a "follow-on" bomber eventually was developed. Furthermore, Brown reminded the president that not building the B-1 would subject him to increased political and military pressure to build the new and more powerful MX intercontinental ballistic missile. Left unstated was Brown's realization that Carter also risked strong political displeasure from all of the supporters who expected him to fulfill his campaign pledge to kill the bomber.

Carter retired to Camp David for the weekend with a two-inch-thick file of memoranda and reports bound together in a red folder indexed with twelve gray tabs. Its contents included the

Defense Department study and recommendations, Utgoff's NSC brief for the cruise solution, and an assortment of articles and editorials. For example, White House aide Stuart Eizenstat, who had staked out Carter's anti–B-1 position during the campaign, sent along a story from the *New Republic* magazine titled "This Bomber Is a Bummer."

Carter pored over the technical data, particularly the material on developing the cruise missile. He concluded that the technology could work and the cruise missile would penetrate Soviet defenses. Furthermore, top-secret research, code-named Have Blue, showed promising signs that cruise missiles—and perhaps airplanes as well—might be given a "stealthy" invisible quality that would make them barely detectable by radar.

Carter felt confident of his own ability to make the technical military decision. On a yellow legal pad he wrote forty-seven different points, pro and con, on the bomber question. Then he rated each one—a modest argument got two points, while a strong one got five. He totaled the points. They added up against the B-1 bomber.

In Jimmy Carter's own mind, the toughest issue of all would be whether he could sustain his decision in Congress. He had known before the election campaign ended that there was no winning political position on the B-1. If he struck down the bomber, he might well be overruled by a coalition of congressmen—southern prodefense conservatives, members whose districts counted on the B-1 for jobs, and Republicans eager to embarrass him—and the highly effective lobbyists for the aerospace industry and the labor unions.

As Carter prepared to rule on the B-1, a larger issue was also at stake—his effectiveness as president. Carter's Washington honeymoon had come to an abrupt end. He had offended western senators when he cut off their important federally funded water projects without even consulting them. He had shown ineptness in his first SALT proposal by making its contents public before the Soviets even received it. The Soviets had responded by rejecting Carter's suggestion of deep cuts in weapons as a propaganda ploy.

The administration's program was not moving in Congress. The toothy smile that had charmed during the campaign was now seen by many in Congress as a fixed mask hiding an enigmatic lone-wolf politician. Even sympathetic Democratic loyalists thought Carter and his Georgia gang showed contempt and insensitivity toward Congress. They didn't return telephone calls. They seemed to be trying to operate the government the way they had run the campaign—by picturing Washington politicians as the problem. On tough issues like the B-1, Carter needed all the help he could get, yet he held himself above the political give-and-take that would produce that help.

To many congressional Democrats, Carter seemed distant and apolitical. Without consulting with them, this president was proposing arms-control deals with the Soviets, lecturing other nations about human rights, signing a nuclear nonproliferation treaty, and signing a controversial treaty ceding U.S. control over the Panama Canal to Panama.

From Carter's perspective, an unfriendly Congress was disregarding his proposals or reshaping them according to its whims. On June 20, 1977, Carter discussed the problem with Mondale and his closest presidential aides.

"The more you comply with congressional changes, the more they will make changes," said the vice-president, an eleven-year veteran of the Senate.

"We'd better defy Congress once and get the test case over with," Carter replied.

That case was clearly the B-1. The president would show that he was both decisive and tough on military spending. But before reaching a final decision, Carter decided to meet once more with Budget Director Lance and with Defense Secretary Brown. In advance of the meeting, Lance sent Carter a paper analyzing the military and political options. Although killing the B-1 outright made sense, Lance wrote, the president might be defeated in Congress. Like Secretary Brown, Lance pointed out that rejecting the B-1 would increase pressure for the controversial MX missile, and could weaken the U.S. SALT bargaining position by giving up a first-line weapon before gaining any Soviet concessions.

Lance recommended a two-year delay in reaching a final decision. Meanwhile, three more prototype B-1s could be built. The program would stay alive and options would remain open. He noted, however, that "the administration could be accused of being indecisive and incurring unnecessary costs" should the B-1 be built later.

Mondale disagreed. "If we're going to kill this plane," he said, "let's do it now. The closer we get to the 1980 election the more difficult it will become."

On Wednesday, June 27, 1977, the president told his cabinet he would make the B-1 decision before the week ended. Harold Brown took the opportunity to complain about another weapons-procurement decision, the administration's approval of production of the F-18 fighter for the Navy (which the Defense Department did not want) to satisfy demands by Senator Edward Kennedy and Speaker of the House Thomas P. (Tip) O'Neill of Massachusetts. It was pork-barrel defense in the old style. General Electric produced the F-18 engines at its plant in Lynn, an important employer for the Massachusetts economy. "We need to make these decisions from a military standpoint," said Brown, who had been lobbied by both O'Neill and Kennedy. "It makes it harder when a senator or congressman announces procurement-policy decisions for their states."

Immediately after the cabinet meeting, Carter called Brown, Mondale, Brzezinski, and Eizenstat into the Oval Office. He would cancel the B-1, he said. Turning to Secretary Brown, Carter gave two reasons for his choice, aside from the military arguments. He had made a campaign promise and wanted to honor it. And he wanted to act decisively. Killing B-1 production would demonstrate his decisiveness, while delaying production or starting it slowly would not.

Brown's face revealed disappointment, but the defense secretary was not surprised. He favored a mixed force that included B-1s, but he had not pushed his view strongly with the president. From the outset he had let Carter know he would not force the president to overrule his own secretary of defense. Now that the decision was made, he would support him fully. Carter wrote in his diary: "Harold Brown has been truly courageous to recommend that the B-1 not be built." Carter misinterpreted Brown's loyal support for his decision as agreement with it. In Brzezinski's view, Brown was adept "in finding ways to let the president satisfy his political needs, without using up his own [Brown's] capital with the Pentagon."

On June 30, Carter startled B-1 opponents and proponents, both of whom had concluded he would build the plane. In his announcement, he called his choice "one of the most difficult decisions I've made." His main reason for canceling the B-1, the president explained, was that the "B-1, a very expensive weapons system, basically conceived in the absence of the cruise-missile factor, is not necessary."

Money intended for the B-1 would be diverted to modernizing and equipping B-52s to carry cruise missiles. Research, development, and production of 3,400 cruise missiles would proceed at maximum speed. Research and development would begin on a possible new widebodied jet to carry cruise missiles. However, Carter said the B-1 program would continue, with $460 million more devoted to research and development to guard against "the unlikely event that more cost-effective alternative systems should run into difficulty."

For Carter, at least, the bomber was dead.

When Carter announced his decision, loud cheers and rebel yells bellowed through the White House West Wing offices and hallways. Carter's Georgia aides, led by chief of staff Hamilton Jordan, press secretary Jody Powell, and domestic adviser Eizenstat, had from the beginning strongly believed that the president must honor his campaign commitments. They also believed that the bomber was unneeded, a waste of money. Jordan, Carter's most influential aide, described the decision as Carter at his best: boldly redeeming a campaign pledge; making his own mark on an old problem; forging a "clean decision" in the face of what Jordan derisively called "the Washington down-the-middle split" on tough issues. Jordan considered that the Pentagon's mixed-force solution was based more on political compromise than on military strategy.

Outside the White House, reaction to the decision varied. Liberal George McGovern praised Carter's "finest hour"; Republican Representative Bob Dornan, in whose district the planes would have been built, fumed, "They are breaking open the vodka in Moscow."

"The decision was bad enough, but what was worse was his betrayal of the workers," said Gerry Whipple, the West Coast regional director of the United Auto Workers. "He didn't think of them at all. He could have at least made some arrangements to help these people." At Rockwell, ten thousand workers immediately lost their jobs. Mary Turner, a fifty-eight-year-old production worker at Rockwell's El Segundo plant, told a *Newsweek* reporter, "God, I'd like to see somebody hang Carter up by the feet."

Representative Jonathan Bingham of New York had again introduced his Economic Conversion Act, which would provide government planning and funds to move both industry and its workers from defense to peaceful needs. Bingham wrote Carter, praising his B-1 decision, but calling for government action to help displaced defense workers. Bingham's bill disappeared from sight without legislative review or attention in the news media. The Carter administration helped set up a special employment office in Los Angeles to help the displaced Rockwell workers find other jobs. But the nation did not have a comprehensive policy, such as Bingham proposed, to deal with the economic dislocation caused by defense-program shutdowns.

Leaders of the National Campaign Against the B-1 and many of the city's antiwar activists celebrated their victory at a party on Capitol Hill. Amidst the congratulations and conviviality, however, a discordant note was sounded by Morton Halperin, a former National Security Council staffer and arms-control expert. "You're going to live to regret this," he said. "It's going to lead to much more dangerous weapons." Once Carter had rejected the B-1, there was no question that the U.S. would develop a cruise missile, and probably the MX missile as well.

Several days after Carter announced his decision, General David Jones received an angry telephone call from Representative William V. Chappell, Jr., a Florida Democrat and ranking member of the House Defense Appropriations Subcommittee. Chappell chewed out Jones for having backed away from what had been his staunch advocacy for the B-1. "How can you justify completely reversing the Air Force's position in three months' time?" he complained.

General Jones told Representative Chappell what he had already told Rockwell executives and his own generals. The commander-in-chief of the United States had made a decision. So long as Jones served as chief of staff, the Air Force would follow and respect that decision. It would not attempt, publicly or secretly, to undermine the president in Congress. Nor would it collaborate with any congressional attempt to overrule the decision. Jones would testify in support of the president's decision even though he had disagreed with it. Unlike LeMay and other of his predecessors, he would not use the congressional forum to challenge a decision after the president had acted. Given Carter's decision, he knew any B-1 victory in Congress would be brief. As a junior party to the Air Force's rebellion against two presidents over the B-70, he had seen that course of action poison the relationship between the Air Force and the administration for eight years. In his view, the real loser had been the Air Force, and its needs.

Furthermore, Jones began to realize that the constant struggle in which each service competed to get its special weapons did not well serve the cause of achieving the most effective national defense. "I am more concerned with our overall strategic posture than with any single weapon system," he told Congress. The continuing B-1 controversy was "diverting attention from our broader strategic needs."

Florida's Chappell, along with some other B-1 supporters in Congress and the Air Force, did not see it that way. To them, General Jones was being "political" in going along with the president. His proper course of action should have been to "fall on his sword" by resigning in protest, or to lead the kind of guerrilla action that the Air Force, in partnership with Congress, often waged against presidents they didn't agree with.

Jones's uncomfortable position demonstrated the severe loyalty test every high-ranking military officer faces within his own service. If he pursues his service's special interests, he is praised. If he serves the president and his definition of the national interest at the expense of the service's central interest, he is considered disloyal or "political." Thus, Jones, at that moment, was considered a pariah by many partisan B-1 supporters. And later, when Carter promoted Jones to chairman of the Joint Chiefs of Staff in 1978, his critics were convinced that he had won the job by going along with the president on the B-1.

• • •

Realizing that he would get no official help from the Air Force, Chappell took over the congressional fight to overturn Carter's decision. With the Air Force on the sidelines, the B-1 lobbying headquarters for Rockwell and its allies moved from the Pentagon to Chappell's office in the Rayburn House Office Building. The vote-counting and the lobbying assignments now took place there.

The congressman's ties to the military went back many years. The fifty-five-year-old Chappell had been a Navy aviator before attending the University of Florida and its law school. He served as a county prosecuting attorney, then won election to the Florida House of Representatives, where he eventually became Speaker. He kept flying in the naval reserve, attaining the rank of captain. His squadron commander, Captain Bud Otto, worked in his congressional campaign and later became his administrative assistant. When Chappell arrived in Congress in 1969, he was thus a natural candidate for membership on the Defense Appropriations Subcommittee.

Bill Chappell knew airplanes from the inside out, and the services saw to it that he got to fly whatever planes they were promoting. The Air Force took him out to Edwards Air Force Base in California, where they invited him to fly a B-1 test plane. For forty-five minutes, Chappell skimmed fifty to a hundred feet above the ground using the plane's terrain-following low-level attack radar, and capped his performance by buzzing the control tower at twenty-five feet. To commemorate the event, the Air Force presented him with a videotape of his exploits.

Chappell maintained a solid relationship with the defense industry. The industry paid special attention to the job needs of his district. At one point, the Grumman Corporation moved one of its aircraft facilities there so the area would suffer no job losses after another aerospace plant closed. Every defense-industry lobbyist in Washington felt welcome in Chappell's office. His own annual financial-disclosure and campaign reports showed that the defense industry expressed its regard for him with substantial speaking fees and campaign contributions. Bill Chappell was a southern conservative to the core, a patriot who belonged to every veterans' organization, a defense expert who had made a specialty of weapons-procurement issues.

Chappell and the B-1's other congressional allies took the initiative even before Carter acted. Two days before Carter announced his decision, the House voted 243 to 178 to continue the B-1 program by building five more bombers in 1978.

Having barely made his decision, Carter now had two major obstacles to overcome in Congress. First, he had to reverse the House decision to build B-1s number seven through eleven in 1978. Second, he needed Congress to agree to rescind the funds it had approved the previous year for B-1s number five and six. Because the White House did not trust the Air Force to lobby for the administration, that job was assigned to the secretary of defense's office. Colonel Grant Miller, who had been the Air Force's chief lobbyist for the B-1 for three years, was transferred to the secretary of defense's office to work for its defeat. Miller knew the B-1 issue in Congress, and the Carter administration wanted his expertise. Colonel Miller was another career public servant who followed orders. He walked into the office of Ron Tammen, Senator Proxmire's aide who had organized the anti–B-1 forces in the Senate, and said, "Well, we're on the same side now. Who's on who?"

Heading the lobbying effort from the White House was Bob Beckel, whom fellow political operatives described admiringly as "tough as a junkyard dog." The Carter White House, which had held itself above politics, now needed to grasp every political lever to convince Congress to change its votes and support the president. Beckel asked the Pentagon for a list of bases that the military had been trying to close. "Throw in a few you don't even want to close," he added. As the House votes approached, Beckel suggested to congressmen they might lose military bases back home if they didn't support the president on the B-1. In return for B-1 votes, he also helped restore water projects and other public-works projects that Carter had vowed to kill. He got sewer grants approved, and arranged to move the rehabilitation of a ship to Newport News to help swing the vote of a Virginia congressman.

The White House played on the expectations of congressmen whose states might benefit from building planes other than the B-1: The Texas delegation was encouraged to think that more FB-111 bombers might be built by General Dynamics in Fort Worth. Congressmen from Georgia and Washington were encouraged to believe that Lockheed and Boeing might build the wide-bodied jet being investigated as a cruise carrier. (Boeing wasted no time rising to the bait. The company put together a task force on a cruise-missile carrier the day after Carter announced his B-1 decision; two weeks later it had a demonstration proposal ready for the Air Force.)

Pro–B-1 forces also played hardball, leaning on members of Congress who were vulnerable on the jobs question. Representative John Anderson, a liberal Republican from Rockford, Illinois, opposed the B-1. But facing a conservative primary opponent, and with hundreds of jobs at stake at the Sunstrand Company's Rockford plant (which made the B-1's rudder-control system), Anderson felt that his political survival was on the line. Reluctantly he switched to supporting the bomber.

Similar pressures pushed Representative Yvonne Braithewaite Burke, a liberal California Democrat, to change her vote. When Vice-President Mondale appealed for her support against the B-1, she told him she couldn't give it. Too many of her Los Angeles constituents depended on Rockwell jobs. She sent a telegram to President Carter, praising him for sticking by his convictions, but asking for action to help the workers who had lost their jobs.

The Rockwell lobby also lost support by bearing down too hard on some members of Congress, who resented the pressure. Republican Senator Henry Bellmon, a former Oklahoma governor, had always supported the B-1, parts of which were made in Rockwell's Tulsa plant. Bellmon, however, was an independent-minded fiscal conservative who saw no point in spending another $500 million for two more airplanes when the Air Force already had four to use for testing.

Bellmon's inclination to terminate the B-1 turned to solid stone the day David Blankenship, a Rockwell executive from Tulsa and later national president of the Air Force Association, came to lobby him. Blankenship argued that building several more planes would let Rockwell keep the production line going and keep Tulsans at work, while leaving the door open to revive the plane at a later date. Nor was that Blankenship's only attempt at persuasion. According to Bellmon, Blankenship began using the telephones in the senator's office to call upon other Oklahomans, including former House Speaker Carl Albert, to lobby him. When he discovered what was happening, Bellmon said, he ordered Blankenship out of his office. At that point, Bellmon was so furious he offered an amendment to eliminate even the continued B-1 research-and-development funds approved by Carter. "I am at a loss to understand why we should spend almost half a billion dollars on a plane that we have already junked," he told a reporter.

Bellmon soon retired from Congress, saying he was disgusted with the pervasiveness of political logrolling, especially in military matters, and the growing influence of political-action committees and their campaign contributions. To illustrate his point, Bellmon described a Senate Defense Appropriations Subcommittee meeting in which Senators Magnuson of Washington and Stennis of Mississippi couldn't decide where three Navy frigates would be built. Each wanted two built in his own state and one in that of the other senator. They finally settled the dispute by agreeing to build four frigates—two in each state.

The Carter administration finally won two razor-thin votes in the House of Representatives—202 to 199 on August 8, and 204 to 194 on October 20—to stop the Air Force from proceeding with five additional B-1 bombers in 1978.

But it had even more trouble trying to rescind the funds already appropriated for the two planes in 1976. If the planes were built, the Rockwell production line would stay open until 1980. At that point Carter might change his mind, or be defeated for reelection. If that should happen, the bomber program would be in a position to move ahead at top speed.

The administration was rebuffed on December 6, 1977, when the House, by a 191–166 vote, refused to kill the two B-1s already scheduled for production. That night, Congressman Bill Chappell celebrated the victory over dinner at Trader Vic's restaurant in Washington with Rockwell lobbyists Doc Watson, John Rane, and Ginger Allen.

Rane and Chappell both recalled later how House Speaker O'Neill approached their table and offered his congratulations. Before he left, however, O'Neill broke open a fortune cookie. Its message, he said, was, "What is done today can be undone tomorrow."

. . .

177

In February 1978, after a seven-month battle, the Carter administration still had not been able to stop funding for the two planes. White House lobbyist Bob Beckel considered the broad aims of the administration in Congress and wondered whether the fight over the B-1 was worth its cost in political capital. In Beckel's view, Carter had made individual decisions on the B-1 and other defense matters in a vacuum, without considering the political effect on other programs and policies. As National Security Adviser Brzezinski described the process, Carter at the outset was inclined to make "pristine decisions."

In addition to killing the B-1, the president further alienated prodefense members of Congress by ordering American troops withdrawn from Korea (although that action later was changed), and vetoing congressional approval of a new U.S. Navy supercarrier.

Beckel couldn't see how killing the B-1, wasteful though the program might be, was worth antagonizing members of Congress whose votes the administration desperately needed on such other issues as approval of the Panama Canal Treaty and a SALT agreement with the Soviet Union. Beckel understood how politically important it is for an administration to look strong on defense; Carter's decisions on the B-1 and other topics were being used to make him appear weak.

"Why are we breaking our pick over this thing?" Beckel asked Jack Stempler, the assistant secretary of defense for legislative affairs. "Who gives a damn?"

Carter did. By that point, his prestige and presidential power were being openly challenged.

On February 22, 1978, the Carter administration finally prevailed. The House voted 234 to 182 to eliminate $500 million for the first two production-model B-1s. At a heavy but still-untallied political cost, President Carter had won a battle on the B-1. The B-1 looked dead. Tip O'Neill had indeed read his fortune cookie correctly.

Speaker O'Neill also helped soften the resistance of congressmen who feared the political repercussions of voting against a weapons system. He asked them to break with the tradition of voting for weapons "just because such endorsements give the political appearance of support to defense of the nation."

The administration finally won because some of the old Democratic congressional warhorses placed their loyalty to the president and their party above their loyalty to the Air Force. Chairman John Stennis of the Senate Armed Services Committee and Chairman George Mahon of the House Appropriations Committee each had supported Air Force causes for decades. Now both defended Carter's position on the B-1.

In a statement about nuclear war, the elderly Mahon said, "We are looking at national defense through a little knothole as though the bomber was everything that was going to save us from war or win the war if war should come. Does not everybody in this House know that the weapon of the future is the intercontinental missile? Do we not know that the only purpose of the bomber is to do the cleanup job? And after the atomic exchange, we could probably do the cleanup job in an oxcart."

14

THE SECRET WAR
TO SAVE
THE B-1

At face value, the final congressional vote on President Carter's decision spelled doom for the bomber. But anyone who assumed that the plane was dead and buried underestimated the forces committed to the B-1. The Air Force, the manufacturers, their allies in Congress, and their supporters in the Carter administration—including some of the president's own high-ranking Pentagon appointees—refused to admit defeat. For those powerful members of the defense network, a battle had just been lost. But the war would go on, with whatever tactics and strategies the situation required.

Watching television in his office in El Segundo, California, Buzz Hello learned of the final congressional vote on February 22, 1978, to eliminate funds for production of the B-1 bomber. The congressional insurrection had ended, but part of his company's legislative strategy had worked.

Although Rockwell had fought tenaciously to overturn the Carter decision in Congress, it never realistically expected to win that fight. Its most important objective now was to protect an additional $442 million in the military budget allocated to B-1 research and development. That money was critically needed to build B-1 research plane number four, which had not even been assembled. Without that plane, Rockwell would lack a bomber fully equipped with the offensive and defensive avionics systems necessary to demonstrate that the B-1 could effectively penetrate the Soviet Union. To Hello's relief, neither Carter nor Congress touched the money.

Behind Hello stood Robert Anderson, the Rockwell president, who had devoted seven years to the B-1 since coming to Rockwell from Chrysler. The fate of Rockwell's aviation division had been tied to the bomber for twenty years. Building 240 B-1s would mean hundreds of millions of dollars in profits. But after Carter's decision against the plane the previous summer, the profits looked less likely, and the value of Rockwell stock had dropped sharply. The company was looking too much like a loser.

Bob Anderson viewed life as a competition. Winning was his tonic—whether the prize was a tennis trophy or a multi-billion-dollar government contract. He set high goals for production and profits, and expected his managers to meet them. He led by example, outworking everyone else. When, at age fifty-one, he assumed responsibility for the aerospace division, he learned how to fly an airplane. When he arrived at an Air Force base behind the controls of a Rockwell executive jet Sabreliner, he intended to show the generals he knew their business. Anderson moved constantly around the Rockwell empire, visiting the B-1 plant in California one day, buttonholing congressmen in Washington the next.

When Jimmy Carter had announced his intention to cancel the B-1 on June 30, 1977, Anderson called Hello from Pittsburgh. "Quiet the troops down, try to be statesmanlike, and don't say anything you will regret," Anderson told him. The Rockwell president then left his office, went to the Concordia Club, and had three martinis with lunch. Then he went back to his desk to plan how he would keep the bomber project alive. He was not about to admit defeat.

Now, with plane number four safe and an infusion of nearly a half billion dollars in government money on its way, Hello and Anderson set about the next step in their plan, hoarding the critical personnel and material already on hand. At government expense, Rockwell put into storage the parts already purchased for eleven airplanes, in addition to 50,000 machine tools and 500,000 pounds of precious aluminum and titanium sheets from which future planes would be built.

Hello managed to keep eleven hundred engineers on the payroll and on the project. Other key personnel were loaned to other companies with the understanding that Rockwell could recall them when needed. Hello rustled up subcontracting jobs from Boeing to keep more workers employed and production facilities open.

Rockwell also engaged in some very fancy bookkeeping. According to government auditors, the company illegally charged some of its B-1 costs to its other government contracts. Although Rockwell never admitted to any guilt, it eventually reimbursed more than $1.5 million to the government and agreed to institute bookkeeping reforms. (Rockwell was not unique. Several other giant defense contractors, including General Dynamics and General Electric, were caught using similar practices.)

The B-1 was in a holding pattern. To proceed further would require help from high levels of the Air Force and the Defense Department.

Help came from two Air Force generals and from two distingushed scientists who were political appointees in the Carter administration. Dr. Hans Mark, the secretary of the Air Force, and Dr. Seymour Zeiberg, deputy undersecretary of defense for research, engineering, and space, were certain that the president had made a bad decision. Both men thought the nation needed a new penetrating bomber, and they were determined to keep the B-1 alive. Allied with them were Lieutenant General Thomas Stafford, Air Force deputy chief of staff for research and development, and Major General Kelly Burke, his director of operations.

Like Defense Secretary Harold Brown, Mark and Zeiberg were members of the elite group of nuclear scientists who had risen to powerful policy-making roles in government after successful academic careers. They exemplified the binding ties between the military, industry, and the nation's most prestigious research universities.

As a scientist as well as a nuclear strategist, Dr. Mark believed strongly in high-performance weapons systems. In his view, both the B-1 and the proposed MX were needed to deter the Soviet Union. A refugee from Nazi Germany who came to the United States at the outset of World War II, Mark was yet another of Edward Teller's protégés at the Lawrence Laboratory. He had chaired the department of nuclear physics at the University of California at Berkeley, and for eight years served as director of NASA's Ames Laboratory, which conducted advanced experimental work on new space weaponry. In 1977 Mark joined the Carter administration as undersecretary of the Air Force, and in 1979, succeeded John Stetson as secretary.

Zeiberg was the second-highest Pentagon official directly involved in research and development of new nuclear-weapons systems. (He served under Undersecretary William Perry.) He had worked on problems of reentry physics at the Aerospace Corporation, an Air Force–funded research center, aimed at improving ICBMs. Tired of theoretical studies, he said he took the Pentagon job because he wanted to do the hands-on work of getting the hardware built.

Bombers, Dr. Zeiberg believed, with their ability to project force rapidly anywhere in the world, could be the global peace keepers of the late twentieth century. The United States ought to play to its strengths—those areas in which it held technological superiority. In bomber technology, U.S. skills far exceeded those of the Soviets, who relied on ICBMs. Aside from their new medium-range Backfire bombers, the Soviet bomber fleet was far older and less capable than the U.S. B-52s.

Generals Tom Stafford and Kelly Burke represented the new generation of Air Force leaders. Starting out as a test pilot, Tom Stafford became one of the most famous American astronauts, commanding both the Apollo 10 flight to the moon in 1969 and the Apollo-Soyuz linkup in space with the Soviet Union in 1975. Later, as commander of Edwards Air Force Base, he had directed the B-1's test-flight program. By 1978 he was in charge of all research and development for the Air Force.

Like Senator John Glenn, Stafford had translated his celebrity as an astronaut into a political power well beyond his military rank. He was sought out to grace political gatherings, and his ideas were welcomed in corporate boardrooms and in congressional offices. After the B-1 cancellation and other administration defense cutbacks, the astronaut general was heard to refer derisively to the president of the United States as "that peanut farmer."

Kelly Burke, a wavy-haired, cigar-smoking Alabaman, had also been a pilot. As an undergraduate at Auburn and graduate student at George Washington University, he earned degrees in history and international relations. Although he had commanded a SAC squadron, his academic background appeared to give him a point of view broader than that of the SAC commanders who had hitherto run the Air Force.

The generals who led the Air Force before the 1970s rose to top command through combat in World War II. The new men came to leadership when the Air Force was already an established, independent institution. They were molded by different experiences; to rise to the top in a huge defense complex, the new leaders needed management skills, and they needed political savvy to defend the Air Force's institutional interests. The modern Air Force had little call for crusty, undiplomatic leaders like Curtis LeMay.

But like SAC pioneers LeMay and Thomas Power, Burke and Stafford both understood how closely the penetrating bomber was linked to the identity of the Air Force. Unlike their predecessors, however, they accepted the fact that the ICBM had forever changed the nature of warfare. If the bomber were to survive, its advocates would have to formulate new reasons for its existence.

Working in tandem with Generals Burke and Stafford, defense officials Mark and Zeiberg managed to inject another $450 million into the B-1 project, most of it earmarked for Rockwell. In the nation's budget the funds usually appeared designated only as research and development for "penetration studies," "advanced avionics," "cruise-missile-carrier studies," "radar-absorbent-material studies," "electronic-countermeasure studies," or "strategic-bomber enhancement." Seldom did they specifically bear the label "B-1." Some of the money Zeiberg delivered to Rockwell came from one of the Air Force's most secret projects, later called Stealth—the effort to develop the technology to make aircraft invisible to radar. The military budget was so vast, and Rockwell perennially received so much research money, that these relatively small individual amounts were easily disguised.

The subterfuge was necessary. President Carter, with his well-known penchant for examining budget documents in the most minute detail, would have spotted, and quickly eliminated, any money overtly designated for the plane. He had staked his prestige and used his political capital to defeat the bomber. To the president and others in the political arena, the B-1 had now become more than an airplane. It was a controversial political symbol, an indicator of where one stood on defense.

Taking the funds patched together from a variety of apparently unconnected programs, Rockwell and the Air Force continued to develop the B-1's avionics. In maneuvers against U.S. fighters and radar systems, they tested its ability to penetrate the Soviet Union. They developed techniques to make the B-1 more "stealthy." A model plane built by Rockwell and the Air Force demonstrated the possibility of remodeling the B-1 to reduce its visibility to radar, by rounding surfaces, using new paints, and changing the engine configurations.

Few members of Congress, even those on the relevant subcommittees, realized how much research money was being funneled to Rockwell to advance the B-1. But several key members of the House Armed Services Committee involved themselves deeply in the project. Their leader was not an elected member of Congress, but a congressional employee, Anthony Battista, staff director of the House Armed Services Subcommittee on Research and Development.

Battista could have served as prototype for the important but obscure congressional staffer, operating behind the scenes, who exercises power far in excess of his official status. These staff members' influence comes from the expertise they bring to subjects that the elected members lack the time (and sometimes the inclination) to master. Battista directed the congressional oversight of more than a thousand military programs. He kept up with the details on all of them. People whose projects he opposed called him a meddling micromanager. However, most members of the subcommittee that employed him relied on his professional judgment as to the merit of military projects.

Battista championed the B-1 and other strategic nuclear weapons. He had worked as a mathematician and aerospace engineer for NASA and for the Surface Weapons Center. His defense views generally were accepted by the subcommittee's chairman, Congressman Richard Ichord of Missouri, and by Congressman William Dickinson of Alabama, the ranking Republican member.

Ichord, an eighteen-year House veteran who started his career as a country lawyer in the Ozarks, rose to Speaker of the Missouri legislature, and through seniority became the leader of the key House subcommittee, which controlled the authorization of new weapons systems. A vehement anticommunist, Ichord said he needed no further evidence beyond Khrushchev's 1960 boast, "We will bury you," to convince him that the nation's survival required maintaining military superiority.

A Navy veteran of World War II, Bill Dickinson served ten years as a judge in the Alabama state courts before his election to Congress in 1964. Dickinson was among the first Republicans elected from the deep south. His views about the threat of communism and need for a strong defense paralleled those of Ichord.

The congressional team of Ichord, Dickinson, and Battista joined Rockwell's Buzz Hello to devise a plan to bring back the B-1 bomber. Battista called it "playing Carter's game." The president had asked Congress to investigate the development of a new airplane whose main role would be to carry and launch cruise missiles. What Carter had in mind was a transport like Boeing's 747 or Lockheed's L-1011, or possibly the Air Force's C-5, also a Lockheed plane. But the B-1 advocates saw an opportunity for their Rockwell bomber to become that cruise carrier—or at least to adopt its disguise until the time was politically ripe for it to emerge once more as a penetrating bomber. The two congressmen and Battista worked on the details of a modified B-1, which they decided to call the Strategic Weapons Launcher, or SWL.

Over lunch at the 116½ Club, a gathering place for lobbyists and politicians near the Capitol, Hello and Ichord discussed how to save the B-1. Ichord agreed with Hello's assessment that at this point, late in 1978, Carter looked politically strong and probably would be reelected in 1980. (Carter's public stature rose in September 1978, when he negotiated the Camp David Accords, a peace settlement between Israel and Egypt.) If Carter were reelected, Hello said, "it would be the bloody end for the B-1."

Clearly, the best way to keep the plane alive was to turn it into the SWL.

A second meeting took place in California. The congressional delegation—Ichord, Dickinson, Battista, and his assistant Tom Cooper—met with Rockwell's Hello and his Washington lobbyists, Doc Watson and John Rane. Hello described plans to convert the B-1's movable swing wings into a simpler fixed wing, to eliminate the bomber's supersonic speed, and to sharply lower its price. He said Rockwell could deliver a hundred of the born-again SWLs for $8 to $10 billion.

It would be Ichord's and Dickinson's job to move the scheme forward in Congress. Everyone in the "cabal" understood that the SWL served as a Trojan Horse for the "real" B-1. "The only way to get the B-1 is to keep it alive for the next president," said Ichord. Staffer Battista put it in technical lingo that spoke volumes to B-1 insiders: "Let's keep the linch pin on the B-1's swing wing well-greased." If the political climate changed, the SWL could quickly be transformed back into the B-1.

But first, the opposition had to be eliminated. Ignoring both a presidential request and a congressional directive, Chairman Ichord and his subcommittee refused to approve funds to study the feasibility of converting a widebody transport plane for use as a cruise carrier. Such a plane was a clear threat to the B-1, and unacceptable in any case to Air Force officers, who regarded modified transport planes as "soft and slow," too vulnerable to Soviet long-range interceptors.

When General Tom Stafford retired in 1979, Kelly Burke, now a lieutenant general, succeeded him as Air Force deputy chief of staff for research and development. Faced with demands from cruise-missile enthusiasts in Congress that a competition be held for a widebodied cruise carrier, Burke pitted a modified B-1 against the designs for a huge new supertransport called C-X. To no one's surprise, the C-X lost.

Another threat to the B-1 came from a different direction. Boeing presented the Air Force with a plan to put new engines on its B-52s, thereby greatly increasing both their longevity and their power as cruise carriers. When Boeing lobbyists began selling that idea to the key congressional committees, top Air Force officials ordered them to stop.

"You have a lot of projects with the Air Force," a general reminded a Boeing executive. "Stop pushing that B-52 proposal. We need a new bomber." Boeing complied, and also stopped advocating its 747 as a cruise-missile carrier. The company had good reason to fear the wrath of the Air Force. Despite fierce competition for contracts, the system also worked to eliminate competition—when the military did not want it.

Rockwell officials were pursuing a dual strategy in Washington. Working with Ichord and Battista, they hoped to introduce the B-1 as a cruise carrier that could fly over congressional hurdles. But with Air Force Secretary Mark and General Burke, they also developed plans to bring the B-1 back in a different guise—as a modified, better penetrating bomber.

By late 1979, the political climate was changing, favoring greater defense expenditures. The shah of Iran had been toppled by a Moslem insurrection, and in early November, sixty-six Americans were taken hostage in the U.S. embassy in Teheran. As they were held month after month by their boastful revolutionary captors, enraged and frustrated Americans at home wanted to retaliate.

In this atmosphere, Dr. Mark thought he might advance a budget proposal for a new bomber. Therefore the Air Force slipped its bomber proposal into the preliminary 1980 defense budget plans sent to the president. The plane was identified by the neutral acronym CMCA, for cruise-missile-carrier aircraft. But when B-1 opponents at the Office of Management and Budget reviewed the budget before forwarding it to the president, they knowingly added the inflammatory identification "(B-1)."

When the president reviewed the budget with Defense Secretary Harold Brown, he spotted the item, as the budget officers expected he would. "I hope I'm dreaming," he said angrily. "Can't we ever get out of this?" Brown tried to explain that the proposal referred only to acquiring a new cruise-missile carrier. The president was not going to resurrect the B-1 in any form. He slashed CMCA(B-1) from the budget he submitted to Congress.

Undersecretary of Defense Bill Perry told Mark how angry the president had been. Perry said that Mark was "walking dangerously close to a forbidden line, trying to bring back the B-1." Defense Secretary Brown, too, was unhappy that Mark kept pushing behind the scenes for the B-1.

Risking the president's fury, Mark, Zeiberg, and Burke decided to forge ahead anyway. If Carter found out what they were doing they might even lose their jobs. To Rockwell's Hello, all three government officials represented profiles in courage, but from the viewpoint of their commander-in-chief, they seemed more like mutineers.

After their CMCA request had been shot down at the White House, Mark, Zeiberg, and Burke decided to try a new strategy for justifying the B-1—complete with still another acronym.

In his first speech as Air Force deputy chief for research and development, General Burke unveiled their creation. Speaking on December 12, 1979, to the National Security Industrial Association, the defense contractors' trade association, he explained that the Air Force needed a new airplane. "I'd like to avoid the much too narrow term, 'penetrating bomber,' " said Burke. "For want of a better term, I'll refer to the concept as a Long Range Combat Aircraft or LRCA."

The LRCA represented a significant change in the way the Air Force perceived the mission of a strategic bomber. Since the beginning of the nuclear age, the SAC-dominated Air Force had single-mindedly promoted the strategic bomber for one exclusive purpose—to penetrate and attack the Soviet Union in a nuclear conflict. During the Korean and Vietnam wars, the Air Force resented using its prized strategic bombers in traditional, nonnuclear combat, and more demeaning yet, in tactical roles supporting ground troops.

A growing number of Air Force officers, led by Generals Kelly Burke and Glenn Kent, realized this narrow vision of the B-1 was militarily anachronistic as well as politically self-defeating. If the issue were the capability to strike the most vital Soviet targets— their highly defended nuclear forces—the bomber could never compete with ICBMs in either military effectiveness or cost. To get a bomber, the Air Force would have to turn its thoroughbred into a workhorse.

Burke therefore outlined a series of roles of the LRCA: It would have its traditional place in the strategic nuclear triad, but would do equal duty in other missions that SAC had previously disdained. Even more significant than the traditional bomber doomsday role, said Burke, would be the LRCA's ability to supplement medium-range nuclear forces. In a large-scale war in Europe, he noted, "a force of LRCA might provide our only means for adding mass firepower at the right spot and at the right time to blunt the massive armored spearhead attack which is a key element of Soviet theater-warfighting doctrine." Such an attack might use nuclear or conventional munitions.

Burke explained that LRCA, for example, could supplement naval forces by providing long-range sea surveillance and interdiction, mine-laying services, and even antisubmarine warfare. For years some Air Force strategists had quietly suggested that the bomber be put to such a broad range of uses. Their ideas had been brusquely rejected not only by the SAC bomber generals but by the Tactical Air Command and by the Navy; neither wanted strategic bombers to encroach on their missions—or their appropriations.

Burke did not raise, much less answer, the question of whether a plane costing $100 to $200 million was needed to perform these more mundane missions—or whether it was wise to risk such an expensive weapon except for the most critical purpose.

The next event to advance the LRCA was more important than anything General Burke and Secretary Mark planned. It was another example of how a provocative Soviet action can provide the rationale for American weapon systems.

On December 27, 1979, Soviet tanks and troops rolled into Afghanistan to take control of that country, strategically located next to Pakistan—and Iran. President Carter was stunned. The event, he said, caused him to reappraise his views on the nature of the Soviet threat. He canceled U.S. grain sales to the Soviet Union and American participation in the forthcoming Olympic

Games in Moscow. In his State of the Union address on January 23, 1980, Carter called the invasion "the most serious threat to peace since World War II." Carter warned the Soviets that any intervention in the Persian Gulf would be considered "an assault on the vital interests of the United States of America, and such an assault would be repelled by any means necessary, including military force."

Most disappointing to Carter, he withdrew the SALT II treaty from Senate consideration. He had signed the treaty with Soviet Premier Brezhnev on June 18, 1979, in Vienna, finally taking that first step towards a nuclear-free world—his greatest objective. But events had not gone as Carter hoped. To win military and congressional approval even to sign the treaty, Carter had reluctantly approved building the more powerful MX and Trident II missiles. Instead of cooperating for peace and arms control, the Soviets had built a new generation of more powerful and accurate missiles— identified by the U.S.-assigned tags SS-17 through SS-20. Because the Soviets moved the intermediate-range SS-20s into Eastern Europe, Carter countered by pledging to put intermediate-range U.S. Pershing and cruise missiles in Western Europe. At home Carter was increasingly perceived by Congress and the public as "weak on defense."

A few days after the Soviets moved into Afghanistan, Air Force Secretary Hans Mark convened a meeting of the Air Force's senior commanders at the Air War College at Maxwell Air Force Base in Alabama to discuss Burke's LRCA concept. His goal was to unite the Air Force in support of another run for the B-1 bomber.

Mark's message was as political as it was military. "Because of Afghanistan, the situation has broken," said Mark. "There now is a climate of public opinion in which we can talk about the bomber." The meeting ended with the Air Force's leaders ready to go public with their demand for a new bomber. Furthermore, Mark felt that Carter would not be reelected, which made it even more imperative to advance the precise case and perfect the technology for what would be a revised version of the B-1—a bomber that could immediately be started up by a new president. But the

technology for the new plane—and a convincing case for it—
would have to be ready by the end of 1980.

Reaching a consensus within the Air Force was not easy. SAC
Commander General Richard H. Ellis and his aides still defined
the bomber in terms of its penetrating role in a nuclear war. For
the long haul, the SAC generals wanted to wait for a new bomber,
the top-secret Stealth, still in the early stages of development. As
a quick fix, they wanted an enlarged version of the small FB-111
bomber. Meanwhile Burke, with assistance from retired General
Glenn Kent, made the case for a general-purpose bomber. The Air
Force would never get a bomber, they argued, if its only mission
was to fill the strategic nuclear role.

The Air Force used the Afghanistan and Iranian crises to dramatize its case for a long-range combat aircraft. In mid-January
1980, three B-52s flew from Guam to buzz Soviet ships in the
Indian Ocean and then back—a round trip of 14,000 miles. In
June, a B-52 flew nonstop around the world in forty-four hours,
refueling in midair. These public-relations efforts were not unlike
those of forty years before, when Lieutenant Curtis LeMay navi-
gated the new B-17s to intercept and photograph an Italian ocean
liner 600 miles out in the Atlantic.

What Mark needed next for his new B-1 was the blessing
of opinion leaders in the military, industry, and science. Toward
that end, he ordered the Air Force's Scientific Advisory Board to
study the bomber question at its annual summer meeting in Monterey, California. The board included distinguished military analysts, aeronautical experts from academia and industry, and Air
Force generals. Dr. Edward Teller and General Jimmy Doolittle,
the elderly World War II air hero, added their prestige to the gathering.

Although the men had come to study bombers in general, the
agenda was carefully planned to advance precisely the revised B-1
that Burke, Mark, and Zeiberg had shaped with Rockwell. The
Stealth bomber was not even considered—it was so secret that
only a few of the participants were even aware of it, although one
MIT scientist, Dr. Eugene Covert, came up with the same idea
out of his own abstract musings. When Dr. Teller, usually a reli-

able bomber supporter, wandered from the prescribed solution with ideas about a long-range cruise-missile carrier, General Kent was assigned to get him off the subject.

The meeting achieved its purpose. The Air Force Science Advisory Board, Dr. Teller included, prepared a report endorsing the modified B-1.

As the 1980 session of Congress unfolded, it quickly became apparent that both the Democrat-controlled Congress and the military services would follow their own agendas, ignoring those of a weakened President Carter, who already looked like a lame duck, even though he was running for reelection.

In the House of Representatives, Tony Battista, Congressmén Dickinson, Ichord, Chappell, and Robert Wilson, the ranking republican on the House Armed Services Committee, moved the B-1 forward, thinly disguised as the strategic-weapons launcher, or SWL. Ichord and Chappell rounded up Democratic support, while Dickinson and Wilson worked on their Republican colleagues, many of whom quickly seized the chance to embarrass Jimmy Carter on the B-1.

On May 14, the House voted overwhelmingly, 297 to 119, to approve $600 million for development and initial production of the SWL. The true purpose of the exercise was colorfully outlined by Representative Robert Dornan, the California Republican in whose district the plane would be built.

"Castrate it, cripple it, call it whatever you want," said "B-1 Bob," but vote for the SWL now "if you want the chassis on the assembly line in January. . . . We can then turn it from a station wagon into a Dino Ferrari!"

House approval of an SWL did not fool President Carter. He told Democratic leaders in the Senate, where the issue had not yet been debated, that he would veto the entire defense bill if it contained the bomber appropriation. In imploring Senator Stennis to stop the B-1 appropriation, Carter wrote him that "any effort to create a second, extremely costly cruise-missile platform is both premature and unnecessarily expensive." The B-1 bomber had come back to haunt Carter, pushing him into a political corner once again. If the president resurrected the bomber now, admitting a mistake, he would look indecisive. If he vetoed the legislation, he would confirm the contention of Republican presidential contenders, including conservative Ronald Reagan, that he was weak on defense.

Senate consideration of the bomber began late in June. After midnight on July 1, Senators Alan Cranston and John Glenn brought onto the Senate floor yet another strategy to advance the B-1. Both Democrats were running for reelection, and their two states contained more B-1 jobs than any others in the country. Glenn and Cranston introduced a clever amendment that would salvage the B-1 while saving face for the president and senators who supported other bomber options. The amendment called for the next president to present plans for a new bomber by February 15, 1981. It could be either the revised B-1 (or LRCA), a "stretched" FB-111, or an entirely new advanced-technology bomber.

Any of the three, that is, so long as it was the B-1. Using a common ploy, Glenn and his legislative aide Robert Andrews drafted the amendment in language so specific that only one airplane would do. The amendment listed multiple missions the plane must accomplish, and it required that at least one squadron be ready for combat by 1987. But the FB-111 could not perform all the missions, and the Stealth, still a paper airplane, would not be ready by 1987. Only the revised B-1 could meet the strict requirements. Yet the apparent options in the bill allowed Carter to save face and offered at least a semblance of hope to congressional advocates of the FB-111 and Stealth. The Glenn-Cranston proposal was approved 53 to 37.

Within hours, John Glenn issued a press release pointing out that the legislation really called for the B-1. In that case, he said, "Ohio would stand to gain thousands of jobs. Ohio would probably dominate production. Some estimates indicate that as many as 16,000 new jobs would be created by 1985."

The House and Senate finally agreed on the Glenn-Cranston plan. The new president would have $350 million and a deadline of March 15, 1981, to come up with a new plane. In 1976 the B-1's opponents in Congress had delayed production in the hope that a new president would kill it. Four years later, B-1 supporters made it possible for a new president to revive the B-1 when he took office in 1981.

The week after the Senate vote, the Republican platform committee called for "accelerated development and deployment of a new manned strategic penetrating bomber that will exploit the $5.5 billion already invested in the B-1 while employing the most advanced technology available." The Air Force itself could not have written a better description. Nor did it have to. Retired Air Force Generals Thomas Stafford and Russell Dougherty, the former SAC commander, were members of the Republican defense advisory committee. Working behind the scenes, Rockwell's Buzz Hello and Air Force General Kelly Burke also sought the GOP endorsement of the B-1.

Ronald Reagan, who won the Republican presidential nomination on July 16, 1980, pounded at President Carter for having weakened American defense. Failure to build the B-1 became one symbol to make his point. Actor Reagan, always skillful with an anecdote, told about how B-52 pilots were younger than their aircraft, and about the pilot who had to repair his ancient B-52 in flight by sticking a fruit-juice can into a broken part.

Speaking at the Veterans of Foreign Wars Convention in Chicago on August 18, Reagan accused Carter of making a "shambles" of the national defense while remaining "totally oblivious" of the Soviet Union's drive toward world domination. Reagan said the United States faced a dangerous "window of vulnerability," exposing the nation to Soviet attack. He called for building the B-1 bomber and new ICBMs to fill the window.

The "window of vulnerability" theory was inspired by studies from SAC, as well as by the Committee on the Present Danger, a group that favored a stronger national defense. Its leaders included Paul Nitze, the lawyer whose views had influenced hard-line nuclear strategy since the Truman administration. Both SAC and Nitze's committee found a narrow and highly theoretical crack in our defenses: a superior Soviet ICBM force might in a surprise attack knock out most of the U.S. land-based ICBM force, weakening U.S. ability to destroy hard targets in a counterforce second strike. According to the theory, the U.S. then would surrender rather than respond with an attack that would lead to mutual annihilation of Soviet and American cities. To critics of the "window theory," it seemed preposterous to think the Soviets would risk an attack, knowing full well that American submarines hidden beneath the seas, not to mention bombers, still would have enough nuclear power to destroy the Soviet Union many times over.

In many ways, 1980 seemed like a replay of 1960. The phrase "window of vulnerability" carried the same political message that "missile gap" had twenty years earlier: the United States urgently needed to build more nuclear weapons. There were other parallels. A political party out of power hoped to regain the presidency, and in both cases, international crises helped fan public opinion to support new weapons.

A Sindlinger poll commissioned by the conservative Heritage Foundation in the fall of 1980 reported that 77 percent of those polled favored restarting the B-1, and thought President Carter had been wrong to stop its production.

The Air Force insurrection on the bomber issue was only one of many actions as the nation's military leaders once again decided to disregard a weakened president. The Navy asked Congress for battleships and aircraft carriers the president had not requested, and the Army pressed for other weapons he opposed, including the Bradley Fighting Vehicle. All five members of the Joint Chiefs of Staff criticized as inadequate a defense budget that Carter had already increased substantially.

Active military leaders met regularly with Senator John Tower, ranking Republican on the Senate Armed Services Committee, providing him with military advice the Republicans could use in the 1980 campaign. In an unprecedented action, army commanders in the field were encouraged to show visiting congressional delegations how poorly prepared and equipped their units were for combat.

During his 1980 budget review, Carter complained to his advisers that Pentagon officials not only refused to rank their priorities, but "treat me like an enemy and try to circumvent me." That included naval officers "running around the Hill pushing the virtues of the battleship." (After Carter had vetoed one authorization of a new supercarrier, the Navy and its congressional allies came back the next year and won it anyway.) Carter spoke angrily about Secretary of Defense Brown, who now increasingly sided with the military in favor of larger defense forces. "Harold's been a horse's ass on defense budgets," Carter told his aides. "He's caused me more work and took a hard line and never yielded."

At a meeting with White House aides in June 1980, Senator Stennis of Mississippi, chairman of the Senate Armed Services Committee, reported that generals were lobbying behind the president's back. Stennis, a southern conservative Democrat of the old school and a consistent supporter of the military, was nonetheless shocked by such behavior. He told one of Carter's aides that if it were up to him, he would block the promotions of the mutinous generals.

Now in serious political trouble and with a revised view of the Soviet threat, Carter embraced new nuclear weapons. He sent Congress a five-year plan proposing an additional $64 billion in defense spending. Carter was now pushing hard for the MX missile, which he had resisted at the beginning of his administration.

The president now sought to fine-tune his position on defense issues to counter the challenge from Republican candidate Reagan. At a White House political strategy meeting on August 12, 1980, on the eve of the Democratic National Convention, Carter told his aides: "We're behind on MX. We need an all-out effort. The GOP went too far to the right and left us the middle. We can't go too far to the left." Carter was no longer making "pristine" military decisions on nuclear weapons, but trying to steer a political course that would get himself reelected.

Carter next made public a secret nuclear war plan called PD-59, spelling out the strategic scenario in which the United States might fight a prolonged, escalating nuclear war. Its implementation required a multibillion-dollar upgrading of the command and control system to fight such a war. Critics suggested that Carter now tried to look tough on defense by making public a nuclear war-fighting plan as grim as any prepared by the most aggressive nuclear strategists.

Bombers again became a problem—not only the B-1 but the Stealth, which the Carter administration was exploring in what was supposed to be top-secret research. Carter and his staff debated whether to make some public announcement of the Stealth development in order to justify not building the B-1. The story leaked into the news, however, before Carter could decide what to do.

Republican candidate Reagan seized the opportunity to criticize Carter both for halting the B-1 and for imperiling national security by letting the Russians know about Stealth. Actually,

Carter probably told the Soviets nothing about Stealth technology they could not have learned much earlier by reading the authoritative and nonclassified publication *Aviation Week and Space Technology.*

Retired General Tom Stafford, who had directed the Stealth program, had warned Senator Tower and Reagan campaign advisers that Carter might reveal a secret weapon to shore up his defense image. Once Stealth leaked, Stafford helped the Republicans fashion their response.

On November 4, California's Ronald Reagan trounced the incumbent president, who carried only six states and the District of Columbia.

The story of the Carter presidency revealed once again how a candidate comes to office committed to one set of goals concerning defense and the arms race, only to be driven by events and politics in a very different direction. Carter's idealistic goals for arms control were undone by the Soviets, by weapons proponents at home, by domestic politics, and by his own political ineptitude.

In January, Jimmy Carter walked out of the White House and back into private life. Other politicians left office at the same time —some through the so-called revolving door that connects the various halls of the defense community.

Congressmen Richard Ichord and Bob Wilson, who led the 1980 fight in the House of Representatives to restore the B-1 bomber, retired from Congress and set up business together as Washington lobbyists. Eight major defense manufacturers immediately signed on as clients. These included Rockwell International—which, thanks in part to their help, now was poised for another chance to build the B-1 bomber—and such planned B-1 subcontractors as Boeing and Hughes.

Bob Andrews, the Glenn aide who drafted the crucial 1980 Senate amendment that helped the cause of the B-1, also went through the revolving door to work for Rockwell in 1982. His new job was to lobby Congress to build B-1 bombers.

Revolving in the opposite direction, Michael K. Deaver, a California public-relations man, became a key aide to President-elect

Reagan. For three years, Deaver and his partner, Peter Hannaford, had represented two major clients, Ronald Reagan and Rockwell International. Their less-than-onerous public-relations duties for Rockwell produced $100,000 in fees over several years. To no one's surprise, Rockwell hoped Deaver and Hannaford would encourage Reagan to support the B-1.

In December 1980, Deaver, in his new capacity as aide to President-elect Reagan, immediately performed a helpful service to Rockwell in its quest for the B-1. He made arrangements for Robert Anderson and Buzz Hello to meet with Reagan's transition team on defense. The Rockwell officials came to sell the new administration on the merits of the revised B-1 bomber. Thanks to three years of preparation, with the secret cooperation of the Pentagon and some members of Congress, they could claim that "the B-1 was ready to roll."

15

THE DEMOCRATIC BOMBER AND THE REPUBLICAN BOMBER

The Reagan administration brought to power a group of hard-line defense strategists who believed that in the face of a hostile and expansionist Soviet Union, the United States must be prepared to fight and win both a nuclear war and a conventional war. Never had so many important positions in the defense establishment been filled by men who believed not only in the importance of building a superior nuclear deterrent, but also in the practicality of fighting a nuclear war. The thinking of these nuclear strategists guided President Reagan and Defense Secretary Caspar Weinberger as they committed the nation to a massive new arms buildup.

The president stressed that superiority over the Soviet Union, rather than sufficiency or parity of nuclear weapons, would be his policy. He said he sought to achieve for the nation "a margin of safety in nuclear weaponry." Weinberger issued a secret directive calling for American nuclear forces that "must prevail and be able to force the Soviet Union to seek the earliest termination of hostilities on terms favorable to the United States."

The Reagan appointees spoke bluntly about the Soviet threat and how they would counter it. Richard Pipes, Soviet-affairs expert in the National Security Council, said that in a Soviet-American nuclear conflict the "country better prepared could win and emerge a viable society." Reagan defense adviser Colin Gray said that, in the face of Soviet aggression, "the U.S. may have no practical alternative to waging a nuclear war." Lieutenant General Edward Rowny, who later became a U.S. arms-control negotiator, said he believed "we have put too much emphasis on the control of arms, and too little on the provision of arms."

These conservative ideologues, who had had only the most marginal influence in earlier administrations, saw "the Russians as the problem, nuclear superiority as the solution, arms control as counterproductive, and the objective of nuclear war-fighting as to win." They frightened a good many Americans and sparked a nationwide nuclear-freeze movement. But for the present, they would clearly prevail.

When Air Force Deputy Chief of Staff Kelly Burke, flanked by a cadre of ranking generals, marched into Caspar Weinberger's office to claim victory in the twenty-seven-year campaign for a new strategic bomber, they expected to be greeted by the most cooperative civilians ever to run the Pentagon, men who held ideas about national defense similar to their own.

The generals had good cause for optimism. Ronald Reagan had swept into office on a wave of promises that the nation's strategic defenses would be rebuilt. He had pledged to close that much-touted strategic window of vulnerability by building new weapons, including the B-1 bomber. Reagan's defense transition team had endorsed every proposal presented to it by the Air Force. In their first days in office, Reagan and Weinberger had agreed to a record $32 billion defense increase for 1981 and 1982—on top of the $20 billion increase already requested by Jimmy Carter before he left office.

General Burke had come to inform Weinberger and Frank C. Carlucci III, his deputy secretary, how the Air Force planned to do its part in closing the window of vulnerability. The generals delivered an Air Force shopping list, confident that the only question to settle was the order in which they wanted their new weapons delivered. The first priority, Burke explained, was to produce a hundred B-1B bombers.

Sweeping away its disguises, the plane reemerged in 1981 with only another *B* to denote its important modifications—elimination of most of its supersonic capability, increase in its weight to include more fuel, weapons, and electronics, and new design features to make it less visible to Soviet radar. Its mission: to penetrate the heaviest defenses and fly deep into the Soviet Union, each armed with forty to sixty tons of devastating nuclear missiles and bombs.

The B-1Bs would be backed up by a fleet of modernized B-52s standing off the edge of Soviet territory and firing cruise missiles. Production soon would follow on 132 advanced-technology bombers, the top-secret Stealths. When they were ready to take over the penetrator role in the 1990s, the B-1Bs would become cruise-missile carriers, freeing some of the B-52s for conventional warfare.

When Weinberger responded, however, it was clear he was extremely skeptical about building two new bombers, especially the B-1B. Weinberger and Carlucci delivered a withering blast of probing, hostile questions that the generals had not anticipated: "Why can't we leapfrog the B-1B and just build the Stealth? How long will the B-1B be able to penetrate the Soviet Union? Why do you need both of these airplanes?"

As the Air Force leaders stumbled over their answers, Weinberger lost his patience and stormed out of the meeting. "They were totally unprepared," Carlucci recalled later. "They didn't have the facts or any good figures on what the planes would cost. They just assumed we would roll over and build it."

Weinberger was not pleased with the notion of spending more than $100 billion on *two* new bombers when many people thought bombers had only a marginal strategic utility anyway. He became fascinated with the idea of skipping the B-1B, thereby saving billions, and opting for the newer technology of Stealth. In this, Weinberger was strongly influenced by conversations with his predecessor Harold Brown and with Stealth advocate William Perry, Brown's undersecretary for research and development, who stayed on for several months as a consultant. Other experts, including former Defense Secretary Melvin Laird, argued persuasively both to Weinberger and Reagan that the B-1B's time had passed. It represented the technology of the 1960s. The country should invest in the plane of the future, they insisted. Moreover, Weinberger, who was not a scientist, was captivated by new technology, and particularly by the idea of a plane that was said to be virtually invisible to radar.

The Air Force had misjudged Caspar Weinberger. The new secretary of defense may have known little about defense issues when he came to office, but he was tough, and he owed them nothing. He had dismissed his political rivals, the weapons advocates on the president's defense transition team, who had approved the Air Force's bomber program. Weinberger would make his own plan. His loyalty ran only to Ronald Reagan, and the money the Air Force leaders had so cavalierly proposed to spend exceeded even the new president's huge defense budget.

Caspar Weinberger, a Harvard-educated lawyer whose political career had begun as state finance director when Reagan was governor of California, had served as head of the Office of Management and Budget in the Nixon Administration. Weinberger was known throughout government as Cap the Knife for his prowess as a budget-slasher. In 1971, he was one of the OMB officials who tried to persuade Nixon to abandon the B-1 or at least to curb its technological excesses. Cap Weinberger wanted to be secretary of state. Instead, his friend Ronald Reagan rewarded his years of faithful service with the command of the nation's defense.

Given the president's desire for a massive defense buildup, Weinberger seemed a strange choice for the job. He was a political moderate with no background in defense. The president wanted Weinberger at the Pentagon, not only because of his unswerving loyalty, but also because Reagan hoped his reputation as a budget-cutter would give the administration's huge defense requests credibility in Congress. Weinberger's appointment annoyed the hard-line defense strategists who had backed Reagan. Moreover, they were outraged when Weinberger chose as his deputy Frank Carlucci, a man who had served in the Carter administration as deputy CIA director.

Weinberger was offended by the effrontery of the Air Force bomber presentation. The generals had not even bothered to offer their secretary of defense a strategic rationale for their extravagant menu of weapons. Carlucci called the briefing an insulting "dog-

and-pony show" which did not begin to make a case for what would be a twenty-year, $100 billion expenditure for strategic air power. The Air Force, he said, made no attempt to analyze or explain how its proposed force would counter the Soviet threat.

After Weinberger stalked out of the meeting, Richard De-Lauer, the newly appointed undersecretary of defense for research and development, took the stunned B-1B advocates to his office. DeLauer, a scientist who worked on the Atlas ICBM, was an executive of the defense conglomerate TRW Corporation before coming to the Pentagon.

"This is nonsense," he said. "You need to put together a program that makes sense." He told them they had to cut the cost of their bomber program by retiring all the B-52s as new planes came on line. Most importantly, they needed to develop a much more convincing rationale for building the B-1B instead of bypassing it for a future Stealth bomber.

Like many new defense projects, the Stealth bomber had its origins not only in new technology, but also in defense politics. When President Carter turned down the B-1 in 1977, General Stafford, the Air Force deputy chief for research and development, decided to create a bomber that Jimmy Carter could like—one the president from Georgia could consider his own. Until 1977, Stealth research had been aimed at developing a fighter plane. Special paints, rounded surfaces, and engines buried in the wings were some of the techniques Lockheed was experimenting with at its secret "Skunk Works" in California. Tiny Stealth fighter planes had been flown at the Air Force's secret installation at Nellis Air Force base in the Nevada desert.

Tom Stafford decided the Stealth research should be directed at a penetrating strategic bomber that would be acceptable within the terms of the SALT II treaty Carter was then negotiating. Stafford put Northrop Aviation and other companies onto the project, which was financed with "black money" hidden within the budget. Only a very few Air Force, Pentagon, and White House officials and heads of the defense committees in Congress knew about Stealth.

When he succeeded Stafford in late 1979, Kelly Burke continued the Stealth bomber research. Fighting desperately for years to get one new strategic bomber, the Air Force now found, much to its surprise, that it had created a brand-new political dynamic: rival political constituencies for two different bombers. The B-1 was backed by Republicans, the House of Representatives, and Rockwell. The Stealth was supported by Democrats, the Senate, and Northrop. Each bomber now had become a political symbol. When Carter canceled the B-1, he made it a symbol for opponents who thought him weak on defense. The Stealth became a symbol for those politicians who had rejected the B-1.

The Air Force would have been grateful for *any* bomber after Carter's rejection of the B-1. Three years later, it suddenly saw the opportunity to get two new bombers. The Air Force wanted both planes. The B-1B was practically a bird in the hand, nearly ready for production, but Stealth held long-term promise as a penetrator far beyond the probable useful life span of the B-1B. Furthermore, the Air Force strategists realized that they now needed both planes for political reasons: to satisfy the rival constituencies.

The generals would have to perform a delicate political and military balancing act to get both bombers. They had to prove to Weinberger and the Stealth enthusiasts that the B-1B still was a strategic necessity. They also had to satisfy the new Stealth advocates. Some Stealth backers truly believed in the military merits of the nearly "invisible" plane; others were driven mainly by economic and corporate interests. For some Democrats, the Stealth provided a convenient radar-proof political shield for their opposition to the B-1B, deflecting criticism of their being soft on defense.

From a military standpoint, the Air Force calculated that the United States could use a force of about 350 to 400 strategic bombers—far beyond any politically acceptable cost. The number of planes actually requested—100 B-1Bs and 132 Stealths—was calculated almost entirely on economic and political factors. The Air Force decided that both Weinberger's and Congress's choke point for the B-1B was $20 billion, and Rockwell's Buzz Hello claimed he could produce 100 B-1Bs for that cost. The Air Force requested more Stealths than B-1Bs to satisfy the Senate—where a coalition of zealous Stealth advocates and B-1B opponents might scuttle the B-1B.

Burke and his staff developed an analysis to show that the cost of building the B-1Bs and Stealths and operating them for 20 years would be only a little more than the cost of reconditioning and operating the aging B-52s—$93 billion for an all-B-52 fleet, $100 billion for all B-1Bs, and $114 billion for the combined B-1B and Stealth force. The analysis was debatable, but it made for a good selling point: "You can buy two new planes for little more than the cost of rehabilitating one old one."

The stage was set not only for a political and military debate but for a bitter economic battle between two industrial combines. Lined up on one side was Rockwell International with its twenty-seven-year effort to build a new Air Force bomber. On the other side were Northrop and its business partr ers in Stealth, Boeing and LTV.

Leading the campaign for the Stealth in Congress was one of the last of the old-style aviation entrepreneurs, Northrop's sixty-one-year-old board chairman Thomas V. Jones, a personal friend of Reagan who knew how to play high-stakes defense politics. Jones put together a potent industry team to lobby for and build the Stealth, as he joined forces with T.A. Wilson, chairman of Boeing, and Paul Thayer, chairman of the LTV Corporation. These executives waged an aggressive campaign to convince the powers in Washington to skip the B-1B and accelerate development of the Stealth. Leapfrogging the B-1B would mean billions in short-term revenue for Northrop, a windfall the company would happily share among its collaborators and subcontractors.

Buzz Hello set up a Washington command center to counter the Northrop challenge. One morning in May, he received an urgent call from a congressional ally on the House Defense Appropriations Subcommittee. "You wouldn't believe what's going on up here," his friend reported. "Northrop's Jones, Boeing's Wilson, and LTV's Thayer are telling the subcommittee that they can produce the first production squadron of Stealths in 1987—and furthermore, they'll do so at a fixed price."

Hello leaped into a taxicab and arrived at the entrance of the committee hearing room just as Thayer, Wilson, and Jones were departing. He tried to speak with Wilson and Thayer, but they ducked past him and out of the Rayburn House Office Building.

Hello had reason to feel betrayed. Boeing and LTV were both major partners with Rockwell in the B-1B program. Boeing would receive more than $2 billion for developing the B-1B bomber's offensive avionics and integrating all avionics systems. LTV would be paid more than $1 billion for manufacturing part of the plane's fuselage. Furthermore, Hello believed the claims being made for the Stealth were preposterous. Jones was proposing a fixed price for a plane whose paper design had not yet been approved, and promising to deliver it in six years. Hello knew that to meet that deadline, Northrop and its partners would have to order machine tools and parts before any blueprints even existed.

Boeing and LTV had valid economic reasons for pushing the Stealth, however, even if it meant sacrificing their B-1B contracts. For Boeing, which would help build the Stealth's revolutionary lightweight composite wing, the Stealth bomber would be a way for the company to acquire, at government expense, the technological expertise to pull ahead of the competition for the next generation of commercial jets. For LTV, and for Boeing as well, income from Stealth contracts would far exceed any possible gains from the B-1B.

During the spring and summer of 1981, as partisans for each plane fought to win the votes of key members of the defense establishment in Congress, they also fought to convince Caspar Weinberger and Ronald Reagan. For the first seven months of 1981, Reagan remained silent and detached from the question of which bomber to choose: Cap Weinberger was making the defense decisions. Those who knew Reagan best said it would not be out of the question for him to reverse himself on the B-1B if Weinberger showed him that such an action made sense. And unlike Carter, Reagan knew how to reverse himself without causing an uproar.

In early May, Weinberger held private sessions with the rival aerospace groups. Tom Jones told Weinberger what he had told members of the congressional subcommittee: Northrop could meet the 1987 date for producing a squadron of fifteen planes, and would commit itself to a fixed price.

Next Weinberger met with Hello and his superiors, Rockwell board chairman Robert Anderson and president Donald Beall. Regarding the meeting as a "shootout" between the Stealth and B-1B, Anderson geared his presentation to showing the improbability of the Northrop promises. "Based on the experience we've had in eleven years working on the B-1," he said, "I don't see how any new concept of an airplane could be ready in 1987. It would take at least until the mid 1990s."

Weinberger wanted to know exactly how much change would be required from the original B-1.

About 20 percent changed, Hello told him.

"How much will it cost to build a hundred planes?" he asked.

Hello said it could be done for about $20 billion—an estimate considered far too low by some Air Force and Pentagon analysts.

"Will you guarantee that price and build the B-1B on a fixed-price contract?" Weinberger asked.

Anderson replied that he would not; there was still too much uncertainty in the plane, and more experience was needed.

"You've had a lot of experience already," said Weinberger. "You ought to be able to do it at a fixed price."

Anderson had told his own associates that he would not "bet the company" on one airplane. He knew that in any huge aerospace venture, costs could be difficult to control. In a $20 billion program, Anderson figured that a 10 percent cost overrun could cause losses for Rockwell of more than three times the value of the company's stock.

Weinberger then pressed the strong B-1B advocates in the Pentagon—Defense Undersecretary DeLauer, Air Force Secretary Verne Orr, and the Air Force generals—for answers to the questions he considered crucial: How soon could the Stealth bomber become operational? How long could the B-1B successfully penetrate Soviet defenses? How much would it cost to build the B-1B?

If the B-1B could serve only briefly as a viable penetrator, until Soviet radar was improved in the late 1980s, and if the Stealths could come on line in the late 1980s, or even the early 1990s, what was the point of spending $20 or $30 billion for a bomber that could at best meet a short-term need? The case for the B-1B was not helped by Rockwell's refusal to match Northrop's offer to build Stealth for a fixed price.

Furthermore, the Air Force itself harbored a strong opponent of the B-1B. In mid-May, just as the service leaders prepared to present their final, unanimous assessment to Weinberger, SAC Commander Richard Ellis flew in from Omaha headquarters to register his dissenting opinion: the B-1B should be bypassed for Stealth, which, he said, had a far greater long-term potential to penetrate the Soviet Union. According to a SAC study, the B-1B could not penetrate what would be vastly improved Soviet defenses after 1988. Ellis, who helped invent the notion of the window of vulnerability, believed that a fleet of F-111 stretch bombers would suffice while the Stealth and MX missile were in development and production.

Ellis lost his case within the Air Force, so he took it to Congress. There, the rest of the Air Force leadership already was pushing the two-bomber program, even though neither Weinberger nor the president had approved it. Angered by the unruly generals, Weinberger ordered them back to the Pentagon. The decision would be difficult enough; Weinberger didn't need the generals feuding in public and trying to preempt his decision.

Weinberger spoke about his dilemma in an interview with Robert Toth of the *Los Angeles Times*:

"If you knew right now you could get an advanced-technology bomber in 1985 or '86 or '87, you could certainly make the B-52 do for a while. And you could put all your eggs in one basket.

"We don't know that [the Stealth bomber] would be ready then, but we do know we could get some increased capacity from an interim bomber [the B-1B]. But how much increased capability? Is it worth the very considerable price of a new airplane?"

Weinberger saw the issue as a classic case study for a business school. "It's got absolutely every element that leads to indecision," he said, "the kind of thing that normally you would put in the hold basket and look at again in five years." But if you were the secretary of defense, you couldn't.

The B-1B advocates thought the penetration issue was given too much emphasis. The plane would be useful later as a cruise-missile carrier, they contended, and would be able to serve for many years doing conventional bomber duty in its newly discovered capacity as a multipurpose long-range combat aircraft. They enlisted former Air Force Secretary Hans Mark and other aerospace experts to convince Weinberger that Northrop could not possibly meet its ambitious schedule, even if money were no object. They pointed out the aeronautical problems that would have to be overcome for an aircraft consisting mostly of wing. There was no such thing as a totally invisible aircraft, DeLauer argued. Rushing the Stealth could cause massive technological problems as well as huge cost overruns.

But the cost overruns on the B-1B were just as difficult a problem for the plane's supporters. For years its soaring costs had been a political sore point. Having been burned repeatedly, the analysts in the Air Force Systems Command now insisted that a hundred B-1Bs could not be built for less than $27 billion in 1981 dollars. When General Kelly Burke argued that this figure was too high, they refused to budge. Burke and Buzz Hello set up their own cost-study group, which came up with a more modest $20.5 billion.

Burke then took his figures to Air Force Chief of Staff Lew Allen. "It's a waste of time to propose the project at $27 billion," he told Allen. At that price neither Weinberger nor Congress would approve it. Allen called Rockwell's Anderson and told him there was a disagreement about the B-1B's cost, and that he should come to Washington.

At a Pentagon meeting, Anderson and Hello argued with the Systems Command officers, led by Lieutenant General Lawrence Skantze, that their $27 billion figure was too high. As Anderson recalled later, the meeting was "very vociferous. It was getting down to life or death for the B-1B and we felt our numbers were right." Eventually, the Systems Command leaders backed down in the face of enormous Air Force pressure to build the B-1B.

Nonetheless, Weinberger appeared ready to make his recommendation to the president that the B-1B should be bypassed. In early June, DeLauer made another appeal to his boss. "If we can get the B-1B for a fixed price, will you go for it?" he asked. Weinberger said that he might. He still had doubts about the need for the B-1B, but a price cap would ease his concern about the enormous uncertainties in the total cost of two different bombers.

DeLauer immediately called Anderson in Paris, where he and everyone else in the aeronautical establishment were attending the Paris Air Show. "Bob, you've got to bite the bullet if you want the plane," DeLauer told him. "It's going to be fixed price or nothing."

Anderson reluctantly gave in. He called Gary Hillary in his Washington office and dictated a letter to Weinberger agreeing to the fixed price. One obstacle to the B-1B was removed. The official price of the plane seemed at least to be settled. The figure of $20.5 billion did not include a number of necessary items that would be billed later, at a cost of several billion dollars; and this "fixed-price" agreement had many loopholes and qualifications, including an indeterminate allowance for inflation. Before Anderson agreed "in principle to a fixed price" on June 9, General Skantze had reassured him in a June 3 letter that "we can do a fixed-price contract that can protect your interests." Even so, Anderson was taking a big gamble.

Anderson's capitulation kept the B-1B in contention, but the battle with the Stealth continued in both Washington and Paris. The Air Show was a perennial favorite of congressional junketeers, and Northrop's Jones was in Paris to collar every federal official who might have any influence on the decision. While Senator Barry Goldwater inspected Northrop's F-20 fighter, Jones lobbied Rhett Dawson, counsel to Goldwater's Senate Armed Services Committee and House legislative aide Tony Battista.

Tom Jones also worked the White House, including the president. In February, he was the only defense-industry official at the president's birthday party. In May he hosted an intimate dinner honoring Reagan at Washington's Georgetown Club. Meanwhile, Rockwell's Bob Anderson called on presidential aides Edwin Meese, Richard Allen, and Michael Deaver to advocate the B-1B. Anderson stressed to Meese both the readiness of Rockwell to build the bomber and the economic benefits for California—home of both Meese and the president.

Congress did not wait for Weinberger and the president to make up their minds. In the House, Congressman Bill Chappell and Tony Battista moved the B-1B forward through the Armed Services and Appropriations Committees.

Joseph Addabbo, a liberal New York Democrat who chaired the House Defense Appropriations Subcommittee, was among the few influential House members still determined to stop the B-1B. Addabbo started an investigation into how the Air Force had slipped Stealth research money to Rockwell to help keep the B-1B alive during the Carter administration—but he stopped after Richard DeLauer pointedly reminded him that Stealth money had been used in an identical fashion to help the A-10 attack plane, manufactured on Long Island by Fairchild Industries—a major employer in Addabbo's district. Addabbo continued to oppose the B-1B, but he was defeated in his own committee. By June the House had authorized $2.4 billion to start production of the B-1B bomber.

The House was responding to a new prodefense political climate. In addition, all the traditional parochial interests were still at play; a congressman's political survival might well depend on his support for the B-1B.

For instance, Representative Martin Frost, a liberal Democrat, represented the 24th congressional district in the Dallas–Fort Worth area, where LTV, the district's largest employer, would employ 2,700 workers on building part of the B-1B's fuselage. The UAW, which represented workers at the plant, was Frost's most important political supporter; his conservative constituents tolerated his liberal voting record—so long as he delivered on locally important issues like the B-1B. Frost voted for the bomber.

By 1981 the B-1B also had become a political symbol for a new force in politics, fundamentalist groups, known as "the religious right." Such organizations as the Reverend Jerry Falwell's Moral Majority, the Religious Roundtable, Christian Voice, and the National Christian Action Coalition began keeping "moral report cards" on the voting records of members of Congress. Voting records were examined for congressmen's positions not only on school prayer and abortion but on defense issues. In 1981, support of the B-1B was on their list. "My instinct was that they were very powerful; they were mobilized," recalled former Representative David Bowen, a Mississippi Democrat who voted for the B-1B. In 1977, liberal Protestant churches had joined the coalition that defeated the B-1; in 1981, the religious right fought to bring it back.

In the Senate, the B-1B faced tougher opposition—from partisans of Stealth, supporters of Northrop, Boeing, and Lockheed, and old B-1 foes who did not want the plane to rise once again from the dead.

On the other side, Ohio's John Glenn continued to lead the fight for the B-1B. At the request of General Kelly Burke, he held a special hearing to show that Northrop's promise to produce the Stealth by 1987 was totally unrealistic. Retired astronaut General Tom Stafford called on numerous senators to push the B-1.

Rockwell, the Air Force lobbyists, and the UAW prepared masses of data showing that Ohio would benefit enormously from production of the B-1B. Contracts worth $7.5 billion would be spread among eight hundred companies in the state, including General Electric's engine plant outside Cincinnati and a principal Rockwell factory in Columbus. Their target was Glenn's fellow senator, liberal Democrat Howard Metzenbaum, who had previously opposed the B-1. Metzenbaum faced a tough reelection campaign in 1982, and the UAW let him know that their support hinged on his backing the B-1B. It was "a tough decision," but Metzenbaum switched to support of the B-1B.

In June, despite six months of intense pressure from the Air Force, Congress, and industry, Secretary Weinberger still hesitated. When it appeared that he might choose the Stealth, Rockwell's stock plunged from $43 to $36.25 a share in ten days.

Worried B-1B supporters stepped up their public advocacy for the bomber. If the Reagan administration did not build the B-1B, declared General Lew Allen, Jr., the Air Force chief of staff, it would not be following through on its earlier defense pledge "to show resolve and determination quickly."

With Weinberger leaning toward the Stealth, the B-1B's hardline supporters focused on President Reagan. One of them reminded the White House that the B-1B was "part of the Republican sacred litany, showing the determination of the Reagan administration to improve our defense posture." Representative Bill Dickinson, still the ranking Republican on the House Armed Services Committee, urged Reagan not to reject a "bird in the hand [the B-1B] for two birds in the bush," particularly when great uncertainties remained about the Stealth. Congressman Chappell sought Reagan's commitment by suggesting that he could deliver the support of forty southern Democrats for the president's tax and budget cuts.

Senator Tower, chairman of the Senate Armed Services Committee, was also pushing hard for the plane. That he had long been a supporter of the B-1 was well known. What was still secret was the fact that he had already received the Air Force's commitment to base a B-1 squadron at Dyess Air Force Base in Tower's home state of Texas.

Most important, a group of Republican senators, led by Majority Leader Howard Baker of Tennessee, came to the White House to deliver a strong message: It would be politically disastrous for Reagan not to build the B-1B. Breaking his campaign promise would be construed as an admission that Carter was *right* when he killed the B-1. It was Carter, they reminded him, not Reagan, who advocated relying on cruise missiles and the Stealth. In the symbolism of Washington politics, Stealth was a Democratic bomber.

Baker had been approached earlier by General Burke and lobbied urgently by Rockwell officials to "get through to the president." He also had a strong parochial interest in the B-1B. The AVCO Corporation had a $1 billion contract to build the B-1B's wings, providing 2,600 jobs at its Nashville plant. For years, AVCO had counted on Baker to push its interest in the plane.

The White House heard increasingly from Reagan's hard-core conservative supporters, who complained that the administration had not taken a single action to close the window of vulnerability. The president had not made a decision on any of the key elements to modernize strategic defenses—the MX missile, a new Trident missile, and the B-1B bomber.

One reason the administration hadn't moved was because Reagan had political problems with the basing of the MX missile. The proposed MX would be a huge land-based intercontinental missile with ten warheads, capable of destroying even the most hardened Soviet targets.

During the 1980 campaign, Reagan had opposed Jimmy Carter's plan to base the new MX missile in multiple shelters spread out over the deserts of Nevada and Utah. The idea, supported by the military and by civilian nuclear strategists, called for shuttling the missiles among 4,600 shelters, thereby protecting them from a surprise Soviet attack. Carter's proposal was attacked by the arms-control movement, by environmental groups, by conservative western ranchers, by the Mormon Church, and by western senators, including Reagan's friend and closest ally in the Senate, Paul Laxalt of Nevada. Candidate Reagan had opposed the multiple-basing plan because Jimmy Carter had favored it, and because it was violently opposed by his own staunchest western political supporters.

The administration seemed hopelessly deadlocked on where to base the MX, so other weapons would have to be used to satisfy nuclear hard-liners. The Trident II would not be ready for several years. The Stealth bomber was further in the future. Reagan and his political advisers began to realize that starting up production of the B-1B was the only dramatic, visible action they could take.

In late July, President Ronald Reagan finally made his decision: to build the B-1B. He told Weinberger, "People vote for you and you make campaign pledges and you keep them." And the B-1B was the best available way to "do something in the here and now." Though Weinberger retained doubts about the B-1B, he was a good soldier, absolutely loyal to the president. He accepted the decision.

On October 3, 1981, Reagan announced his strategic modernization program: the U.S. would build 100 B-1B bombers, to be followed by 132 Stealth bombers (exactly what the Air Force had proposed from the beginning); 100 MX missiles would be located in hardened underground silos, at least until a better basing mode was found; the improved submarine-fired Trident II missile would be developed; the nuclear command and control system would be upgraded. The whole package was estimated to cost $180 billion.

As he announced his long-awaited strategic program to the news media, Reagan revealed an embarrassing lack of understanding of the military rationale underlying his decisions. Asked why the MX would be less vulnerable to Soviet attack in fixed rather than multiple silos, Reagan answered haltingly, "I don't know but what maybe you haven't gotten into the area that I'm going to turn over to the Secretary of Defense."

Questioned a few moments later whether the revived B-1B could penetrate Soviet defenses, Reagan hastily fled the press briefing room, saying, "I think that my few minutes are up and I'm going to turn that question over to Cap [Weinberger]."

Reagan may not have understood the strategic issues, nor how to explain them smoothly without a script, but he fully understood how to meet his own basic political needs. The B-1B met them. On the MX issue, he had deflected a barrage of criticism from opponents, including some of his own strongest political supporters in the West. With Rockwell ready to roll, he could demonstrate his resolve to take immediate action to produce new strategic weapons.

Reagan finally closed the window of vulnerability when he simply stopped talking about it, just as John F. Kennedy stopped talking about the missile gap after he took office. The president also settled the MX controversy by appointing a committee headed by Lieutenant General Brent Scowcroft, which decided that submarine-based missiles and bombers were an adequate threat to keep the Soviets from exploiting any "window." So much for the window of vulnerability.

The president still had to justify to Congress his choice of the B-1B over Stealth. When Weinberger appeared before the Senate Armed Services Committee on November 5, 1981, he still revealed a lack of confidence in the B-1B. He testified that the B-1B would not be able to penetrate the Soviet Union at all after 1990, and even by 1988 or 1989 could not penetrate "unless someone wants to direct suicide missions." He also said the Stealth would be ready by 1990. Robert Huffstutler, a CIA analyst, told the Senate Defense Appropriations Subcommittee that the old B-52s could do as well as B-1Bs in penetrating the Soviet Union until 1990.

The General Accounting Office and Congressional Budget Office both reported to Congress that the B-1B would cost far more than the Air Force estimate. The cost of the hundred-plane force would be $35 to $40 billion, counting inflation and the costs conveniently omitted by the Air Force, rather than the figure of $20.5 billion in 1981 dollars that Rockwell and the Air Force had agreed on.

Taken at face value, all this information supported Weinberger's business-school case that skipping the B-1B might result in little strategic loss and would save billions of dollars. Influential senators, even including staunch Republicans, had reached this same conclusion.

To head off congressional opposition, the Air Force and the administration quickly reworked their testimony to justify the two-bomber program. Secretary Weinberger and William Casey, director of the CIA, issued a joint letter on November 11, 1981, refuting both Weinberger's and the CIA's earlier testimony. They now stated that the B-1B "would have the capacity to penetrate anticipated Soviet air defenses well into the 1990s."

The Air Force once again improvised a new mission for the plane to quell political opposition. At the beginning of 1981, the Air Force plan called for B-1s to be converted to carry cruise missiles once the Stealths were ready. By the end of 1981, the Air Force was explaining how both planes would be used together as penetrators, creating a "synergistic effect," thereby compounding problems for Soviet defenders. Air Force officers admitted privately that the new synergism had more to do with politically justifying the B-1B than with attacking the Soviet Union.

When Republican Senator Ted Stevens of Alaska, the deputy minority leader, questioned the worth of the B-1B, Reagan defended it with an argument often used to support new strategic weapons. At the outset of arms negotiations, Reagan wrote Stevens, not building the B-1B would send the Soviets "a dangerous and misleading signal of weakening American resolve in the face of an ever-growing Soviet challenge." Resolve was more important than rationality.

The late 1981 congressional debates over the bomber became irrelevant. A majority of members accepted as gospel that Reagan had won a mandate for massive new defense spending. The Air Force was getting two bombers because it had persevered doggedly enough and long enough, until the politically opportune moment finally arrived.

And the opposition fell apart. The grass-roots coalition that effectively opposed the B-1 in 1976 and 1977 had fragmented. Some groups now fought the MX; others worked on a national nuclear-freeze movement. The bomber was yesterday's cause. Congressman Downey of New York, a passionate B-1B opponent in 1976 and 1977, acknowledged its political inevitability in 1981. Pragmatically shrugging off the B-1B as merely a waste of money and at least not a destabilizing weapon, he joined his liberal colleagues in focusing on the MX, a more dangerous weapon as well as a possibly more winnable political fight.

But the forces that sustained the B-1B remained intact. For Rockwell and the Air Force, the B-1B constituted a permanent interest. The bomber also represented a permanent interest to the states and communities which benefited economically from its production. Together they constituted the permanent B-1 lobby.

On November 18, 1981, the House of Representatives approved the two-bomber program by a vote of 335 to 61. On December 4, the Senate followed suit, defeating by 66 votes to 28 an effort to delete the B-1B's funds.

The final victory reflected the decisive power of the president of the United States to shape nuclear weapons policy. Presidents Eisenhower, Kennedy, Johnson, and Carter did not want to build a new strategic bomber, and under them none was built, although billions were spent in development. Because they approved it, the B-1 was started under Nixon and completed under Reagan. Over the course of almost thirty years, as individuals came and went and administrations changed, the Air Force and its allies kept the bomber alive. The federal funds that were the plane's lifeblood never stopped flowing. The ultimate strategy was patience, survival, and perseverence. Once the huge defense project developed momentum, it became as hard to stop as a driverless freight train, rolling downhill.

FOUR

Hooked on Defense

16

BUT DOES
IT FLY
WELL ENOUGH?

With parts from hundreds of subcontractors flowing into the huge desert plant at Palmdale, Rockwell finally began to build B-1 bombers, slowly at first, then with increasing speed and efficiency. The world's most expensive airplanes were assembled in a beige stucco plant taller than a seven-story office building and larger than six football fields. By the fall of 1986, seven bombers at a time were rolling down the final assembly line, and four a month were being delivered to the Air Force. The hundredth bomber was scheduled to fly to McConnell Air Force Base in Wichita in April 1988.

Each bomber started its journey down the production line at the fuselage-mating station, where parts were joined to the wing carry-through section. First came the forward fuselage sections, manufactured by Rockwell in Palmdale and at Columbus, Ohio. Next came the middle and rear fuselage, built by LTV on a $1.5 billion subcontract in Dallas. Workers then connected the tail section, built by Martin Marietta in Baltimore. The main landing gear built by the Cleveland Pneumatic Company in Ohio, and the nose landing gear from Menasco Corporation of Burbank, California, were then attached, along with wheels and tires from Goodrich Rubber Company of Akron, Ohio.

The assembled fuselage was then rolled forward to the wing-mating station, where workers fitted on the wings manufactured by AVCO at its Nashville plant on a $1 billion subcontract. Next the swing controls, built by Sunstrand Aviation Corporation at Rockford, Illinois, were inserted into the wings. Added next were the engine shrouds from Aeronca, Incorporated, in Middletown, Ohio. Then each plane was fitted with four powerful F-101 engines, manufactured by General Electric at its factory in Evendale, Ohio.

At the next assembly point, workers added the four Weber ejection seats built by McDonnell Douglas in Ontario, California. The two in front would be occupied by the pilot and copilot; behind and slightly below them would sit the offensive and defensive avionics officers. They would operate the "black boxes," the critical electronics installed in the forward fuselage. Boeing of Seattle and Wichita was prime contractor for the offensive avionics, while the AIL (Air Instruments Laboratory) division of Eaton Corporation built and assembled the defensive avionics at Deer Park on Long Island.

For years, the Air Force and its allies in industry and labor had sought political support for the plane by stressing jobs and contracts, by trying to persuade members of Congress that its production would boost the economies of their states and congressional districts. During the seven years of construction, from 1982 through 1988, an average of about 40,000 workers kept busy on the B-1. Almost half of them were on the Rockwell payroll; the rest worked at several thousand companies in forty-eight states. In 1985, the peak production year, 60,000 persons worked on the bomber.

The B-1 program indeed had economic impact, particularly in southern California, and in several dozen other communities with major work on the project. In retrospect, though, it appears that B-1 supporters had exaggerated the total economic benefits of the project, particularly in overstating the number of jobs created directly and indirectly, just as opponents had exaggerated the extent to which Rockwell cleverly placed subcontracts for their political effect. But no one can doubt the impact on Rockwell International itself, whose corporate slogan boasts that it is the place "where science gets down to business."

Rockwell delivered the bombers on schedule and at the agreed price of $20.5 billion—plus an additional $8 billion allowed for inflation from 1981 to 1988. Rockwell Vice-President Sam Icobellis directed the program, taking over in 1982 from Buzz Hello, who moved to head the corporation's Washington office. As an engineer who had spent thirty-two years developing military weaponry at Rockwell, Icobellis took great pride that his company had met its goals.

How much profit Rockwell made on the B-1 depended on the ability of Icobellis and his team to improve its production performance with every airplane. The first bomber required 1.2 million man-hours to construct; the fiftieth bomber, only 150,000. It took Rockwell ninety-two days to check out the thousands of complex parts in the first bomber, but only twenty days for the fiftieth. The improvements produced profits. In 1986, Rockwell International earned $516 million on total sales of $5.6 billion, with the B-1 bomber accounting for two-thirds of the income. Since Ronald Reagan revived the bomber in late 1981, Rockwell's stock had doubled in value. After all the crises and setbacks, the B-1 story seemed to be crowned with success.

Then, in early 1987, Congress discovered that the bomber was not all it was cracked up to be. The Air Force had in fact withheld $300 million in payments to the principal contractors because of shortcomings in the plane. It could not perform all the technological feats in its specifications, and therefore might not be able to carry out its deadly mission of penetrating the Soviet Union.

It had problems of flight-control stability, which caused difficulty with aerial refueling—which in turn limited its range. The terrain-following radar navigation system malfunctioned, limiting the bomber's ability to attack at ground-hugging altitudes—so it would be vulnerable to Soviet radar. The mechanism for firing the bomber's twenty-four nuclear-armed short-range attack missiles did not work well. Added weight kept the B-1 from cruising at an altitude high enough for best fuel consumption.

Most troubling, however, were problems with the bomber's defensive avionics system, a complex computerized method of detecting and deceiving enemy defenses. The Soviets had spent billions of dollars developing a bomber-defense network that consisted of thousands of radar units, ground-to-air missiles, and fighter interceptors. The ALQ-161 defensive avionics system, developed and manufactured by AIL on Long Island, was designed to provide the electronic countermeasures to protect the B-1 from enemy attack. This complex gear, housed in 118 black boxes in the plane's forward fuselage, serves as the plane's computer brain for processing and reacting to intelligence information. The devices are intended to warn the plane's crew of enemy radar signals, including those emitted by missile sites on the ground, and to allow the bomber to jam the signals, confusing the enemy.

"That capability is far less than we hoped it would be," admitted Air Force Major General Peter W. Odgers, in an early-1987 interview with Molly Moore of the *Washington Post.* "To tell the truth, we haven't got that far to really understand how serious [the problem] is."

Odgers was quickly replaced as the officer responsible for supervising the B-1 program. In the view of admiring fellow officers, Odgers, a respected former commander of the Air Force's testing program, had angered his superiors with his public candor—he had committed the cardinal sin of revealing embarrassing weaknesses in the plane.

The defensive avionics had multiple problems. To begin with, it was unable to simultaneously identify and counter many enemy radars seeking out the bomber. Second, the defensive avionics and the offensive avionics—the radar that guides the bomber to its target—actually jammed each other on certain frequencies. Third, the defensive avionics sometimes created a "beacon effect"—instead of confusing the enemy about the bomber's location, the system's radar signals caused the bomber to stand out like a lighthouse.

The Air Force acknowledged to Congress that the defensive avionics did not work well enough to counter Soviet defenses that were already in place in 1987. It would take two to four years to fix the problem—which means that the system would not be operating properly during any of the time period, the "window of vulnerability," during which the Air Force had so strenuously argued that the plane was most needed. Even after they solved this problem, Air Force officers said, they still would have to spend several billion dollars to improve the system further—to match new Soviet defenses now in development.

A few critics within the Air Force had foreseen problems with the defensive avionics. They had argued unsuccessfully that the planned bomber mission had relied too heavily on complex and hard-to-perfect electronic countermeasures. The GAO reported to Congress that some of AIL's difficulties stemmed from the fact that the company's principal experience had been in research and development, rather than in volume production of avionics equipment. Some Air Force officers privately questioned the choice of AIL, speculating that the company may have been chosen because of its strategic political location in New York.

News of flaws in the B-1 made headlines, stimulating renewed political controversy over the bomber. Predictably, the Democrats, newly in control of both houses of Congress, leapt at the opportunity to attack Ronald Reagan's "Republican" bomber. Longtime B-1 critics such as Representative Les Aspin, chairman of the House Armed Services Committee, immediately launched an investigation. His committee announced that the defensive-avionics problems would cost $3 billion and four years to remedy —if the Air Force could find a solution. "The biggest problem confronting the B-1 is not its weight growth, its fuel leaks, or its uncertain electronics countermeasures," said Aspin. "The greatest problem is the Air Force itself, which exerts more effort to obscure the B-1's problems than to correct them."

Seeking to refute the criticism—or at least defuse it—the highest-ranking officers in the Air Force appeared before Congress and described the bomber's flaws as normal growing pains in new aircraft. After flying the B-1 himself in January 1987, Air Force Chief of Staff Larry Welch issued an assessment: "The central fact is that the B-1, the most advanced bomber in the world, is today on alert at Dyess Air Force Base, Texas, fulfilling its intended mission of deterring conflict by being capable—this moment—of carrying out its mission. As is the case with most new aircraft or other weapons systems at this stage of their lives, there are some deficiencies in the B-1 that require correction to realize the full, long-term potential. Most will be corrected in the short term. One or two will take longer."

Echoing Welch's comments, SAC Commander John T. Chain, Jr., declared, "The B-1 is the best bomber in the world today, on anybody's side."

"It might be the best bomber ever made," retorted Frank L. Conahan, the GAO official responsible for overseeing defense programs, "—except it can't do its job." He further criticized the Air Force for failing to inform either Congress or top Defense Department officials about the B-1's problems.

In another effort to stem the tide of adverse publicity, the Air Force invited reporters to Dyess in March 1987 to see the bomber and speak with its SAC crews, who knew the airplane best. The pilots declared that the B-1, even with its imperfections was a great airplane, far superior to the old B-52.

To the dismay of the Air Force, the nation's major newspapers and the television networks largely ignored the pilots' glowing testimony. SAC Commander Chain complained bitterly that the news media had "trashed" the B-1 by printing "outright falsehoods," while not reporting any of the Air Force's own positive stories. Without doubt, the negative news coverage in 1987 owed something to the media's general penchant for "bad" news, but it also reflected the skepticism bred in many reporters and members of Congress by years of hearing Air Force officials make rosily misleading statements about the bomber.

Whatever its flaws or its capabilities, the B-1's advocates have won their long and arduous battle. The money has been spent, the airplanes are being delivered to SAC bases, and military planners are incorporating the B-1 into the nation's strategic nuclear war plans.

How much the B-1 is truly handicapped is a matter of conjecture. No one knows how it would perform in the chaos of a nuclear war. But if the Soviet Union believes that the B-1 could penetrate and cause horrible destruction, it will presumably have served its deterrent role—to help prevent a war from starting.

Nonetheless, the flaws remain an important issue. The Air Force billed the defensive avionics as the critical key to the B-1's ability to do its job—penetrating the heaviest defense to attack the Soviet heartland. And those critical avionics are defective. As Congress sees it, they must be perfected if the $28 billion B-1 investment is to pay off. The costs of the B-1 were high and the politics often questionable, and both caused widespread and justified concern. If the B-1 does not fulfill its requirements, then the nation has added cause for concern about the effectiveness of the Pentagon's defense-procurement system.

In September 1987, one year after the first fifteen-plane squadron was scheduled to join the nuclear force, only a single B-1 stood a lonely and symbolic alert. The other sixty-six bombers already delivered were undergoing testing, repairs, and revisions. GAO auditors criticized the Air Force for shortages of spare parts, lower-than-expected reliability, and lower-than-expected alert rates for the bomber. At times, parts were borrowed from some bombers so that others could fly. The cost of operating a B-1, $21,000 an hour, was much higher than planned for. The Air Force said the bombers could be readied for action in an emergency, but no one pretended that they were fully ready for combat.

And on September 28, 1987, tragedy struck the program when one of the B-1s crashed while flying a low-level training mission over southeastern Colorado. One of the four demonstration-model B-1s had crashed in 1984, with the death of two crew members, in a loss that the Air Force attributed to pilot error. But the 1987 accident marked the first crash of the new production-model B-1s. Of the six crew members and instructors on board over Colorado, three parachuted to safety. Killed in the crash were Major James T. Acklin, First Lieutenant Ricky M. Bean, and Major Wayne D. Whitlock. The plane had plowed through a flight of migratory birds, a number of which were sucked into the jet engines. A crew member reported "multiple bird strikes," and radioed that the plane had "lost engines three and four with an engine on fire." His final transmission was, "We're going down."

It is common for both commercial and military aircraft to hit birds; several thousand such incidents are reported each year. Most of the bird incidents occur while planes are flying at low altitudes—a thousand feet or less. And low altitudes are where the B-1 must function: its strategy is premised in large part on a low-level attack, on flying only two hundred to five hundred feet above the ground for more than a thousand miles as it penetrates to its Soviet target.

A spokesman for General Electric, manufacturer of the B-1 engines, said they had been built and tested to withstand strikes by one or two large birds. Experts said, however, that there is no way to prevent catastrophic damage if a plane rams through a whole flock of birds.

The tragedy provided immediate new grist for B-1 critics. In a lead editorial titled "The B-1 Fiasco," the *New York Daily News* questioned, "What good is a plane that may elude Russian missiles—but can't cope with one of the most common hazards of low-level flying?"

Days later, the B-1 fleet was temporarily grounded, to permit inspection of the emergency escape systems. Air Force spokesmen said the inspection was an "outgrowth" of the crash.

The Air Force had been caught in a dilemma partly of its own making. In its zeal to justify the continued role of the bomber in the missile age, it called for a plane with almost miraculous capabilities, to meet every need, to answer every criticism. The B-1's original and unnecessary "goldplated" requirements, including its Mach 2.6 supersonic speed, resulted in delays, cost overruns, and a series of changes in the bomber design. Even when performance requirements such as speed were gradually reduced, however, it was too late to change the basic design of the plane.

The Air Force must assume additional responsibility because it chose to serve as its own general contractor, rather than putting one defense firm in charge of the project. Instead, it supervised and coordinated the four companies it had selected for specific roles: Rockwell to build and assemble the plane, General Electric for the engines, Boeing for the offensive avionics, and AIL for the defensive avionics. The Air Force said it played this coordinating role in an effort to save money. As a result, however, the GAO said the Air Force could not play its proper and critical role of supervising the overall work of the defense contractors.

Some of the problems revealed in 1987 might have been averted if in 1981 the Reagan administration had followed a more cautious development procedure—"fly before you buy"—and built several B-1 test models before starting the hundred-plane production run. Instead, the bomber was developed and built on a rush schedule with considerable "concurrency"—that is, design changes were introduced as the bombers were being manufactured: engine modifications, added weight in weapons and fuel, updated defensive avionics, and redesign of various parts to be less visible to radar. The Air Force hoped that the new features would lower the bomber's cost while increasing its range, lethality, and ability to penetrate the Soviet Union. For Rockwell, the changes meant increasing the complexity of an already difficult engineering and production challenge. For AIL it meant producing defensive avionics to install in the first bombers as it struggled to improve the system that would go into the next batch of planes on the production line. As a result, the planes contained several different avionics systems.

Congressional critics said the B-1 dramatized the problems inherent in trying to produce a new weapon before completing research, development, and testing to find and correct defects and inadequacies. But the Air Force, Rockwell, and their congressional allies had deliberately chosen this rush production schedule. At their instigation, legislation was passed in 1980 requiring initial deployment of a new bomber by 1987—largely to head off competition from the experimental Stealth, which could not be built that quickly. If the Air Force had been more cautious and delayed the deployment several years, Defense Secretary Weinberger and Congress would probably have bypassed the B-1 and waited for the more advanced Stealth. In short, the B-1 was politically vulnerable, and its vulnerability compelled the Air Force advocates knowingly to undertake a riskier production schedule.

Rigid efforts to control the B-1's costs also lessened its capability. Considering the project's long history of rising costs, Weinberger had good reason to prohibit any design or equipment changes that would further drive up costs. An ironic result, however, was that the B-1 bombers were not equipped with an advanced new infrared navigation system that became available. Instead, it was installed on thirty-year-old B-52 bombers—making them in some ways more advanced than the B-1s.

.   .   .

The political and industrial competition between the B-1 and the Stealth was not halted by President Reagan's decision to build the B-1. With one contract finally in hand, Rockwell immediately began lobbying to build a second hundred B-1s. Northrop, which had the Stealth contract, fought to block any additional B-1s and to rush its bomber ahead faster.

In the midst of still another aerospace lobbying war, several key former government officials went through the defense community's revolving door to Rockwell. Michael Deaver, the White House aide considered closest to President Reagan, left government in 1985 to open his own Washington lobbying firm. Rockwell immediately hired him at $100,000 a year to persuade his former associates to buy the second hundred B-1s. (Deaver's efforts to lobby Reagan administration officials for the B-1 excited the attention of the special prosecutor investigating whether he had violated federal conflict-of-interest laws.)

Rockwell also hired a new Washington consulting firm formed in 1982 by three retired Air Force generals—Kelly Burke, Tom Stafford, and Guy Hecker. Before retiring, all three had held high positions from which they helped to revive the B-1 after President Carter canceled it. They were only three among the hundreds of officers who annually retire, then take jobs with defense-related industries—often working on the same projects that were their responsibility in the military.

The revolving door has its legislative side, too. Robert Andrews, John Glenn's Senate aide, has been mentioned; he went onto Rockwell's payroll in 1982 to seek congressional approval for more B-1s. In the rival camp, Northrop retained as consultants recently retired Representative Jack Edwards, the ranking Republican on the House Defense Appropriations Committee, and Kenneth M. Duberstein, Reagan's former director for congressional relations. Northrop also hired James Roche, who previously served as an important staff aide on the Senate Armed Services Committee.

With billions of dollars at stake, the competing aerospace corporations sought the expertise of the former military officers and politicians most familiar with the bomber issue—and with an insider's knowledge of the Washington defense network.

. . .

Despite Rockwell's efforts, Defense Secretary Weinberger repeatedly rejected the proposal to build more B-1 bombers. Instead, he pushed ahead with the Stealth. The B-1 backers felt they were at a disadvantage, since the Stealth was being developed in almost total secrecy, with its hidden funds scattered throughout the defense budget. Rockwell wanted to show that building more B-1s would be a bargain, costing a fraction of the Stealth, but as Buzz Hello said, "I can't make a comparison with the [Stealth] because I'm not allowed to know anything about it."

Secrecy about the technology of the Stealth is justified on grounds of national security. But total secrecy about the plane's cost and performance is not justified on any grounds; it serves principally as a political shield to protect the plane from criticism. The Stealth program is symptomatic of the Pentagon's growing tendency to shelter an increasing percentage of the defense budget in "black programs," hidden from public scrutiny. Only a few defense programs deserve total secrecy, says Thomas Amalie, an outspoken civilian Air Force missile expert, "and Stealth isn't one of them." If Congress permits actual construction of a force of Stealth bombers without publicly examining the cost and worth of the plane, then it will have taken a giant step toward abdicating its responsibility to oversee major defense expenditures and priorities.

The only aggressive attempts in Congress to puncture Stealth's veil of secrecy came from the B-1's principal advocates, particularly Ohio's Senator John Glenn, Representative Bob Dornan of California, and Representative Mike Synar of Oklahoma. They demanded that Congress be informed of the cost and development progress of the Stealth. Not surprisingly, the three represented places with the greatest economic stake in continued production of B-1 bombers.

One reason the Stealth escaped critical congressional inquiry is that it had become the "Democratic bomber." Dozens of congressional Democrats who voted against the B-1 had early embraced the Stealth. Some truly believed in the airplane's promise, but other B-1 opponents endorsed it primarily to protect their political flanks, to deflect accusations that they were antibomber or antidefense. Only with great political difficulty could they now disown the newer bomber that they had claimed would outclass the B-1.

A few members of Congress privy to information about the Stealth's progress estimated that the newest bomber might cost an astronomical $450 to $600 million a plane, or $60 to $80 billion for a fleet of 132 bombers. By 1987, several billion dollars had reportedly already been spent on research and development—and the first test model was still not in the air. Senator Barry Goldwater, the Air Force's most faithful bomber advocate, told the author that not only does the Stealth "face some very grave problems, both structural and aerodynamic, but the cost is climbing so high that I have begun to believe we may never be able to afford it for our fleet."

Misgivings about both the B-1 and the Stealth once again raise the same doubts that have haunted the concept of the strategic bomber ever since the advent of the intercontinental ballistic missiles in the late 1950s.

Some defense analysts dismiss the bomber as an anachronism in the age of ICBMs. Bombers can attack very few targets more successfully than ICBMs can. Bombers are more vulnerable than ICBMs during every phase of the attack. Furthermore, bombers are slower, and therefore are useless for certain "time-urgent" targets—such as enemy missiles before they are launched. Bombers are more expensive to build, to maintain, and to operate.

Many others insist that the idea of the nuclear triad—the bomber, land-based ICBMs, and submarines with missiles—remains valid. According to this view, a bomber strengthens the U.S. strategic deterrent by making it virtually impossible for the Soviet Union to destroy the United States' ability to retaliate. Bombers are recallable, and therefore they may be launched to send a very clear signal of resolve to aggressors without actually launching an irrevocable attack. Bombers also can perform more roles, and may thus provide important capability in conventional war, if not the military decisiveness claimed by their most avid proponents.

Let us assume, then, that the United States needs a strategic bomber. Does it need a penetrating bomber—one with the capability to get through the Soviets' most sophisticated air defenses?

The Air Force always insisted that in a nuclear war, penetrating bombers are needed to search out and destroy mobile targets, including missiles.

Other analysts who support the bomber role in the triad believe the need for the enormously expensive penetrator is far less certain. As George Mahon, a supporter of the military throughout his forty-four years in the House of Representatives, put it, there would be no air defense left to be penetrated after a nuclear missile attack—on either side. These analysts doubt the need for bombers to linger after an attack, identify "targets of opportunity," and destroy them. They consider the scenario unlikely and unworkable. They resist expensive outlays for a capability of arguably minor importance. The penetrating strategic bomber today is so expensive that even a defense budget that runs to a trillion dollars in five years can support only a small number of them.

Those who see the strategic bomber as a "backup weapon," valuable mostly as insurance against a surprise Soviet attack, argue that a standoff bomber with long-range cruise missiles is an adequate deterrent. Those advocates agree that at some point, a new plane will be needed. And the U.S. now has the new planes —a hundred B-1 bombers, designed to serve either as penetrators or as cruise-missile carriers.

After studying the strategic deterrent issue, one must conclude that the bomber remains a valid part of the triad, and that a standoff cruise missile carrier is adequate for the job. The conventional bomber role is important, but it can be filled by a plane less costly than either the B-1 or Stealth. The Stealth technology is worth pursuing, but the reported cost of the bombers seems vastly disproportionate to the marginal benefits they would add to the strategic deterrent. The Air Force has yet to demonstrate that they are worth the cost. The proven problems of the one plane and the uncertainties of the other ensure that the role of the bomber will remain a critical issue for years to come.

17

OUT
OF
CONTROL

By now the B-1 is more than a bomber. It has become a cause whose history sheds great light on how the nation's defense decisions are made. Our huge defense establishment is driven by powerful dynamics other than mere difference of opinion about the relative merit of various weapons or military strategies. Decisions about the American defense arsenal are influenced at least as much by psychological, political, and economic factors as by military analysis. The nation has built dozens of expensive weapons systems in a disorderly and wasteful process buffeted by erratic political and economic currents, and influenced by questionable, self-interested assessments of military need:

- The U.S. Navy, dominated by advocates of supercarriers, continues to win approval for more carrier groups, despite compelling evidence that these expensive and vulnerable armadas are the product of flawed military strategy, and divert huge sums that could be better spent on other defense and national needs.
- The U.S. Army presently is seeking $60 to $80 billion worth of new helicopters for transporting troops and providing them

with close air support. These vehicles are highly vulnerable to enemy attack. Numerous seasoned military leaders have contended that the helicopters not only are ineffective and wasteful, but that their role could best be performed by Air Force planes.

The nation now has embarked on what could become the most expensive defense program in human history: the Strategic Defense Initiative (SDI), or Star Wars. Dozens of scientists and nuclear strategists are convinced Star Wars will not work—that is, it cannot prevent a determined or desperate foe from making a devastating nuclear attack on both American cities and military targets. Yet SDI spending already runs into the billions, and plays a vital part in the economic well-being of hundreds of defense companies and research universities.

The self-interested politics and economics of many parties—the armed services, Congress, the president, the defense industry, and large chunks of the American public—intrude into almost every aspect of a weapon system's conception, development, manufacture, and deployment. The total effect is to warp the defense process in ways that serve neither the defense needs nor the overall well-being of the nation. When these special interests assert themselves—through the democratic process or on its margins—the results are predictable: billions wasted on weapons and military facilities we don't need, weapons deployed at strategically impractical locations, a defense strategy that lacks coherence, and mindless acceleration of the arms race.

Individual defense decisions are not made in isolation. There is a multiplier effect as the different military services, members of Congress, presidential administrations, and defense industries trade support for each other's projects. The cumulative effect of many special interests battling to get their way is further distortion of the entire national defense effort. After a continuous thirty-year defense buildup, marked by such repeated excesses, the military program is totally out of control.

This lack of control came about almost innocently, rather than out of any directed malevolence. Most of the defense programs originated from the legitimate and decent motivations of people who thought they were serving the country's best interests. Presidents, congressmen, defense contractors, union leaders, and civic groups all worked for what they thought should be done. They all believed in the need for a strong national defense.

The scope of each party was narrow, perhaps, but each saw a natural concurrence between its own legitimate self-interest, and the broader national interest. But widely diverse interests in defense seldom automatically combine to form a coherent national interest. Problems arose because so many self-interests had to be served, and inevitably this tangled web of self-interests began to dominate the political process, and the interested parties began to manipulate it.

The people of northern Michigan or of central Texas have a legitimate right to seek a defense base important to the local economy. When one community's desire for a base is multiplied too many times across the country, however, we end up with too many unneeded bases. And when the Air Force, Navy, and Army play politics by trading bases for civilian support for their prized military programs, we get even more bases. And no one wants any of them to close.

Several years ago, Senator Goldwater sent the members of his Armed Services Committee an impressive list of bases that military leaders had long thought were unneeded and should be closed. Goldwater asked each senator to volunteer one base for closing in his state; this might make it possible to share, and balance, the losses caused by the closings. Not a single senator responded.

Similarly, local communities seek defense jobs for their citizens. It is legitimate for the Georgia legislator to look out for workers at Lockheed and the California senator to look out for those at Rockwell—that is, until those narrow interests begin to distort the overall defense equation and the use of national resources. Unfortunately, most members of Congress somehow manage to rationalize that building a particular weapon in their own districts serves both the local and the national interest well. However, meeting the needs of 435 congressional districts and fifty states leads to more defense spending than the country needs, and to a less-effective allocation of resources.

Rockwell's Bob Anderson and other defense-industry executives are properly performing their jobs as they seek contracts to earn profits. In the consumer marketplace, their salesman would have to compete for customers to earn those profits. But in the highly specialized defense field, that kind of competition does not exist. There is only one customer—the U.S. government. Salesmen are not enough. Lobbyists must try to influence the various government officials who share the power to award contracts.

Lobbying by interest groups is a legitimate form of representation, but it gets out of line when an industry continues to press for a weapon that the nation's leaders have turned down. It is important for citizens to support political candidates, but the democratic process becomes distorted when defense industries, along with other special interests, funnel large sums of money through their political-action committees to the politicians who can do the companies the most good. It's also questionable for industry to place subcontracts where they will have the highest political value, instead of the highest quality or profit.

Furthermore, the profits and the economic impact are so huge that the shape of defense economics almost inevitably becomes a political issue. Winning or losing a single large contract may determine the fate not only of companies but of communities. Who gets the profits and who gets the dislocated economy often depends on who has the most clout—rather than on which company has the best product, or even on whether the weapon is needed at all.

Political leaders from the president on down have avoided facing the consequences of the enormous role defense spending has assumed in the nation's overall economy. In an unwritten, unstated policy, a succession of administrations have divided up weapons contracts among the nation's major defense contractors. Privately, government officials explain that they do it to ensure that the country maintains its defense-industrial base. The nation could not create these enterprises overnight in an emergency, they say, so it is important to keep them economically healthy and in business.

Protecting the defense industry is a sensible policy, but it should not be executed informally and secretly, while the government pretends it is choosing contractors for having presented the best and most cost-effective proposal for particular defense requirements. The problem with passing contracts around—either to fulfill a vaguely defined need for national defense preparedness, or to protect the nation's general political and economic health— is that it often results in higher costs, poorer products, or unneeded weapons. Defense programs are sometimes sustained primarily because no one has sought out economic alternatives to cushion the blow to workers and communities when a defense program is eliminated.

In the American political economy, defense spending has become a staple that we believe we cannot do without. Communities throughout the country have developed a severe defense dependency; they feel that their economic well-being depends on a particular military base or defense plant. Defense spending has become a narcotic, and the country is hooked.

Each military service believes that it makes a vital contribution to national defense. Fulfilling its own role, each has promoted the weapons that best justify its own existence and contribute most to that service's independence, rather than placing primary emphasis on a coherent interservice strategy. From its inception, the Air Force has justified its independence on the theory of strategic airpower: the belief that bomber strikes can cripple an enemy's vital interests, thus ending wars quickly. In its determination to get an unbeatable new strategic bomber, the Air Force gave short shrift to other vital missions, such as transporting troops to battle and providing close air support on the battlefield.

In the interservice competition between the Army, Navy, Air Force, and Marine Corps, the national defense interest too often has been lost. Shortchanged, for example, is the ability of the United States to fight a sustained conventional war in Europe, or to rapidly move an effective fighting force to a distant trouble spot such as the Middle East. Such critical but mundane needs as air and sea transport, minesweepers, ammunition, aviation fuel, spare parts, and training are crowded out of the budget as the Air

Force pushes to get a bomber that costs $200 or $500 million, and the Navy another supercarrier. Why is the emphasis so often misplaced?

There are strong reasons for high-ranking military officers to neglect the needs of national defense when those needs conflict with other priorities within their own services. The services compete fiercely for the military missions that will give them a larger share of the defense budget. Even when serving in the hypothetical neutrality of the Defense Department, officers are keenly aware that their promotions depend on loyalty to the goals of their own service. In the Air Force, loyalty has for decades been measured by support for a new bomber.

General David C. Jones worked after his retirement to cope with military special interests, which he encountered constantly as chairman of the Joint Chiefs of Staff from 1978 to 1982. "A great problem is that each service takes its own narrow parochial view, looking at the weapons it wants in isolation from everything else," said Jones. "The lack of a broad view is the biggest problem in the defense business today."

David Packard had a similar experience as deputy secretary of defense in the Nixon administration. In 1970, Packard gave the Air Force free rein to choose its own weapons. After experiencing and studying the distorting dynamics of defense politics, however, Packard reflected that he had given the services too much independence in making weapons decisions—one result being a too costly, goldplated design for the B-1.

After heading the Reagan administration's Blue Ribbon Commission on Defense Management in 1986, Packard reported on the shortcomings of the defense process: "There are strong perverse incentives for Congress, the military services, and defense contractors to play games with the budget to accommodate pet projects," he said. "Programs are kept alive to satisfy parochial, not national, interests and are introduced without realistic notions of future costs. In this environment, coherent long-range budget planning has become impossible."

And what happens when a president chooses not to follow the counsel of the military? Every military officer sometimes finds that his own service's view of the best course of action differs from that of the president. In these conflicts, the officer's clear duty is to obey the commander-in-chief. Yet when Presidents Eisenhower, Kennedy, Johnson, and Carter disagreed with the Air Force's desire for a new bomber, the Air Force teamed up with its allies in Congress and industry to try to overturn what they saw as a bad, even dangerous, decision. General Jones, then Carter's Air Force chief of staff, drew the intense anger of many fellow officers because he insisted on obeying the president's decision, rather than leading the traditional guerrilla war to overturn it.

The military has a responsibility to provide its candid advice to Congress, even when its views differ from those of the president or secretary of defense. But offering a respectful dissenting military opinion has too often been followed by an endless, aggressive campaign to reverse the presidential decision. The military is clearly acting improperly when it teams up with industry (as the Air Force did with Rockwell) to lobby a program through Congress. When service leaders defy the president, not only do they violate the constitutional provision of civilian control; they also weaken presidential authority, and confuse the whole decision-making process.

On reflection, a number of Air Force officers involved in the long bomber fight have acknowledged the excesses of their own service. "I was a young officer with a narrow view caught up in a crusade," said retired Air Force General James Allen, who as a major was assigned by General Curtis LeMay to try to overturn President Kennedy's decision not to build the B-70.

Given the incessant Washington power struggles over defense programs, it is not surprising that the military services get caught up in political machinations and push their own causes. The military is under constant pressure both from the executive branch and from members of Congress, who seek political favors in the awarding of defense contracts or maintaining military bases. Military officers rationalize that they also must play the political game in order to procure the weapons they think are necessary. But when military programs are manipulated for political purposes, one effect is to corrupt the most important values of military leadership—the integrity of its officers in making honest, professional judgments about defense needs.

When military officers mix political calculations into those professional judgments, their advice becomes suspect, even to their staunch supporters. "The 'window of vulnerability' has blown over like a cloud of smoke," said Representative William Dickinson, ranking Republican on the House Armed Services Committee. "The military keeps changing its rationalizations for what it wants."

Politics in Congress also distorts effective defense policy. Congress often seems shortsighted in its focus—it is perennially unable to come to grips with the broad issues of national defense, its members continually place parochial interests above national ones, and it has a tendency to "micro manage" the fine details of the defense budget.

Congress most often deals with the military budget by focusing on hundreds of individual items, rather than overall military needs. In examining programs such as the B-1 bomber or MX missile, congressional debate usually is framed in terms of stopping one weapon only by supporting another weapon that is said to do the same job better. The broad problems of adequate defense, national priorities, and arms control cannot be dealt with adequately on such a weapon-by-weapon basis.

It is important for Congress to oversee and examine the budget, but it too often enmeshes itself in the details, resulting in annual and often unpredictable changes in ongoing programs. Erratic funding changes often make good military management even more difficult.

The committee system of Congress further politicizes defense decisions. Members with military assets join the defense committees to protect those interests, just as legislators from farm states seek membership on the agriculture committees. Once they are sitting on the defense committees, their favor is sought by presidents, by the military, and by industry lobbyists who seek to win their support by providing their districts with more bases and defense plants. By the time committee members trade support for each other's projects, the military has solid, continuing backing for its major programs.

The political dynamics within the defense committees also discourage dissenting or independent viewpoints. Long Island Representative Thomas Downey decided to relinquish his seat on the House Armed Services Committee after his opposition to the B-1 evoked retaliatory attacks by other committee members on defense projects of interest to Downey's constituents.

The military committees too often become centers of defense advocacy rather than forums for establishing defense priorities. The House Armed Services Committee never once wavered in supporting the Air Force's bomber quest from 1954 until victory finally was achieved in 1981. Congress has managed to maintain a number of questionable weapons programs, irrespective of whether the president—or even, sometimes, the services— wanted them.

In this atmosphere, congressmen respond to a wide range of influences—the interests of their constituents, the persuasion of special-interest groups, the lure of campaign contributions and gifts, the promises and implicit promises of employment in retirement. And, of course, the congressman's own views of the national interest.

The toughest balancing act is faced by the president, who has all these forces to contend with, as well as a commitment to his own ideology and the promises he made to get elected. Like members of Congress, presidents are enmeshed in defense politics. Both candidates Kennedy and Reagan created political momentum for new weapons by proclaiming "gaps" or "windows," only to decide once in office that the threat was not so pressing as they had depicted it. Carter campaigned for arms control only to find that events and politics pushed him toward increased armaments. Once elected, presidents must make compromises as they deal with other power centers in government, including the military and Congress.

In theory, the United States' system of representational democracy should produce the kind of national defense that the people want. But representation does not end at the ballot box. Defense issues often are decided by whatever pressure groups can most effectively manipulate the levers of government power. Unfortunately, the system is tilted in favor of a panorama of special interests—from local chambers of commerce to presidential candidates—who benefit from more defense spending. And those interests have been adept at manipulating public fears to win approval for weapons that are not needed.

The prospect of nuclear war, irrespective of the weapons to be used, frightens American voters and people throughout the world. That fear reflects legitimate concerns; no one wants to die in a nuclear conflagration, or see it put an end to human civilization. Americans also fear aggression by a Soviet Union armed with nuclear weapons, just as the Soviets unquestionably fear the United States.

Instead of addressing those fears candidly and calmly, politicians and military leaders have followed two quite different and equally unsatisfactory courses. Either they have avoided discussing nuclear realities entirely because they didn't want to arouse fears and irrational opposition, or they have exploited public anxiety in order to justify more nuclear weapons. Consequently, the fate of the B-1 and other weapons has swung back and forth as the public lurches between periods of hyperactive fear of the Soviets and periods of desire for arms control.

Public fears are heightened and channeled into support for newer and more costly weapons in two ways:

First, fears about various kinds of nuclear vulnerability are repeatedly used to exploit latent public anxiety about the Soviet threat. Most people are understandably confused by the experts' mind-numbing debates over esoteric nuclear war-fighting theories. Nevertheless, they can be aroused to support new weapons by the shrill warnings of weakness and danger.

Retired General Andrew Goodpaster, who served Dwight Eisenhower as military aide during World War II and later in the White House, reflected on this problem: "I've seen history repeating itself over and over again—bomber gaps, missile gaps, windows of vulnerability. They all come from us and the Soviets drawing a worst-case scenario of what might happen. The result is endless pursuit of the arms race. The window of vulnerability is but the latest case of someone with a narrow view drawing a narrow, arcane case to show how one element of our nuclear deterrent might be vulnerable."

Dr. Bernard Brodie, the father of nuclear-war strategy, finally decided that nuclear war-fighting plans, with their requirements for more and still more weapons, made no sense. President Eisenhower reached that conclusion early on, as did Robert McNamara after serving as secretary of defense.

Second, international incidents often have the same unsettling effect, and can be fully exploited. General Goodpaster recalls how the nation's first encounter with the "balance of terror," the launching of Sputnik, caused a national panic, despite President Eisenhower's attempts at rational reassurance. Sputnik and the downing of the U-2 stirred public fears and gave the faltering B-70 a much needed boost. Twenty years later, events in Iran and Afghanistan provided the Air Force with its best chance since 1960 to win approval of a new strategic bomber. None of those incidents in themselves actually increased the military need for a B-70 or a B-1, yet they created a climate of public opinion in which weapons proponents could win support for their long-cherished projects. Such experiences only begin to show how much the nuclear struggle, in General Goodpaster's words, "is political and psychological as well as military."

Perhaps the most dangerous psychological effect is a numbing of our senses about the basic issues of war and peace. As George F. Kennan, diplomat and historian, describes the dilemma: "Over the years, the competition in nuclear weaponry has proceeded steadily, relentlessly, without the faintest regard for all those warning voices. We have gone on piling weapon upon weapon, missile upon missile, new levels of destructiveness upon old ones. We have done this helplessly, almost involuntarily; like the victims of some sort of hypnotism, like men in a dream. . . . And the result is that today we have achieved, we and the Russians together, in the creation of these devices and their means of delivery, levels of redundancy of such grotesque dimensions as to defy rational understanding."

How do we regain control of a reasonable national defense, one that protects us without sapping our resources and carrying the world closer to Armageddon?

When a politician or citizen calls for bringing the arms race under control, or for crafting a leaner, more effective defense, that person—no matter how knowledgeable or gifted—is too often dismissed as an impractical, naïve idealist. What such defense reformers and arms control advocates usually lack is a significant power base in the defense network. And they'll never develop such a base if they're perceived as antidefense. It's a vicious circle that keeps them on the outside.

Most people in this country support a strong national defense and want their political leaders to do so. The military-industrial complex is not a conspiracy imposed on the country, but a community of interests, backgrounds, professions, and ideologies. The defense community—with its members spread throughout the military, industry, government, and, increasingly, universities— tends to look at issues with a common view. Bonds are reinforced by the natural movement of individuals from job to job. The members of this broad defense network believe they are contributing to a strong national defense. And they all work hard on their contributions.

The common denominator in these endeavors is that everyone —everyone who is involved, that is—benefits. Any potential new multibillion-dollar weapons system provides a golden opportunity for every special interest. The sponsoring military service, politicians, defense contractors, scientists, and engineers all have a chance to get new technology that can win wars, enhance the service, increase profits, score scientific breakthroughs, boost the economy—and incidentally advance the careers of everyone associated with the project.

But there are too few people looking out for the pitfalls. The politicians too seldom examine whether the weapon is needed or the resources might be better spent for other purposes. The operations people who propose projects too often do not understand the technological constraints. The scientists and engineers are willing to take on impractical projects because they want the challenges—and the jobs. The result is needless or harmful gold-plating, and weapons that work poorly and are too complicated to use.

What is missing in this defense process is independent thinking, fresh ideas, and truly dispassionate advice—ingredients that the president, the Pentagon, the Congress, and the American public all sorely need. Dwight Eisenhower sought to address this problem in 1957 when he created the position of presidential science adviser and the President's Science Advisory Committee.

Meeting with his new science advisers, Eisenhower told them he never received suggestions for arms control. Instead, he was fed only recommendations calling for more nuclear weapons, and tougher strategies for nuclear war. "You can't have that [nuclear] war," Eisenhower told them. "There aren't enough bulldozers in the country to scrape the bodies off the street. Why don't you help me prevent it? Neither the Defense Department nor the AEC [Atomic Energy Commission] will give me any help. They have other interests."

The advisory committee did offer independent views that led to approval of the Partial Test Ban Treaty—and to denial of several unneeded weapon systems. As a result, though, the committee antagonized the defense network, which hastened the committee's demise in the Nixon administration. Dr. Jerome Wiesner, science adviser to President Kennedy and a member of the committee under four administrations, contends that the voice of independent scientific advice has been undercut by the power of the military community. In addition, Wiesner says, "increased technological complexity and the imposition of military secrecy have shut out public understanding and participation from decision-making."

Reviving a science advisory committee is obviously only a small step toward curing the weaknesses in the defense decision-making process. But any measure that stimulates independent study and advice, and increases public education, must be encouraged. A better-informed citizenry would be less swayed by psychological manipulation in favor of nuclear weapons.

Despite political constraints, the president is the one participant in the defense process who undeniably has the mandate and ability to address the broad issues of national security. More than any other politician, the president can shape the national agenda, balancing defense and other national needs. And the president can prevail. Four presidents did not want to build a new bomber, and their actions stopped or slowed the bomber program. Two supported the B-1, with the result that the program started and came to fruition in their presidencies.

The president faces no challenge greater than the one of defining a sound national defense policy and providing the leadership to implement it. An essential part of that role is public education. Presidents—like the entire military community—have failed to speak candidly on the issue of defense in the nuclear age. Every president since Truman has adopted a war plan that calls for the United States to use nuclear weapons in certain circumstances when deterrence fails. Yet few have had the courage to explain these plans to the country. Neither have they tried to explain the consequences of a nuclear war for the planet.

If leaders would clearly discuss nuclear strategy and weapons, and the consequences of their use, the American public could evaluate for itself whether these plans make sense. The nation is not better off, nor the world safer, when nuclear issues are kept as the esoteric province of the military community.

Government leaders must also face the unacknowledged but important role that defense plays in maintaining the nation's economic health—a role that grows larger as the country's basic heavy industry declines. If the nation cuts back defense spending, it needs to be prepared to fill the resulting gap in the economy.

The United States has always shunned any semblance of government economic planning, which would move workers and industrial resources out of defense to fill other needs. Granted, there are good reasons to doubt the government's wisdom and ability to allocate major private economic resources. But if the nation does not develop alternatives to defense programs, the pressures of defense dependency will make unnecessary weapons projects even more difficult to stop.

Furthermore, the nation needs to address the challenge of using its high-tech abilities, now unduly concentrated in the defense industry, to compete in more peaceful and rewarding pursuits. The nation has the ingenuity and resources to compete technically and commercially with Japan and other countries. The question is whether it will exercise the courage and develop the concrete options for breaking its defense dependency.

The Strategic Defense Initiative is a test case. With billions of dollars at stake just in preliminary research and development, virtually every aerospace company in the country and many research universities already have a piece of the SDI action. Star Wars has brought together in a single project more members of the defense network than any earlier endeavor. And they are all excited by the challenges and rewarded by the funding. They want more of both. But the decision on whether to proceed with SDI, and at what pace, should be based on defense needs, not economic needs.

In one hopeful development, Congress has taken action designed to curb the parochialism of the individual armed services, and to strengthen the national interest in Pentagon decision-making. Senators Barry Goldwater and Sam Nunn co-authored the 1986 Defense Reorganization Act, which gives more authority to the chairman of the Joint Chiefs of Staff in setting policies, drafting military strategies, devising Pentagon budgets, and promoting officers assigned to his staff. No one expects organizational tinkering to solve the deep-rooted problems of military parochialism, but the new law is a positive step.

Also needed is a renewal of military leadership values, which instill loyalty to national rather than service interests, and keep officers out of the corrupting practices of defense politics. With the awesome challenges of high technology and the horrendous dangers of nuclear war, the nation needs military advice that is not filtered through a political prism.

If the armed services are not to compromise their military judgments in the political arena, then Congress and the executive branch must also rise above narrow self-interest. Members of Congress must also show they can choose national goals, even at the peril of offending their constituents.

"We have to get this whole sense of personal responsibility extended beyond the military into all aspects of government and society," said retired Admiral James D. Watkins, the former chief of naval operations. "Congress has to feel it. When we say, 'Let's shut down an air station,' can they stand up and say, 'That's in my district, but I agree we've got to do what's right for the country'?"

From its initial conception as the B-70 to its completion as the B-1B, the Air Force's new strategic bomber has been pushed and pulled around to serve the needs of too many masters. The bomber had to pass many tests: the need to match the Air Force's conception of air power and serve as the symbol of that institution's prestige; the trial of presidential elections and the political agendas of ideologues on both the left and the right; the parochial political needs of members of Congress; the political maneuverings between the United States and the Soviet Union from the height of the Cold War to the midst of détente.

Thirty years after the Air Force started seeking a new bomber, the B-1 has finally emerged as a real weapon, one component of the military machine we trust to defend our nation. Hopefully, the B-1 will never have to prove itself in nuclear combat, but will defend our lives by helping to deter nuclear war.

But the B-1 falls short in many areas, from the design of initial specifications to defects in the final product. It is disturbing that in 1987 its performance is substandard. This is not only a matter of getting the most bang for the buck, mere cost-effectiveness. We are risking our lives and safety, in some measure, upon the performance of the B-1 bomber; for our past investment of money and present investment of trust, we should have a bomber that works as well as possible.

The B-1's development has been marred by political indecisiveness, bureaucratic obsessions, Air Force overreaching, parochialism, partisan demagoguery, and an utter lack of consensus on defense priorities and procurement strategies.

Despite these weaknesses, one could take the view that the democratic system did work in its own messy way, finally producing a new bomber, perhaps at just about the time that one could be justified.

A harsher view is that the defense network, pursuing its goal with relentless determination, can wear down and outlast any opposition. And the bomber cannot be judged in isolation. Every delay or cutback in the B-70 and B-1 programs had a political cost that resulted in production of other deadly nuclear weapons which expanded the arms race. C. Wright Mills concluded in *The Power Elite* that the military-industrial complex has "succeeded within the American system of organized irresponsibility."

More is wrong than the squandering of taxpayers' dollars. The American people have been needlessly frightened and unfairly manipulated by politicians of both parties. The credibility of both civilian and military leaders has been continually compromised in the eyes of the public and those who serve under them by the need to play politics with national-security assets. The priceless time and talent of the nation's government officials has been squandered playing the defense game. The abilities of highly skilled scientists and engineers are wasted in pursuit of unrealistic or unneeded weapons, and the nation's economy has been destructively skewed.

Those are some of the costs of "providing for the common defense" that must be added onto the $28 billion price tag of the B-1. We deserve a political process that defends our lives but also is not drawn out, divisive, and costly beyond reason. If American defense decisions were not fractured by so many conflicting voices of political, military, and economic self-interest, it is possible that we would develop and produce new weapons that were militarily sound as well as cost-effective—and only weapons that were really needed. But we have not done so. The result of our failure is a defense system that is spinning madly out of control.

THE
DEFENSE NETWORK
1957–87

Office	1957	1958	1959	1960
PRESIDENT				
	Dwight D. Eisenhower			
OFFICE OF THE SECRETARY OF DEFENSE				
Secretary of Defense	Charles E. Wilson	10/57 Neil H. McElroy		12/59 Thomas S. Gates, Jr.
Deputy Secretary of Defense		4/57 Donald A. Quarles	6/59 T. Gates	1/60 James H. Douglas, J
Secretary of the Air Force	DAQ	5/57 James H. Douglas, Jr.		12/59 Dudley C. Sh
MILITARY LEADERS				
Chairman, Joint Chiefs of Staff	Adm. A. W. Radford	8/57 Gen. Nathan F. Twining (AF)		10
Chief of Staff, Air Force	Gen. Twining	7/57 Gen. Thomas D. White		
Commander, SAC	Gen. C. LeMay	7/57 Gen. Thomas S. Power		
HOUSE OF REPRESENTATIVES				
Chairman, Armed Services Committee	Rep. Carl Vinson (D-Ga.)			
Chairman, Defense Appropriations Committee	Rep. George H. Mahon (D-Tex.)			
SENATE				
Chairman, Armed Services Committee	Sen. Richard B. Russell (D-Ga.)			
Chairman, Defense Appropriations Committee	Sen. Dennis Chavez (D-N.M.)			
NORTH AMERICAN AVIATION				
President	J. Leland Atwood			
Chairman of the Board	James (Dutch) Kindelberger			

1 John F. Kennedy | 11/63 Lyndon B. Johnson

1 Robert S. McNamara

1 Roswell L. Gilpatric | 1/64 Cyrus R. Vance

1 Eugene M. Zuckert | 10/65 Harold Brown

. Lyman
emnitzer (Army) | 10/62 Gen. Maxwell D. Taylor (Army) | 7/64 Gen. Earle G. Wheeler

6/61 Gen. Curtis E. LeMay | 2/65 Gen. John P. McConnell

12/64 Gen. John D. Ryan

1/65 Rep. L. Mendel Rivers (D-S.C.)

1/63 Sen. Richard B. Russell (D.-Ga.)

8/62 J. Leland Atwood

Office	1967	1968	1969	1970
PRESIDENT				
	Johnson		1/69 Richard M. Nixon	
OFFICE OF THE SECRETARY OF DEFENSE				
Secretary of Defense	McNamara	3/68 Clark M. Clifford	1/69 Melvin R. Laird	
Deputy Secretary of Defense	Vance	7/67 Paul H. Nitze	1/69 David Packard	
Secretary of the Air Force	Brown		2/69 Robert C. Seamans, Jr.	
MILITARY LEADERS				
Chairman, Joint Chiefs of Staff	Wheeler			7/70
Chief of Staff, Air Force	McConnell		8/69 Gen. John D. Ryan	
Commander, SAC	2/67 Gen. Joseph J. Nazzaro	8/68 Gen. Bruce K. Holloway		
HOUSE OF REPRESENTATIVES				
Chairman, Armed Services Committee	Rivers			
Chairman, Defense Appropriations Committee	Mahon			
SENATE				
Chairman, Armed Services Committee	Russell		1/69 Sen. John C. Stennis (D-Miss.)	
Chairman, Defense Appropriations Committee	Russell			
NORTH AMERICAN AVIATION	11/67 merger creates **NORTH AMERICAN ROCKWELL**			
President	Atwood			1/70 Robert Anderson
Chairman of the Board	Atwood	11/67 Willard F. Rockwell, Jr.		

'1	1972	1973	1974	1975	1976

8/74 Gerald R. Ford

		1/73 *	7/73 James R. Schlesinger		11/75 Donald H. Rumsfeld
	2/72 Kenneth Rush	1/73 William P. Clements			12/75 Robert Ellsworth
		7/73 John L. McLucas		†	1/76 Thomas C. Reed

•mas H. Moorer (Navy)   7/74 Gen. George S. Brown (AF)

7/73 Gen. G.S.Brown   7/74 Gen. David C. Jones

5/72 Gen. John C. Meyer   8/74 Gen. Russell E. Dougherty

71 Rep. L. Edward Hebert (D-La.)   1/75 Rep. Melvin Price (D-Ill.)

71 Sen. Allen J. Ellender (D-La.) | 8/72 Sen. John L. McClellan (D-Ark.)

2/73 name changed to **ROCKWELL INTERNATIONAL**

* Elliot L. Richardson   †James W. Plummer

255

Office	1977	1978	1979	1980	19

PRESIDENT

	1/77 Jimmy Carter				1.

OFFICE OF THE SECRETARY OF DEFENSE

Office					
Secretary of Defense	1/77 Harold Brown				1.
Deputy Secretary of Defense	1/77 Charles W. Duncan			8/79 W. Graham Claytor, Jr.	
Secretary of the Air Force	Reed	4/77 John C. Stetson		7/79 Hans Mark	

MILITARY LEADERS

Office					
Chairman, Joint Chiefs of Staff	Brown		7/78 Gen. David C. Jones (AF)		
Chief of Staff, Air Force	Jones		7/78 Gen. Lew Allen, Jr.		
Commander, SAC	Dougherty	8/77 Gen. Richard H. Ellis			

HOUSE OF REPRESENTATIVES

Office					
Chairman, Armed Services Committee	Price				
Chairman, Defense Appropriations Committee	Mahon		1/79 Rep. Joseph P. Addabbo (D-N.Y.		

SENATE

Office					
Chairman, Armed Services Committee	Stennis				1/
Chairman, Defense Appropriations Committee	McClellan	1/78 Sen. John C. Stennis (D-Miss.)			1/

ROCKWELL INTERNATIONAL

Office					
President	Anderson		2/79 Donald R. Beall		
Chairman of the Board	Rockwell		2/79 Robert Anderson		

ald W. Reagan

par Weinberger

| k C. Carlucci III | 1/83 Paul Thayer | 2/84 William H. Taft IV | | | |

| e Orr | | | | 12/85 Roarke | 6/86 Edward C. Aldridge, Jr. |

| 7/82 Gen. John W. Vessey, Jr. (Army) | | | 10/85 Adm. William J. Crowe (Navy) | | |

| 7/82 Gen. Charles A. Gabriel | | | | 7/86 Gen. L. D. Welch | |

| 1 Gen. B. L. Davis | | | 8/85 Gen. L. D. Welch | 7/86 Gen. John T. Chain, Jr. | |

1/85 Rep. Les Aspin (D-Wis.)

4/86 William V. Chappel, Jr. (D–Fla.)

| . John G. Tower (R-Tex.) | | | 1/85 Sen. Barry M. Goldwater (R-Ariz.) | | 1/87 Sam Nunn (D–Ga.) |

| Ted Stevens (R-Alaska) | | | | | 1/87 J. Stennis |

MAJOR
B-1
CONTRACTORS

Political support for the $28 billion B-1 bomber program came in part from expectations that it would create thousands of jobs all over the country. Between 1982 and 1988, an estimated forty thousand workers a year at several thousand companies provided supplies or parts for building the one hundred bombers. The jobs were spread throughout forty-eight states. Earlier research and development on the plane also involved thousands of jobs and $5 billion in contracts. In lobbying members of Congress, the Air Force and its industrial allies emphasized the jobs and dollars flowing into each member's state or congressional district. The following partial list of contractors and subcontractors on the B-1 indicates how the project reached into many areas of the American economy:

Manufacturer	Place	B-1 Construction Role
AIL Div., Eaton Corp.	Deer Park, N.Y.	defensive avionics
Aeronca, Inc.	Middletown, Ohio	engine shrouds
Aircraft Porous Media	Pinellas Park, Fla.	air and fuel filters
ARMCO Corp.	Middletown, Ohio	stainless steel
AVCO Corp.	Nashville, Tenn.	wings
Bendix Corp.	Teterboro, N.J.	speed indicator components
Boeing Co.	Seattle, Wash., and Wichita, Kan.	offensive avionics

Manufacturer	Place	B-1 Construction Role
Brunswick Corp.	Marion, Va.	radomes
Chem-tronics Inc.	El Cajón, Cal.	engine casings
Cincinnati Milacron	Cincinnati, Ohio	industrial machines
Cleveland Pneumatic Co.	Cleveland, Ohio	main landing gear
Cyber Systems, Inc.	Anaheim, Cal.	testing systems
Garrett Corp., AiResearch Div.	Torrance, Cal.	air data computer
Garrett Corp.	Los Angeles, Cal.	weapons door drive
Garrett Turbine Eng. Co.	Phoenix, Ariz.	secondary power system
General Electric Co.	Binghamton, N.Y.	engine thrust control
General Electric Co.	Evendale, Ohio	engines
General Electric Co.	Wilmington, Mass.	engine instruments
General Electric Co.	Syracuse, N.Y.	attack radar system
B.F. Goodrich Co.	Akron, Ohio	tires
Goodyear Aerospace Corp.	Litchfield, Ariz.	side and upper windows
Goodyear Aerospace Corp.	Akron, Ohio	brakes
Goodyear Tire and Rubber Co.	Akron, Ohio	nose landing gear assembly
Hamilton Standard Div. of United Technologies Corp.	Windsor Locks, Conn.	environmental controls
Harris Corp.	Melbourne, Fla.	electrical multiplex system
Hercules Inc.	Taunton, Mass.	fairing seals
Hughes-Treitler Mfg. Co.	Garden City, N.Y.	heat exchangers
Hughes Aircraft Co.	Irvine, Cal.	computer connectors
Hydroaire Div. of Crane Co.	Burbank, Cal.	braking system
IBM Corp.	Oswego, N.Y.	computers for defensive avionics
Kaman Aerospace Corp.	Bloomfield, Conn.	doors, rudders and fairings
Kearfoot Div. of Singer Co.	Little Falls, N.J.	flight instrument signal converter
Kelsey Hayes Co.	Springfield, Ohio	launcher components
Kidde and Co.	Bellsville, N.J.	fire protection system
Link Div. of Singer Co.	Binghamton, N.Y.	flight simulators
Litton Ind.	San Carlos, Cal.	radio and radar tubes
Lockhart Ind., Inc.	Paramount, Cal.	defensive electronics parts
LTV Corp.	Dallas, Tex.	fuselage sections
Martin Marietta Corp.	Baltimore, Md.	tail section
McDonnell Douglas Corp.	Long Beach, Cal.	ejection seats
Menasco Corp.	Burbank, Cal.	nose landing gear strut
Normalair-Garrett, Ltd.	Somerset, England	oxygen system
Parker Hannifin Corp.	Cleveland, Ohio	liquid cooling system
Pittsburgh Plate and Glass Ind. Inc.	Huntsville, Ala.	windshield glass
Parker Hannifin	Irving, Cal.	liquid cooling loops
Raymond Eng.	Middletown, Conn.	data entry unit
Rockwell Intl.	El Segundo, Cal.	head office, test labs
Rockwell Intl.	Palmdale, Cal.	bomber construction, assembly and testing
Rockwell Intl.	Tulsa, Okla.	wing flaps, overwing fairings

Manufacturer	Place	B-1 Construction Role
Rockwell Intl.	Columbus, Ohio	wing, nacelle and fuselage parts
Rockwell Intl., Collins Radio Div.	Cedar Rapids, Ia.	flight director computer
Sedco Systems	Melville, N.Y.	electronic countermeasures
Shultz Steel Co.	South Gate, Cal.	steel structural forgings
Simmonds Precision Co.	Vergennes, Vt.	fuel management system
Singer-Kearfott	San Marcos, Cal.	data processor
Sperry Corp.	Phoenix, Ariz.	vertical situation display
Sperry Corp.	Albuquerque, N.M.	automatic flight controls
Stainless Steel Products Co.	Burbank, Cal.	air ducts
Sierracin Corp.	Sylmar, Cal.	windshield
Sterer Eng. & Mfg. Co.	Los Angeles, Cal.	steering and damping
Sundstrand Aviation Corp.	Rockford, Ill.	rudder and wing controls
Sunstrand Data Control Inc.	Redmond, Wash.	test system recorder
Support Systems Assoc., Inc.	Northport, N.Y.	test systems
Swedlow, Inc.	Garden Grove, Cal.	windshield
Systron Donner Co.	Concord, Cal.	flight control systems
Telephonics Co.	Huntington, N.Y.	integrated test system
Tetrafluor Inc.	El Segundo, Cal.	piston and rod seals
TRW Inc.	Cleveland, Ohio	fuel pumps
United Aircraft Products Inc.	Dayton, Ohio	heat exchangers
Vickers Aerospace Co.	Jackson, Miss.	emergency electrical system
Westinghouse Corp.	Lima, Ohio	terrain-following radar
Western Gear Corp.	City of Industry, Cal.	gear boxes
Wyman-Gordon Co.	Worcester, Mass.	airframe forgings

ACKNOWLEDGMENTS

Many persons contributed to this book. My debt begins with the leaders—military, political, industry, labor, academic, and civic —who generously provided more than two hundred interviews. In their candid and knowledgeable recollections and critiques, these Americans shared a common concern about their country's well-being, and about the distorting effect of narrowly self-interested politics on national defense programs. A number of these persons made available their personal papers, including Stuart Eizenstat, assistant to President Carter, who permitted me to read his daily diary of the Carter White House years.

The information in the book comes from a wide variety of sources: interviews, books, magazine and newspaper stories, television reports, doctoral dissertations, and official documents obtained from the Defense Department, the National Archives and other official sources. I have tried to carefully document sources in the footnotes, although in some cases, the interview source asked not to be identifed. The book contains numerous direct quotations of conversations. Some of these are taken from notes made at the time of the conversations; others are based on the recollections of the participants or their close associates. My intent was to capture the immediacy and flavor of the dialogue of national-defense politics.

Research for the book began at the American University

School of Communication, where as an adjunct professor I have been encouraged to lead students in ambitious examinations of public-policy issues. A study of American military leadership preceded and led to this exploration of defense politics. Our objective was to explore, understand, and explain how Americans make important defense decisions. The AU study team in 1985 included Stephen Koff, Tobby Hatley, David Barnes, Alexandra Clough, Mary Colby, Mary Gabriel, Gail Henzel, Stephanie Holmes, Caroline Huang, Lynn Rickman, and Tamara Thompson. In 1985–86, Brad Clemenson, another AU graduate student, contributed essential help in research and shaping of the book.

In 1986–87, Douglas Fox, a student at Duke University, made major contributions to all aspects of the book, including research and editing. His work began while fulfilling an internship for Duke's Institute of Policy Sciences and Public Affairs.

Traci Lester, a student at Georgetown University, carried out valuable research during 1985–87 while working as a part-time assistant.

Many journalists generously and unselfishly helped. Frank Greve of the Knight-Ridder newspapers suggested the projects that led to the book. Jack Limpert, editor of the *Washingtonian* magazine, encouraged, supported, and published the first American University study. Fred Kaplan of the *Boston Globe* donated to the National Security Archive the government documents he got declassified for *The Prophets of Armageddon.* George Wilson, defense reporter of the *Washington Post* and author of *Supercarrier*, patiently answered my many questions.

The scholars and authors whose work directly contributed to my own include most importantly Stephen E. Ambrose, military historian and biographer of President Dwight Eisenhower; and Thomas M. Coffey, biographer of General Curtis LeMay.

A critical source of information was the National Archives, one of our greatest treasures. For their unfailing cooperation and skill, I am indebted to the archivists in Washington, and at the Eisenhower, Kennedy, Johnson, Ford, and Carter Presidential Libraries, the Nixon Project, and the Watergate Special Prosecution Force.

Different drafts of the manuscript were read and commented on by generous friends: Gar Alperovitz, Jerry H. Booth, Robert H.

Booth, my son Jack Kotz, David Lasser, Stuart Loory, Jay Jefferson Miller III, Robert Ward, and Lewis Wolfson. Barbara Wolfson sharpened the book's focus in editing the first draft. Sheila Harvill met all the deadlines with her word-processing skills.

With good humor and patience, Karen Wilson and George Wiser took on added responsibilities so that I would have the time to write.

My agent, Arnold Goodman, believed in and guided this project from the outset. He helped make the book a reality.

André Schiffrin, editor in chief of Pantheon Books, and David Frederickson of Pantheon provided wise guidance and editing skills that greatly improved the manuscript. With integrity and high standards, they constantly challenged me to get closer to the truth and to write it clearly and fairly.

My wife, Mary Lynn Kotz, lovingly contributed her journalistic and literary talent to every aspect of the book.

To all those who helped and believed in the book, I am grateful. I alone am responsible for the book's contents, its point of view, and its inadequacies. My goal was first to understand, and then to explain, how Americans make defense decisions. My hope is that the book will help us as citizens to play a more active and informed role in seeking both a secure defense and a safer world.

Washington, D.C.
October 1987

PEOPLE INTERVIEWED

The following is a partial list of the more than two hundred persons who were interviewed for the book. The author conducted most of the interviews, assisted in some by his students from the American University School of Communication. The students conducted fourteen interviews without the author present.

David Aaron, National Security Council (NSC) staff, Carter administration.
Brig. Gen. Richard Abel, USAF, ret., former director of public affairs, USAF.
Gordon Adams, director Defense Budget Project, Washington, D.C.
Madeleine Albright, NSC staff, Carter administration.
Herbert Alexander, director, Citizens Research Foundation.
Gen. James Allen, USAF, ret., B-1 officer, HQ, USAF, 1974.
Richard V. Allen, NSC director, Reagan administration, 1981–82.
Col. Kenneth Anderson, USAF, ret., congressional liaison staff, 1983–85.
Robert Anderson, board chairman, 1979–88, and president, 1970–79, Rockwell International.
J. Leland Atwood, president, 1948–62, and board chairman, 1962–67, North American Aviation; president, 1967–70, North American Rockwell.
Maj. William Austin, USAF, ret., former public affairs officer.
Peter Barrer, former staff, American Friends Service Comittee.
Anthony Battista, staff, House Armed Services Committee.
Sen. Birch Bayh (D-Ind.), 1961–79.
Robert Beckel, special assistant to the president, Carter administration.

Sen. Henry Bellmon, (R-Okla.), 1967–79.

Barry M. Blechman, former research associate, Brookings Institution.

Col. Charles Bock, USAF, ret., Rockwell test pilot, 1973–81.

Lt. Gen. Marion L. Boswell, USAF, ret., assistant vice chief of staff, 1974–76.

Rep. David Bowen (D-Miss.), 1973–81.

John Bohn, chief historian, Strategic Air Command, USAF.

Sen. David Boren (D-Okla.), 1979 to present.

Carter Bradley, aide to the late Sen. Robert Kerr (D-Okla.).

Zbigniew Brzezinski, national security adviser to President Carter.

McGeorge Bundy, special assistant for national security affairs, Presidents Kennedy and Johnson.

Lt. Gen. Kelly Burke, USAF, ret., deputy chief of staff, 1979–82.

Frank Carlucci, deputy secretary of defense, 1981–82.

Rep. William Chappell (D-Fla.), 1969 to present.

R. Michael Cole, former Washington lobbyist, Common Cause.

Sen. Alan Cranston (D-Cal.), 1969 to present.

Sen. John Culver (D-Ia.), 1975–81.

Rhett Dawson, former staff director, Senate Armed Services Committee.

Richard DeLauer, undersecretary of defense, 1981–84.

Rep. William Dickinson (R-Ala.), 1965 to present.

Rep. Norman Dicks (D-Wash.), 1977 to present.

William Dodds, former legislative and political director, United Automobile Workers.

Ed Dodson, businessman, East Tawas, Michigan.

Rep. Robert K. Dornan, (R-Cal.), 1977 to present.

Gen. Russell Dougherty, USAF, ret., SAC commander, 1973–77, executive director, Air Force Association, 1979–86.

Rep. Thomas Downey (D-N.Y.), 1975 to present.

James Drake, former engineer, North American Aviation.

Gen. Richard Ellis, USAF, ret., SAC commander, 1977–81.

Stuart Eizenstat, White House staff, Carter administration.

Jeff Ethell, airplane historian.

Rep. Martin Frost (D-Tex.), 1981 to present.

Jaques Gansler, former Defense Department official.

Charles Gifford, official of United Automobile Workers union.

Lt. Gen. Otto Glosser, USAF, ret., deputy chief of staff, 1970.

Alfred Goldberg, chief historian, Department of Defense.

Sen. Barry Goldwater (R-Ariz.), 1953–65, 1969–87, correspondence.

Gen. Andrew J. Goodpaster, USA, ret., staff secretary to President Eisenhower.

Lawrence P. Greene, former Washington staff, North American Aviation.

Morton Halperin, former Defense Department official.

Gary Hillary, former Washington staff, Rockwell International.

Hubert Harris, congressional liaison, Carter administration.

Lt. Col. Thomas Hobbs, USAF, ret., USAF B-1 contract management office at Rockwell International, 1970–73.

John Holum, assistant to former Sen. George McGovern (D-S.D.).
Purvis Hoyt, former assistant to Sen. Robert Byrd (D-W. Va.).
Paul Hoeven, Project on Military Procurement.
Rep. Richard Ichord (D-Mo.), 1961–81.
Sam Icobellis, vice-president, Rockwell International.
Gen. David C. Jones, USAF, ret., chief of staff, 1974–78; chairman, Joint
    Chiefs of Staff, 1978–82.
Hamilton Jordan, chief of staff to President Carter.
Lt. General Glenn Kent, USAF, ret., Rand Corporation, 1972 to present.
William W. Kaufmann, adviser to four secretaries of defense.
Gordon Kerr, assistant to Sen. Carl Levin (D-Mich.).
Walter Krause, chief historian, Systems Command, USAF.
Thomas Mackin, former Washington staff, North American Aviation.
Michael Mann, former staff, National Campaign Against the B-1.
Roger McIntosh, businessman, East Tawas, Michigan.
Robert McNamara, secretary of defense, 1961–67.
Brig. Gen. Michael McRaney, USAF, director of public affairs.
Walter Mondale, vice-president of the United States, 1977–81.
Dr. Hans Mark, secretary of the Air Force, 1979–81.
Melvin Laird, secretary of defense, 1969–73.
Donald Mansfield, assistant to former Rep. John Seiberling (D-Ohio).
Col. William O. McCabe, USAF, special assistant for B-1B in 1985.
Sen. George McGovern (D-S.D.), 1963–81.
Sen. Howard Metzenbaum (D-Ohio), 1977 to present.
Richard Moe, staff of Vice-President Mondale, 1977–81.
Frank Moore, White House congressional liaison, Carter administration.
Robert Moot, comptroller, Department of Defense, Nixon administration.
Robert Murphy, General Accounting Office, Dayton, Ohio.
Warren Nelson, assistant to Rep. Les Aspin (D-Wis.).
Ron Nesson, press secretary to President Ford.
Sen. Sam Nunn (D-Ga.), 1972 to present.
Col. Robert J. O'Brien, USAF, deputy assistant secretary of defense, Reagan
    administration.
Verne Orr, secretary of the Air Force, Reagan administration.
David Packard, deputy secretary of defense, 1969–72.
Steven Pearlman, former staff, National Campaign Against the B-1.
Hans Peot, assistant B-1 program director, USAF systems command.
Valerie Pinson, White House staff, Carter administration.
Jody Powell, press secretary to President Carter, 1977–81.
Sen. William Proxmire (D-Wis.), 1957 to present.
Terry Provance, former staff, National Campaign Against the B-1.
Senator David Pryor (D-Ark.), 1977 to present.
John Pulliam, auditor, General Accounting Office, Washington, D.C.
John Rane, retired marketing representative, Rockwell International.
Thomas Reed, secretary of the Air Force, 1976; NSC staff, 1982–83.
Willard Rockwell, Jr., former board chairman, Rockwell International.

Henry Ritter, former vice president, Avco Corporation.

David Rubenstein, White House aide, Carter administration.

Paul Schrade, former West Coast regional director, United Automobile Workers.

Barry Schneider, former staff, Members of Congress for Peace Through Law.

William Schneider, undersecretary of state, Reagan administration.

James R. Schlesinger, secretary of defense, 1973–75.

Lt. Gen. Thomas P. Stafford, USAF, ret., deputy chief of staff, 1978–79.

Charles Stevenson, assistant to former Sen. John Culver (D-Ia.).

Strategic Air Command headquarters, briefing officers, 1985: Maj. Steven Hafner, Lt. Col. Jerry Reynolds, Capt. Steven Sword, Maj. Joseph Mc-Nichols, all USAF.

Ivan Selin, Defense Department staff, Johnson and Nixon administrations.

Rep. John F. Seiberling (D-Ohio), 1971–87.

Walter Slocombe, NSC staff, Nixon administration; Defense Department, Carter administration.

David Smith, aerospace analyst, Stanford C. Bernstein Corporation.

Richard Stubbing, former assistant director, OMB.

Harrison Storms, former chief engineer, North American Aviation.

Rep. Mike Synar (D-Okla.), 1979 to present.

Ronald Tammen, assistant to Sen. William Proxmire (D-Wis.).

William R. Van Cleave, director, defense transition team, Reagan administration, correspondence.

Ralph J. Watson, former Washington lobbyist, Rockwell International.

Caspar Weinberger, secretary of defense, 1981 to present, correspondence.

Maj. Gen. Jasper Welch, USAF, ret., assistant deputy chief of staff, 1981–83.

Pat Wilson, chairman, Little Rock Air Force Base Community Council.

Rep. Robert Wilson (R-Cal.), 1953–81.

Col. Archie Wood, USAF, ret., cruise-missile development, 1969–71.

Seymour Zeiberg, deputy undersecretary of defense, Carter administration.

SOURCE NOTES

1 BUT WILL IT FLY?

3. Skantze quote   Molly Moore, "Air Force Activates B1B Bomber Unit," *Washington Post*, Oct. 2, 1986, p. A17.

3. Rather quote   *CBS Evening News with Dan Rather*, transcript of Oct. 1, 1986.

4. Air Force testimony   Molly Moore, "Fixing B1B May Cost $3 Billion," *Washington Post*, Feb. 13, 1987; and "Officials Say Air Force Understates B1 Problems," *Washington Post*, Feb. 26, 1987, p. A6.

4. Weinberger misled   Testimony of John E. Krings before House Armed Services Committee, Mar. 4, 1987.

4. Odgers quote   Molly Moore, "B1 Bomber Repair Fund Is Requested: New Weapon Suffers from Major Defects," *Washington Post*, Jan. 7, 1987, pp. A1, A7.

5. House A.S.C. report   The Subcommittee on Research and Development and the Subcommittee on Procurement and Military Nuclear Systems of the House Committee on Armed Services, *The B-1B: A Program Review*, Mar. 30, 1987.

5. Aspin quote   Molly Moore, "Air Force Management of B1 'Screwed It Up,' Aspin Says," *Washington Post*, Mar. 31, 1987, p. A1.

5. "Flying Edsel"   David Evans, "The B1: A Flying Edsel for America's Defense?" *Washington Post*, Jan. 4, 1987, p. C1.

5. Nunn quote   "A Trillion for Defense: What Have We Bought?" *An NBC News Report on America*, transcript, Apr. 21, 1987, p. 24.

5. **Stratton quote** Molly Moore, "Air Force Sees Hyperbole in B1 Praise, Criticism," *Washington Post*, Feb. 27, 1987, p. A4.
5. **Welch testimonial** Transcript of news conference of Larry D. Welch, Air Force chief of staff with Pentagon press corps, Jan. 16, 1987.
7. **Cost of Stealth** Hearings of the House Appropriations Defense Subcommittee on the Department of Defense Authorization for Fiscal Year 1982, part 6, July 8, 1981, *Strategic Bomber Proposals* (Washington, D.C.: Government Printing Office, 1981), pp. 1098–99.
9. **Eisenhower quote** "Farewell Radio and Television Address to the American People," Jan. 17, 1961, *Public Papers of the Presidents: Dwight D. Eisenhower, 1960* (Washington D.C.: Government Printing Office, 1961), p. 1038.

2 THE BEST BASES POLITICS CAN BUY

11. **Wurtsmith Chamber of Commerce meeting** Jim Dunn, "Base Closing," *Oscoda Press*, June 29, 1983, p. 1; interviews with Ed Dodson (president of the Michigan Bank–Huron), Robert McIntosh (East Tawas car salesman), and others.
11. **O'Loughlin at Chamber of Commerce meeting** Dunn, "Base Closing," p. 4.
12. **Air Force speaker program** Interviews with Gen. James Allen and others.
13. **Bob Davis and B-1 politics in Michigan** Interview with Chris Jewell.
13. **Detroit News editorial** "Michigan and the Pentagon," July 11, 1983.
14. **Levin and the Air Force apology** Interviews with Levin staff including Gordon Kerr; letter from Gen. James P. McCarthy to the Hon. Carl Levin, July 1, 1983; Levin staff notes on special congressional hearings.
15. **McIntosh quote** Interview with Robert McIntosh.
15. **Dodson quote** Interview with Ed Dodson.
15. **Dyess B-1 celebration** Jim Conley, "Abilene Celebrates Arrival of B-1B," *Abilene Reporter-News*, June 30, 1985, p. A1.
16. **Air Force promise to John Tower** Interviews with Air Force officers and Senate Armed Services Committee staff.
16. **Air Force base criteria** Hearings before the Committee on Armed Services, United States Senate, *Department of Defense Authorization for Appropriations for Fiscal Year 1985*, Mar. 9, 1984, part 7 (Washington, D.C.: Government Printing Office, 1984), p. 3359.
16. **Weaknesses of Dyess as a SAC base** Interviews with Air Force officers.
17. **Wichita citizens and McConnell Air Force Base** Dave Bartel, "Kansas Out of Running as MX Site," *Wichita Eagle-Beacon*, Dec. 4, 1981, P. A1; and "Whittaker Wants B-1s for McConnell," *Wichita Eagle-Beacon*, Dec. 12, 1981, p. D1.
17. **Air Force reluctance to "reward" Kassebaum and Glickman** In-

terviews with Air Force officers; Angela Herrin, "Right Stuff Won Out," *Wichita Eagle-Beacon*, Feb. 2, 1984.

18. **Dole on Meet the Press** "Dole Hints Budget Ax may Fall on B-1," *Chicago Tribune*, Nov. 2, 1981, p. 9.

18. **Dole and the B-1 basing announcement** Andrew Miller, "Bombers to Be Based in Wichita," *Kansas City Star*, Feb. 1, 1984, p. 1.

18. **Weaknesses of McConnell as a SAC base** Interviews with Air Force officers and GAO officials.

18. **Reopening of Smokey Hill Air Force Base** Interview with Air Force officer.

19. **Johnson and Brown threatening to close bases** *Interview with Harold Brown*, Jan. 17, 1969 (Lyndon B. Johnson Library, Oral History Collection), pp. 14–16.

19. **Johnson helping Abilene and Hughes quote** Brenda Zobrist, "Community Persistence Brought Dyess to Abilene," *Abilene Reporter-News*, June 29, 1985, p. E15.

19. **Little Rock Air Force Base** Interviews with Pat Wilson (chairman of the Little Rock Community Base Council) and others.

20. **Pryor meeting with General McCarthy** Interviews with Pryor, his aides Anne Lesher and Knox Walkup, and Col. Anderson; Air Force Document "Senator Pryor: Floor Statements and News Items."

22. **Title 18** U.S. Code, Title 18—Crimes and Criminal Procedure, chapter 93: Public Officers and Employees, section 1913: Lobbying with Appropriated Moneys.

23. **Gen. Russ quote** Hearings before the Committee on Armed Services, U.S. Senate, *Department of Defense Authorization for Appropriations for Fiscal Year 1985*, Mar. 9, 1984, part 7 (Washington, D.C.: Government Printing Office, 1984), p. 3358.

3 EISENHOWER AND THE POLITICS OF FEAR

27–28. **Eisenhower's early foreign policy** See Stephen E. Ambrose, *Eisenhower: The President* (vol. 2) (New York: Simon and Schuster, 1984), pp. 224–25, 618–27.

27. **Eisenhower quote** Ambrose, *Eisenhower*, p. 239.

28. **Dulles quote** Stephen E. Ambrose, *Rise to Globalism: American Foreign Policy Since 1938* (New York: Penguin, 1983), p. 194.

28. **Eisenhower quote to Dulles:** Personal and Confidential letter from Dwight D. Eisenhower to John Foster Dulles, Mar. 26, 1958 (Eisenhower Presidential Library, DDE Diary Series, Box 31, Folder: DDE Dictation, Mar. 1958), p. 1.

28. **Eisenhower press conference on Sputnik** "The President's News Conference of Oct. 9, 1957," in *Public Papers of the Presidents, Dwight D. Eisenhower, 1957*, pp. 719–32.

29. **Reaction to Sputnik** See Ambrose, *Eisenhower*, pp. 423–35; see Her-

bert York, *Race to Oblivion: A Participant's View of the Arms Race* (New York: Simon and Schuster, 1970), pp. 106–24.

29. Khrushchev quote "The News of the Week in Review," *New York Times*, Oct. 13, 1957, sec. 4, p. 1.

29. York quote York, *Race to Oblivion*, p. 106.

30. Aide to Lyndon Johnson quote Memorandum from George Reedy to Lyndon Johnson, Oct. 17, 1957 (Johnson Presidential Library, Senate Office Files of George Reedy, Box 420, Folder: Reedy Memos—Oct. 1957), p. 1.

30. Extra defense spending and Eisenhower quote Memorandum of Conference with the President Following NSC on Dec. 5, 1957, by Gen. Andrew Goodpaster (Eisenhower Presidential Library, DDE Diary Series, Box 29, Folder: Staff Notes—Dec. 1957), p. 2.

31. WS-110 and LeMay quote Ed Rees, *The Manned Missile: The Story of the B-70* (New York: Duell, Sloan, and Pearce, 1960), p. 99.

32. Eisenhower rejecting defense budget increases and Killian quote Memorandum of Conference with the President, Mar. 20, 1958, by Gen. Andrew Goodpaster (Eisenhower Presidential Library, DDE Diary Series, Box 31, Folder: Staff Notes—Mar. 1958 [1]), p. 1.

32. Eisenhower's Queen Elizabeth quote Ambrose, *Eisenhower*, p. 550.

33. Dyna-soar and other futuristic bombers Richard Witkin, "Two Teams Bidding on Space Glider," *New York Times*, May 11, 1958.

33. Eisenhower increasing B-52 production and quote Ambrose, *Eisenhower*, p. 454.

33. Eisenhower: "I don't know how many times you can kill" Notes on Meeting of Mar. 24, 1958 (Eisenhower Presidential Library, Records of the Staff Secretary, Legislative Meeting Series, Box 5, Folder: L-50 [1], June 24 and July 1, 1958), p. 8.

33. Eisenhower on growth of target list Ambrose, *Eisenhower*, pp. 493–94.

33. Eisenhower quote on his move for peace Ambrose, *Eisenhower*, p. 537.

34. Augusta meeting with President on B-70 and other weapons George B. Kistiakowsky, *A Scientist at the White House: The Private Diary of President Eisenhower's Special Assistant for Science and Technology* (Cambridge, Mass.: Harvard University Press, 1976), pp. 157–63; Memorandums of Conference with the President, Nov. 16, 18, and 21, 1959, Augusta, Georgia, by Gen. Andrew Goodpaster (Eisenhower Presidential Library, DDE Diary Series, Box 45, Folder: Staff Notes—November, 1959).

35. Eisenhower New Year's Eve quote Ambrose, *Eisenhower*, p. 553.

36. Eisenhower telephone call to Gates Telephone Calls, Jan. 12, 1960 (Eisenhower Presidential Library, DDE Diary Series, Box 47, Folder: Telephone Calls—Jan., 1960).

36. Eisenhower quote to Republican leaders Notes on Meeting of Feb. 9, 1960 (Eisenhower Presidential Library, Records of the Staff Secretary,

Legislative Meeting Series, Box 6, Folder: L-60 [1] Feb. 9, 1960), pp. 30–31.

4 CURTIS LeMAY AND STRATEGIC AIR POWER

37. *LeMay, defense advisers, and the SAC demonstration* Fred Kaplan, *The Wizards of Armageddon* (New York: Simon and Schuster, 1983), pp. 132–34.

38. *LeMay on civilian authority* See Gen. Curtis E. LeMay, with Gen. Dale O. Smith, "Civil Control of the Military," *America Is in Danger* (New York: Funk and Wagnalls, 1968), pp. 1–9.

38. *LeMay: "silent silo sitters"* Herbert York, *Race to Oblivion: A Participant's View of the Arms Race* (New York: Simon and Schuster, 1970), p. 53.

38. *Theory of strategic air power* See Robert Frank Futrell, *Ideas, Concepts, Doctrine* (New York: Arno, 1980); Lee Kennett, *A History of Strategic Bombing* (New York: Scribner's, 1982); Lt. Col. Barry D. Watts, *The Foundations of U.S. Air Doctrine: The Problem of Friction in War* (Maxwell AFB, Ala.: Air University Press, 1984).

39. *Army Air Corps before World War II* See Ronald H. Spector, *Eagle Against the Sun: The American War with Japan* (New York: Free Press, 1985), pp. 9–32.

39. *LeMay's interception of the* Rex Thomas M. Coffey, *Iron Eagle: The Turbulent Life of General Curtis LeMay* (New York: Crown, 1986), pp. 241–42.

39. *Army Air Corp's plans for the war in Europe* Watts, *Foundations of U.S. Air Doctrines*, pp. 17–23.

40. *Effect of Allied air supremacy* See Albert Speer, *Spandau: The Secret Diaries* (New York: Macmillan, 1976), pp. 339–40.

40. *LeMay's role in World War II* See Coffey, *Iron Eagle*, pp. 3–182; see also Gen. Curtis E. LeMay with MacKinlay Kantor, *Mission with LeMay: My Story* (Garden City, N.Y.: Doubleday, 1965).

41. *LeMay and the fire bombing of Japan* Coffey, *Iron Eagle*, pp. 171–73.

41. *LeMay: "Once you make a decision"* Coffey, *Iron Eagle*, p. 306.

41. *LeMay at Strategic Air Command* See Coffey, *Iron Eagle*, pp. 270–346; LeMay, *Mission with LeMay*, pp. 425–500.

42. *Eisenhower and LeMay defense priorities* York, *Race to Oblivion*, p. 53.

43. *LeMay on "human control"* Andrew Wilson, *The Bomb and the Computer* (New York: Delacorte, 1968), pp. 131–32.

43. *LeMay's relations with Congress and visits to Johnson* Coffey, *Iron Eagle*, pp. 282–83, 347–48.

43. *Eisenhower: "What you want is enough"* "The President's News Conference of Feb. 3, 1960," *Public Papers of the Presidents: Dwight D. Eisenhower, 1960* (Washington, D.C.: Government Printing Office, 1961), p. 145.

43. **LeMay: "Military men think"** LeMay, *America Is in Danger*, p. 52.
44. **LeMay: "Our general war policy"** LeMay, *America Is in Danger*, p. 117.
44. **LeMay: "It is the same kind of arms race"** LeMay, *America Is in Danger*, p. 94.
44. **LeMay: "They may feel they should"** Quoted in Michael Krepon, *Strategic Stalemate: Nuclear Weapons and Arms Control in American Politics* (New York: St. Martin's, 1984), p. 53.
44. **LeMay: "I would never be happy"** Krepon, *Strategic Stalemate*, p. 31.
44. **LeMay: "How can we dress and"** Krepon, *Strategic Stalemate*, p. 93.
44. **National war plan and SIOP** See Peter Pringle and William Arkin, *SIOP* (London: Sphere Books, 1983).
44. **LeMay resisting changes in the war plan, and quote: "hands were being tied"** Gen. LeMay's Diary, Jan. 23, 1951 (Library of Congress, Manuscript Division, LeMay Papers, Box B-64, Folder: Diary, 1951), p. 2.
45. **LeMay: "SAC was the USA Sunday punch"** Commanding General's Diary for July 22, 1950 (Library of Congress, Manuscript Division, LeMay Papers, Box B-64, Folder: Diary, 7–12/50), p. 2.
45. **LeMay ordered to reveal details of the war plan** Letter from Gen. Nathan Twining to Gen. Curtis LeMay, June, 9, 1955 (Library of Congress, Manuscript Division, LeMay Papers, Box B-60, Folder: Twining), p. 2.
45. **Navy adding targets to play a role in the war plan** Interview with Navy officer.
45. **LeMay and the Navy admiral assigning nuclear targets** Coffey, *Iron Eagle*, p. 341.
46. **SAC celebration following failed missile test** George B. Kistiakowsky, *A Scientist at the White House: The Private Diary of President Eisenhower's Special Assistant for Science and Technology* (Cambridge, Mass.: Harvard University Press, 1976), p. 396.
46. **Army general and Eisenhower** Richard A. Stubbing, with Richard A. Mendel, *The Defense Game: An Insider Explores the Astonishing Realities of America's Defense Establishment* (New York: Harper and Row, 1986), p. 131.
46. **Arleigh Burke: "the prescription for . . ."** Unclassified Summary of NAVWAG Study No. 5—National Policy Implications of Atomic Parity (Eisenhower Presidential Library, White House Office Files, Office of the Staff Secretary, Subject Series, Alpha Subseries, Box 21, Folder: Nuclear Exchange [1]), p. 2.
46. **LeMay on the role of ICBMs** "SAC Position on Missiles, Nov. 26, 1955" (Library of Congress, Manuscript Division, Nathan F. Twining Papers, Box 76), p. 2.
46. **Kistiakowsky visit to SAC** Kistiakowsky, *Scientist at the White House*, pp. 413–16.

5 DUTCH KINDELBERGER AND THE NEW DEFENSE POLITICS

48. *Atwood meeting with Kistiakowsky* George B. Kistiakowsky, *A Scientist at the White House: The Private Diary of President Eisenhower's Special Assistant for Science and Technology* (Cambridge, Mass.: Harvard University Press, 1976), p. 218.

49–51. *North American dealings with Kerr* Interviews with former North American officials, including J. Leland Atwood and former Kerr aides. See also Robert Gene Baker, *Wheeling and Dealing: Confessions of a Capitol Hill Operator* (New York: Norton, 1978); Robert Pack, "One Deal Too Many," *Washingtonian*, Feb. 1986, pp. 100–103, 150–55.

51. *Political division of space contracts* Interviews; see also *Toward the Endless Frontier: History of the Committee on Science and Technology, 1959–79* (Washington, D.C.: Government Printing Office, 1980).

52–55. *Early history of North American aviation* See Ralph B. Oakley, "North American Goes to War, Part II," *American Aviation Historical Society*, vol. 20, no. 1, 1975, p. 46–57; see also John Leland Atwood, *North American Rockwell: Storehouse of High Technology* (Princeton: Princeton University Press, 1970).

55. *Sen. Jackson on B-70 cancellation* "Boeing Losing Contract," *New York Times*, Dec. 2, 1959.

55. *Sen. Engle on B-70 cancellation* Jack Raymond, "Air Chief Scores B-70 Cut; Plans Appeal to Congress," *New York Times*, Jan. 12, 1960, p. 12.

56. *Competition for the ICBM* Herbert York, *Race to Oblivion: A Participant's View of the Arms Race* (New York: Simon and Schuster, 1970), pp. 83–104.

56. *Competition for the IRBM* Desmond Ball, *Politics and Force Levels: The Strategic Missile Program of the Kennedy Administration* (Berkeley; University of California Press, 1980), p. 253.

56. *McCloy quote* Stephen E. Ambrose, *Eisenhower The President*, vol. 2 (New York: Simon and Schuster, 1983), p. 476.

57. *McElroy quote* Kistiakowsky, *Scientist at the White House*, p. 161; see also Memorandum of Conference with the President, Nov. 16, 1959, Augusta, Ga., by Gen. Andrew Goodpaster (Eisenhower Presidential Library, DDE Diary Series, Box 45, Folder: Staff Notes—Nov. 1959 [3]), p. 6.

58. *Eisenhower: "I see no reason" and "would be an almost imperceptible"* "The President's News Conference of Apr. 27, 1960," *Public Papers of the Presidents: Dwight D. Eisenhower, 1960* (Washington, D.C.: Government Printing Office, 1961), p. 363.

58. *Kent visit to North American Aviation* Interviews with Glenn Kent.

6 POLITICS AND THE MISSILE GAP

59. *U-2 incident* See Michael R. Beschloss, *Mayday: Eisenhower, Khrushchev, and the U-2 Affair* (New York: Harper and Row, 1986).

60. *Eisenhower: "Soul-searching concern" and "I have one"* Stephen E. Ambrose, *Eisenhower: The President* (vol. 2) (New York: Simon and Schuster, 1983), p. 568.

60. *Eisenhower conversation with Kistiakowsky* George B. Kistiakowsky, *A Scientist at the White House: The Private Diary of President Eisenhower's Special Assistant for Science and Technology* (Cambridge, Mass.: Harvard University Press, 1976), p. 375.

61. *Johnson and Preparedness Subcommittee Report* "The B-70 Program," *Report of the Preparedness Investigating Subcommittee of the Committee on Armed Services* (Washington, D.C.: Government Printing Office, 1960).

62. *Twining quote* Testimony before the Senate Aeronautical and Space Sciences Commitee, Feb. 9, 1960, quoted in *Selected Quotations from Public Speeches, Press Conferences, and Congressional Testimony by Key Government Officials from January 1959 through February 1962 on the B-70* (Bolling AFB, Office of Air Force History, Washington, D.C.: prepared by Research and Analysis Division, SAFAA, 1962), p. 139.

62. *1960 Democratic platform quotations* "Democratic Platform: 1960," quoted in *National Party Platforms; Vol. II, 1960–76* (Urbana: University of Illinois Press, 1978), p. 575.

62. *Kennedy endorsing bomber during 1960 campaign, and quote: "I wholeheartedly . . ."* Desmond Ball, *Politics of Force Levels: The Strategic Missile Program and the Kennedy Administration* (Berkeley: University of California Press, 1980), pp. 236–37.

63. *Nixon-Rockefeller joint statement on defense* Ambrose, *Eisenhower*, p. 597.

63–78. *Eisenhower authorizing additional $500 million in defense spending* Memorandum of Conference with the President, July 19, 1960, by Gen. Andrew Goodpaster (Eisenhower Presidential Library, DDE Diary Series, Box 51, Folder: Staff Notes—July, 1958), pp. 5–6.

63. *Eisenhower telephone call to Jones* Telephone Calls, Aug. 8, 1960 (Eisenhower Presidential Library, DDE Diary Series, Box 52, Folder: Telephone Calls—Aug., 1960), p. 1.

64. *Eisenhower releasing $155 million for B-70* John W. Finney, "B-70 Program Expanded in a Pentagon Policy Shift," *New York Times*, Nov. 1, 1960, pp. 1, 6.

64. *Kennedy: "We could not get"* *Selected Quotations on the B-70*, Nov. 2, 1960, p. 45.

64–65. *Eisenhower quotations from his farewell address* Farewell Radio and Television Address to the American People, Jan. 17, 1961, *Public*

Papers of the Presidents: Dwight D. Eisenhower, 1960 (Washington, D.C.: Government Printing Office, 1961), pp. 1038–39.

65. **Eisenhower quote from Waging Peace** Dwight D. Eisenhower, *Waging Peace: 1956–1961* (Garden City, N.Y.: Doubleday, 1965) pg. 615.

66. **Ambrose: "great tragedy" through "to override his own"** Ambrose, *Eisenhower*, p. 621.

66. **Ambrose: "In a limited and halting"** Stephen E. Ambrose, *Rise to Globalism: American Foreign Policy Since 1938* (New York: Penguin, 1983), p. 234.

7 THE WHIZ KIDS AND THE BOMBER GENERALS

67. **Kennedy: "We shall pay any price"** Inaugural Address, Jan. 20, 1961, *Public Papers of the Presidents, John F. Kennedy, 1961* (Washington, D.C.: Government Printing Office, 1962), p. 1.

67. **McNamara and Gilpatric examining photos** Interview with McNamara; Fred Kaplan, *The Wizards of Armageddon* (New York: Simon and Schuster, 1983), pp. 286–87.

68. **McNamara meeting with Kennedy and offering his resignation** Interviews with McNamara and others.

68. **Kennedy's supplemental defense budget** Text of President Kennedy's Special Message to Congress on Defense Spending, *New York Times,* Mar. 29, 1961, pp. 16–17.

68. **Kennedy defense policy and "flexible response"** Stephen E. Ambrose, *Rise to Globalism: American Foreign Policy Since 1938* (New York: Penguin, 1983), pp. 245–52.

69. **McNamara background** David Halberstam, *The Best and the Brightest* (New York: Random House, 1969), pp. 215–40.

69. **Schlesinger: "humane technocrat"** Arthur M. Schlesinger, Jr., *A Thousand Days: John F. Kennedy in the White House* (Boston: Houghton Mifflin, 1965), p. 312.

70. **McNamara, the "whiz kids," and systems analysis** Interview with William Kaufmann.

70. **Enthoven overwhelming Air Force officers with systems analysis** Interview with Air Force Gen. James Allen.

70–71. **White: "I am profoundly"** Jack Raymond, *Power at the Pentagon* (New York: Harper and Row, 1964), p. 289.

71. **LeMay: "like a hospital"** Thomas M. Coffey, *Iron Eagle: The Turbulent Life of General Curtis LeMay* (New York: Crown, 1986), p. 370.

71. **LeMay: "Would things be much worse"** Kaplan, *The Wizards of Armageddon*, p. 256.

71. **Kennedy and appointment of LeMay as chief of staff** Schlesinger, *A Thousand Days*, p. 912.

71. **Gilpatric: "would have a major revolt" and "ended up in sort of"** Quoted in Coffey, *Iron Eagle*, p. 357.

71. **McNamara's opinion of LeMay in World War II, and quotes: "Who was the" and "the greatest fighting"** Interview with McNamara.

72. **LeMay and the Bay of Pigs Invasion** See Coffey, *Iron Eagle*, pp. 353–56.

72. **B-52s training for low-altitude attacks** See Michael Edward Brown, "Flying Blind: Decision Making in the U.S. Strategic Bomber Program," Ph.D. thesis, Cornell University (Ann Arbor, Mich.: University Microfilms International, 1983), p. 274.

73. **LeMay: "With manned systems"** Testimony before the Senate DOD Appropriations Subcommittee, Fiscal Year 1962 Budget, quoted in *Selected Quotations on the B-70*, p. 52.

73. **McNamara and Gilpatric: "processing and display"** "Text of McNamara Statement on the B-70 Bomber," *New York Times*, Mar. 16, 1962, p. 12.

73. **Taylor: "Is it worth several"** Quoted in "Memorandum for the President, the B-70 Program," by Robert McNamara, *Draft Presidential Memorandum, Nov. 20, 1962*, p. 21.

74. **North American working on RS-70 designs** Interviews with North American Aviation engineers, including Jim Drake and others.

74. **McNamara ordering LeMay not to testify on the B-70** Interviews with McNamara and Gen. James Allen.

74–75. **Background on Carl Vinson, and quote: "Aw shucks"** Raymond, *Power*, p. 296.

75. **Vinson challenge to McNamara and Kennedy, and quote: "ordered and directed"** Jack Raymond, "House Unit Directs Production of B-70," *New York Times*, Mar. 2, 1962, pp. 1, 3.

75. **Committee report: "If this language"** Jack Raymond, "President Backs Limitation of B-70," *New York Times*, Mar. 8, 1962, pp. 1,10.

75. **Vinson: "We don't want to run"** Jack Raymond, "McNamara Wary on B-70 Conflict," *New York Times*, Mar. 9, 1962, pp. 1, 14.

75. **Rose Garden agreement** Interviews with McGeorge Bundy and others; see also John G. Norris, "Rep. Vinson Drops Fight on RS-70," *Washington Post*, Mar. 22, 1962; and Russell Baker, "B-70 Dispute Ends as Vinson Yields on Fund Demand," *New York Times*, Mar. 22, 1962, pp. 1, 21.

76. **Proposals on the number of Minuteman missiles, and conversation between McNamara and Kennedy** Halberstam, *The Best and the Brightest*, p. 72; also interview with McNamara.

76. **McNamara: "The secretary must understand"** Interview with McNamara.

76. **Kennedy: "I used the Skybolt"** Herbert York, *Race to Oblivion: A Participant's View of the Arms Race* (New York: Simon and Shuster, 1970), p. 155.

77. **Schlesinger on bartering of weapons, and quote: "risking public conflict"** Schlesinger, *A Thousand Days*, pp. 499–500; also interview with McGeorge Bundy.

77. **Largest peacetime defense budget in history** Michael Krepon, *Strategic Stalemate: Nuclear Weapons and Arms Control in American Politics* (New York: St. Martin's, 1984), p. 95.

77. **Kennedy speeches in Fort Worth, Texas** "Remarks at a Rally in Fort Worth in Front of the Texas Hotel, Nov. 22, 1963"; "Remarks at the Breakfast of the Fort Worth Chamber of Commerce"; and "Remarks Prepared for Delivery at the Trade Mart in Dallas," *Public Papers of the Presidents: John F. Kennedy, 1963*, pp. 87–94.

8 VIETNAM AND THE TEST OF AIR POWER

79–80. **Johnson, LeMay, and McNamara in Texas discussing AMSA** Thomas M. Coffey, *Iron Eagle: The Turbulent Life of General Curtis LeMay* (New York: Crown, 1986), pp. 431–32.

80. **Reappointment of LeMay, and Johnson quote: "I don't know"** Coffey, *Iron Eagle*, pp. 433–35.

81. **LeMay request for AMSA, and Bundy quote: "any serious political"** Memorandum to the President, Subject: Letter to General LeMay, September 2, 1964, by McGeorge Bundy (Johnson Presidential Library, NSC File—Aide File: Bundy, vol. 6, July 1–Sept. 30, 1964), p. 1.

81. **Decision to deepen involvement in Vietnam** See Rowland Evans and Robert Novak, *Lyndon B. Johnson: The Exercise of Power* (New York: New American Library, 1966) pp. 530–40.

81. **LeMay: "bomb [North Vietnam] back"** Gen. Curtis E. LeMay, with Mackinlay Kantor, *Mission with LeMay* (Garden City, N.Y.: Doubleday, 1965), p. 565.

81. **JCS recommendation for air war against North Vietnam** See Lyndon B. Johnson, *The Vantage Point: Perspectives of the President, 1963– 1969* (New York: Popular Press, 1971), pp. 128–30; see also, Gen. William W. Momyer, *Air Power in Three Wars: World War II, Korea, and Vietnam* (Washington, D.C.: Government Printing Office, 1978), p. 15.

82. **Rolling Thunder** See Years 1965 through 1968 in J. C. Hopkins, *The Development of Strategic Air Command, 1946–1981: A Chronological History* (Office of the Historian, Headquarters Strategic Air Command, July 1, 1982), pp. 128–52.

82. **Momyer: "To wait until [the enemy]"** Momyer, *Air Power in Three Wars*, p. 338.

83. **Johnson: "I'm not a LeMay"** Evans and Novak, *Lyndon B. Johnson*, p. 539.

83. **LeMay: "In Vietnam we dropped"** Coffey, *Iron Eagle*, p. 429.

83. **Criticisms of Vietnam bombing strategy** See Momyer, *Air Power in Three Wars*; see also Gabriel Kolko, *Anatomy of a War: Vietnam, the United States, and the Modern Historical Experience* (New York: Pantheon, 1985).

84. **LeMay: "It takes a long time here"** Coffey, *Iron Eagle*, p. 438.

84. **McNamara's changing views on nuclear strategy** Memorandum for the President by Robert McNamara, *Draft Presidential Memorandum*, Dec. 3, 1964.

85. F-111 transformation offered to Johnson Memorandum for the President by Robert McNamara, *Draft Presidential Memorandum, Nov. 1, 1965.*

86. B-70 crash John G. Norris, "XB-70 Loss on Publicity Flight," *Washington Post,* June 11, 1966; Howard Simons, "The Anatomy of a Fatal Plane Collision in Midair," *Washington Post,* June 23, 1966.

9 THE GREENING OF CALIFORNIA

90. Atwood: "All of Mr. Nixon's" Bernard D. Nossiter, "Arms Firms See Postwar Spurt," *Washington Post,* Dec. 8, 1969, p. A18.

90. North American Aviation in trouble "Rockwell Trims the Giant," *Business Week,* Jan. 10, 1970, p. 33.

91. Hillary: "There was an expectation" Interview with Hillary.

91. Nixon on "security gap" "The Security Gap," radio broadcast on *CBS Radio Network,* Oct. 24, 1968.

91. Rooting out whiz kids Alain Enthoven and K. Wayne Smith, *How Much Is Enough: Shaping the Defense Program, 1961–1969* (New York: Harper and Row, 1971), p. 333.

91. Laird's key goals Richard A. Stubbing, with Richard A. Mendel, *The Defense Game* (New York: Harper and Row, 1986), p. 290.

91. Laird's "treaty" with the military Enthoven and Smith, *How Much Is Enough,* pp. 333–34.

93. Packard conversation with Ryan Interview with Ivan Selin.

93. LeMay bomber proposal of 1963 Interviews with Air Force Generals David Jones and James Allen.

93. Selin's views on the B-1 Interview with Selin.

93. Packard's views on the B-1 Interview with Packard.

94. Atwood and the F-15 contract Interviews with Atwood, Anderson, and Storms.

94. Discussion about quitting the B-1 competition Interviews with Rockwell, Anderson, and Storms.

94. Anderson: "We can't quit" Interview with Anderson.

94. Rockwell promotional campaign, and quote: "Where did we fail" "Cheers and Tears," *Nation,* June 22, 1970, pp. 740–41.

95. Intercession of Reagan and Murphy "Happy days for North American," *Business Week,* June 13, 1970, pp. 28–29.

95. Role of Lipscomb Interview with Laird.

95. Packard encouraging Atwood to bid on B-1 Interview with Anderson.

95. Conversation between Packard and Anderson on the state of major defense contractors Interview with Anderson.

95. Packard: "You could just throw darts" Interview with Packard.

96. Effect of political contributions Interviews with North American Aviation officials and Nixon administration officials.

96. Award announcement by Murphy Interview with Watson; "North

American Rockwell Receives B1 Bomber Award," *Wall Street Journal*, June 8, 1970.

96. **Headline: "43,000 New Jobs"** *Los Angeles Times*, June 8, 1970, p. 1.

96. **Rockwell: "We knew as a company"** "The 'One More Chance' Bomber," *Fortune*, July, 1970, p. 27.

96. **Air Force response** "Air Force says North American had Lowest Bid for B-1 Bomber," *New York Times*, June 9, 1970.

97. **Congressional challenge to ABM development** Richard Harwood, "Hill Wises Up to Pentagon," *Washington Post*, Aug. 10, 1969, p. B1.

97. **Seiberling, McGovern, and MCPL challenge to B-1** Interviews with McGovern, Seiberling, and Don Mansfield (Seiberling aide); also Sen. George S. McGovern and Rep. John F. Seiberling, "Report on the B-1 Bomber," *Congressional Record—Senate*, May 6, 1971, pp. 13887–90.

97. **Seiberling visit to SAC** Interview with Seiberling.

98. **Anderson conversation with McGovern** Interview with McGovern.

98. **Moore: "If the government provided"** Bernard D. Nossiter, "Defense Firms Leery of Civilian Work," *Washington Post*, Dec. 9, 1968, p. A6.

99. **B-1 opposition growing within the Nixon administration** Interviews with Stubbing, Laird, Packard, K. Wayne Smith, Walter Slocombe, and Ivan Selin; Stubbing, *The Defense Game*, pp. 84–85.

99. **Stubbing on the pattern of defense contract awards** Interview with Stubbing; see also Stubbing, *The Defense Game*, pp. 34–36.

100. **Cost of building B-1** National Archives Nixon Project WHSF-Krogh, Box 10, Memorandum Peter Flanigan to Egil Krogh, Dec. 5, 1969.

100. **Packard threatens to resign over B-1** Interviews with Laird and Packard; see also James M. Naughton, "Budget Cutters Outmaneuvered," *New York Times*, Apr. 9, 1971.

101. **Ehrlichman's "Sun Belt" strategy for Nixon's reelection** Malcolm McConnell, "T Minus," *Washingtonian*, Feb. 1987, p. 125.

101–103. **"Keep California Green"; and the "Industrial State Unemployment Project" drawn up by John Rose** Memorandum from John Rose to Peter Flanigan, re: Industrial State Unemployment Project, Apr. 22, 1971, Internal White House Document.

101. **Goals of "Keep California Green"** White House Memorandum from Don Derman to Ellis Veatch, Aug. 26, 1971.

102. **Involvement of William Howard Taft IV** Memorandum from Taft, Aug. 9, 1971, in which Taft asks an OMB official to "check out . . . the possibility of reprogramming funds for these action [sic] from areas where there is less need for direct employment or from less job intensive activities."

102. **Considering closing East Coast bases** White House Memorandum, "California Employment, Sept. 10, 1971," p. 2.

102. **Rose on B-747 command post** Rose Memorandum to Weinberger and Flanigan, Nixon Project WHSF-SMOF, Flanigan, Box 19.

102. **Fitzgerald on the B-1, and quotes: "bigger boondoggle" and "to make jobs"** Jerry Landauer, "The Costs Are Jumping on the New

B-1 Aircraft, a Secret Report Says," *Wall Street Journal*, May 3, 1971, pp. 1, 21.

103. **Schultz Memo to Nixon**   Nixon Project WHSP-WHCS, Box 50.

103. **Weinberger Memo to Haldeman**   Nixon Project, WHSF-SMOF, Box 96.

103. **Stans and Mitchell campaign solicitations**   Interviews with North American Rockwell officials

103. **Rockwell contributions**   Memorandum from John G. Koeltl to Thomas F. McBride, Subject: Rockwell International, Dec. 21, 1973, Watergate Special Prosecution Force, Department of Justice. Released by petition under the Freedom of Information Act from the National Archives, Washington, D.C., Record Group 460, Records of the Watergate Special Prosecution Force, Campaign Contributions—Rockwell. [Watergate Special Prosecution Force papers are referred to hereafter as National Archives, Watergate, F.O.I.A.]

104. **Daniell trip to Washington, Apr. 6, 1972**   Memorandum from John G. Koeltl to File #406, Subject: Interview with James L. Daniell, Jan. 17, 1974, Watergate Special Prosecution Force, Department of Justice, p. 3 (National Archives, Watergate, F.O.I.A.).

104. **Quote: "partial payment of our pledge"**   Letters from James L. Daniell (North American Rockwell) to Hugh W. Sloan, Jr. (Committee for the Re-Election of the President), July 6, Apr. 7, and Apr. 17, 1972 (National Archives, Watergate, F.O.I.A.).

104. **Rose Mary Woods's list**   Rose Mary Woods List of Political Contributions (National Archives, Watergate, F.O.I.A.).

104. **Nixon to Rane: "hang in there"**   Interview with Rane.

104. **Nixon to Rockwell: "I'm sorry I can't"**   Interview with Rockwell official.

105. **Rockwell and Anderson Meeting with Flanigan**   Interview with Anderson.

105. **Fulbright on post-SALT defense budget**   Murrey Marder, "Rogers and Fulbright Clash on New Arms," *Washington Post*, June 20, 1972, pp. A1, A10.

105. **Laird on the need for B-1 and Trident**   John W. Finney, "Support of Pacts Is Linked by Laird to New Arms Funds," *New York Times*, June 7, 1972, pp. 1, 11; see also George C. Wilson, "Laird's SALT Stand May Delay Funds," *Washington Post*, June 8, 1972; George C. Wilson, "House Votes Against Cutoff of War Funds," June 28, 1972, *Washington Post*.

105. **Laird: "to raise the white flag"**   "Washington Roundup," *Aviation Week and Space Technology*, July 10, 1972, p. 11.

106. **Effect of Linebacker II**   Gabriel Kolko, *Anatomy of a War: Vietnam, the United States, and the Modern Historical Experience* (New York: Pantheon, 1985), pp. 439–44; Gen. William W. Momyer, *Air Power in Three Wars: World War II, Korea, and Vietnam* (Washington, D.C.: Government Printing Office, 1978), pp. 242–43; J. C. Hopkins, *The*

Development of Strategic Air Command (Office of the Historian, Headquarters Strategic Air Command, 1982), pp. 175–78.

10 THE GOLDPLATED BOMBER

108. Problems with the B-1 as reported by Air Force program managers Letter to AFCMD (CC/Brig. Gen. Nunn) from Capt. Robert C. Hawkins (SAIMS Surveillance Office), Subject: Status of the B-1 Program, Mar. 16, 1972 (Department of the Air Force, Air Force Plant Representative Ofc., Air Force Contract Management Division, Air Force Systems Command).

108. Captain threatened by Rockwell employee Letter to CC/Col. Hoag from Capt. Malcomb C. Edelblute (Chief, Production Administration Division), Subject: Possible Conflict of Interest, Apr. 20, 1971 (Department of the Air Force, Air Force Plant Representative Ofc., Air Force Contract Management Division, Air Force Systems Command).

109. Gen. Nelson on the status of the B-1 program "North American Rockwell, Air Force Defend B-1 but See Fight Ahead," *Wall Street Journal,* June 4, 1971.

109. Dayton orders bad news to be relayed outside of normal reporting procedures Letter to Air Force Plant Representative Office, attn. Col. Hoag, from Lt. Col. Robert L. Zambenini (Dir., Program Control, Deputy for B-1), Subject: SAIMS Surveillance Report," May 15, 1972 (Department of the Air Force, Headquarters Aeronautical Systems Division, Wright-Patterson Air Force Base, Air Force Systems Command).

109. Hoag reply, and quotes: "tenor and substance" and "what deficiencies" Letter to ASD/YHPE/Lt. Col. Zambenini from Col. Earl A. Hoag (Air Force Plant Representative, Subject: SAIMS Surveillance Report, May 26, 1972 (Department of the Air Force, Air Force Plant Representative Ofc., Air Force Contract Management Division, Air Force Systems Command).

109. Quotes: "those in the highest" and "they were building on" Letter to Sen. William Proxmire from Air Force officer, July 17, 1973.

109. Removal of Lt. Col. Hobbs Letter to ASD (YH/Gen. Nelson) from Lt. Col. Thomas H. Hobbs, Subject: Clarification of Issues, Apr. 12, 1972 (Department of the Air Force, Air Force Plant Representative Ofc., Air Force Contract Mangement Division, Air Force Systems Command).

110. Rockwell fee award upgraded to 95 percent Interview with Glosser.

110. Problems in the development of the B-58 and B-70 See Michael Edward Brown, "Flying Blind: Decision Making in the U.S. Strategic Bomber Program," Ph.D. thesis, Cornell University (Ann Arbor, Mich.: University Microfilms International, 1983), pp. 186–88, 250–57.

111. Covington: "The Air Force wanted" Interview with Defense Department official.

111. 1963 origin of B-1's requirements Interviews with Jones and Allen.

112. **Storms on the B-1** Interview with Storms.
112. **Rockwell contract award and General Electric** Interviews with Rockwell officials; William Beecher, "Air Force Plans for Prototypes of New Bomber," *New York Times*, June 6, 1970, pp. 1, 62.
112–113. **GAO 1973 report** U.S. General Accounting Office Staff Study: "B-1 Weapon System," Feb. 1973 (Department of the Air Force).
113–114. **Rockwell on problems with the B-1** Interviews with Rockwell officials and engineers, including Robert Anderson and Sam Icobellis (Rockwell vice-president).
114. **Boyd on variable-sweep wing** Interview with Air Force officer.
114. **Recommendations of Generals Glosser and Kent** Interviews with Glosser and Kent.
115. **Kent: "never backing" and "I always back"** Interview with Kent.
116. **Ferguson: "A lieutenant at Systems Command"** Interview with Defense Department official.
116. **Problems with escape capsule** Interviews with Generals David Jones and Jasper Welch, Rockwell chairman Robert Anderson, and others.
117. **Anderson quote: "Why can't bomber pilots"; and reply: "Because bomber pilots"** Interview with Robert Anderson.
117. **Welch on B-1** Interview with Welch.
117. **Glosser: "You guys have got your way"** Interview with Glosser.
118. **GAO 1974 report** U.S. General Accounting Office Staff Study: "B-1 Weapon System," Mar. 1974 (Department of the Air Force).
118. **Schlesinger: "Major technical risks" and "fully assured that the"** "Remarks by the Honorable James R. Schlesinger, Secretary of Defense, at Rollout Ceremony for B-1 Bomber, Palmdale, California, Saturday, Oct. 26, 1974" (Washington, D.C.: News Release, Office of Assistant Secretary of Defense [Public Affairs]), p. 4.
118. **General Jones's position on the B-1** Interview with Jones and other Air Force sources.
119. **General Ellis's position on the B-1 at Corona Quest** Brown, "Flying Blind," pp. 322–25.
119–120. **Corona Quest meeting** Interviews with Air Force participants.
120. **Two sets of books on the B-1** Interviews with Air Force and congressional sources.
121. **Changes in B-1 specifications** Michael Getler, "Air Force to Modify B-1 to Cut Costs," *Washington Post*, Aug. 24, 1974; "USAF Cuts B-1 Maximum Speed," *Aviation Week and Space Technology*, June 16, 1975, p. 18.

11 WHO'S ON WHO?

123. **Description of lobbying assignments** Interviews with Ralph Watson, John Rane, and others.
123–124. **Lobbying of Howard Baker** Interview with Henry Ritter (retired vice-president for marketing, AVCO, Nashville, Tenn.).

126. **Title 18 of the U.S. Code**   U.S. Code, Title 18—Crimes and Criminal Procedure, Chapter 93: Public Officers and Employees, Section 1913: Lobbying with Appropriated Monies.

126. **$100 million cut from B-1 authorization**   Michael Getler, "Senate Panel Cuts B-1 Fund, Bars New ABM," *Washington Post*, Aug. 3, 1973.

127. **Congress asserting itself in defense matters**   Interviews with Rep. John Seiberling (D-Ohio) and others.

128–129. **Rockwell subcontracting strategy**   Interviews with Lawrence P. Greene (former Rockwell official in Washington, D.C., office) and other Rockwell officials.

129. **Role of United Automobile Workers Union**   Interviews with UAW officials, including Charles Gifford (Iowa) and Paul Schrade (former West Coast representative).

129. **UAW quits liberal coalition against the B-1**   "UAW Secedes," *Philadelphia Inquirer*, May 7, 1975.

130. **Role of Gen. James Allen**   Interview with Allen.

131–132. **Lobbying Glenn**   Interviews with Air Force officers, Rockwell officials, and UAW officials.

132. **Schlesinger letter to Glenn**   Quoted in *Congressional Record—Senate*, June 5, 1975, pp. S 9851–52.

132. **Nunn lobbied by Dr. Daniel Callahan**   Interviews with Nunn, Air Force sources, and Dr. Daniel Callahan.

133. **Rockwell brochure on Akron**   Letter from John Rane, to Mel Brown (Director, AED, Inc.), June 23, 1973; "14th District, Akron, Ohio—B-1 Jobs—Economic Impact" (B-1 Division, North American Rockwell), p. 2.

134. **Whipple: "California has been built"**   Anthony Sampson, *The Arms Bazaar: From Lebanon to Lockheed* (New York: Viking, 1977), p. 207.

134. **Rockwell analysis of economic impact of B-1**   Peter J. Ognibene, "The Air Force's Secret War on Unemployment," *Washington Monthly*, July–Aug. 1975, pp. 58–61.

134. **Seiberling economic impact study**   Ognibene, "The Air Force's Secret War on Unemployment," p. 60.

134. **University of Michigan economic impact study**   Ognibene, "The Air Force's Secret War on Unemployment," p. 61.

134. **"Operation Common Sense"**   Interviews with Ralph Watson and others; also Minutes of Meeting of OCS [Operation Common Sense] Executive Committee, Dec. 5, 1973, and Minutes of Meeting of OCS Executive Committee held at the B-1 and Autonetics Division Offices, Jan. 15–16, 1974 (confidential documents of the Rockwell corporate office in Washington, D.C.).

135. **Washington Alert *article and payment***   Martha Rountree, "Why the B-1 Is Vital to Our Defense," *Washington Alert*, special report, April 1976, p. 3; "Urgent SOS from Martha Rountree" (Washington, D.C.: Presbrey Associates, Inc., 1976); "Annual Review of Washington, D.C., Office of Operation and Other Expenses: Rockwell International Cor-

poration," prepared by the Defense Contract Audit Agency, Chicago Region, Pittsburgh Branch Office (audit report no.: 3191-99-6-0318; Apr. 6, 1976), pp. 13–14.

135–136. Watson and Rane lobbying activities Interviews with Watson and Rane.

136. Rockwell campaign contributions "Committee Index of Candidates Supported, 1974–84: Rockwell International Corporation Good Government Committee" (Federal Election Commission).

136. Admiral Television letters to Aspin Interview with Aspin aide.

136–137. Downey on B-1 lobbying, and quote: "they figured if they built" Interview with Downey.

137–138. Proxmire Senate hearings "Hearings on Entertainment Practices, Feb. 2, 1976," *Joint Committee of Defense Production* (Washington, D.C.: Government Printing Office, 1976), pp. 24–54; John W. Finney, "Rockwell Names Pentagon Guests," *New York Times*, Mar. 18, 1976, pp. 1, 74.

137. Anderson conversation with Watson about hunting lodges Interviews with Anderson and Watson.

138. Conte at Wye Island Interview with Watson.

12 JIMMY CARTER AND THE ANTI–B-1 COALITION

140. Brammer-Carter encounter in Waterloo Interview with Brammer; also Linda Kettner, "Campaign 'No Bed of Roses' for Kraft," *Cedar Falls* (Iowa) *Record*, Aug. 23, 1975, p. 10.

141. Role of Barrer in the campaign against the B-1 Interview with Barrer.

142–143. AFSC and CALC involvement and alliance Interview with Terry Provance (campaign organizer).

142. Rockwell annual stockholders meeting Byron E. Calame, "Rockwell Listens to Roar of Holders over Its B-1 Bomber," *Wall Street Journal*, Feb. 13, 1976.

143. Common Cause involvement Interview with David Cohen, president of Common Cause.

143. Role of Brammer in campaign against the B-1 Interview with Brammer.

146. Rep. Yatron lobbied Newsletter of the National Campaign to Stop the B-1, Apr. 9, 1976, p. 1.

146–147. Seiberling decision to pursue the delay tactic Interview with Seiberling.

148. Culver role in the B-1 campaign Interview with Culver.

148. Culver meeting with UAW, and quote: "I know why you are here" Interview with Charles Gifford (UAW official in Des Moines, Iowa).

149. Culver meeting with anti–B-1 activists Interview with Brammer.

150. Ford reactions to Reagan criticisms Herbert Scoville, *MX: Prescrip-*

tion for Disaster (Cambridge, Mass.: MIT Press, 1981), p. 94; "B-1 Politics," *New York Times*, Apr. 26, 1976.

151. Ford decision to build B-1 Elizabeth Drew, *American Journal: The Events of 1976* (New York: Random House), p. 245.

151. Carter spring campaign troubles Martin Schram, *Running for President: A Journal of the Carter Campaign* (New York: Pocket Books, 1976), pp. 120–21.

151. Shrum statement and Carter confronted by Mohr Jules Witcover, *Marathon: The Pursuit of the Presidency, 1972–76* (New York: Viking, 1977), pp. 324–26.

151. Eizenstat on Carter's B-1 statements Interview with Eizenstat.

152. Eizenstat: "The next President is" "Final Decision on B-1 Delayed to 1977 by Senate," *Wall Street Journal*, May 21, 1976, p. 1.

153. Downey: "It's impossible in Congress" Interview with Downey.

153. Brookings report Alton H. Quanbeck and Archie L. Wood, *Modernizing the Strategic Bomber Force* (Washington, D.C.: Brookings Institution, 1976).

154. Dougherty: "There is no weapons delivery system" Letter to the Hon. Barry Goldwater from Gen. Russell E. Dougherty, Feb. 23, 1976, in *Hearings on Military Procurement, Fiscal Year 1977, Before the Senate Committee on Armed Services*, Mar. 10, 1976, p. 2834.

154. "National Campaign to Stop the B-1" tactics with regard to the cruise missile Interviews with Pearlman and other campaign leaders.

155. Reasons for Magnuson's vote switch on B-1 Interviews with Air Force and congressional sources.

156. Anderson asking employees to write to Congress "Anderson seeks Employee Support," *Rockwell International News*, Aug, 1976, p. 1.

156. Anderson meeting with Eizenstat Interview with Anderson.

156. Ford visit to Rockwell plant Lou Cannon, *Washington Post*, Oct. 8, 1976; also interview with Robert Anderson.

157. Carter campaign meeting with defense contractors Interview with Anderson.

157. Carter visit to Oklahoma Interview with Senator David Boren; also Virgil Gaither, "Many Tulsa Jobs Hinge on Carter's Bomber Decision," *Tulsa Tribune*, Nov. 8, 1976.

157. Carter in Plains, Georgia Interview with Provance.

13 THE POLITICS OF A NUCLEAR ENGINEER

158. Carter meeting with Joint Chiefs of Staff Interview with Richard Stubbing.

159. Carter meeting with defense advisers Interview with Richard Stubbing; see also Richard A. Stubbing, with Richard A. Mendel, *The Defense Game* (New York: Harper and Row, 1986), pp. 343–44.

159. Ramsey: "If Carter builds the B-1" George C. Wilson, "One B-1 for $100 Million," *Washington Post*, May 19, 1977, pp. A1, A7.

160. Rockwell lobbyists' meeting in Pentagon Interview with Watson.

161. Brown letter to Proxmire Nicholas Wade, "Death of the B-1: Events Behind Carter's Decision," *Science*, vol. 197, p. 538.

161. Brown's defense views Harold Brown, *Thinking About National Security: Defense and Foreign Policy in a Dangerous World* (Boulder, Colo.: Westview, 1983).

161. Joint Strategic "BS" Richard K. Betts, ed., *Cruise Missiles: Technology, Strategy, Politics* (Washington, D.C.: Brookings Institution, 1981), pp. 370–71.

162. Air Force giving preliminary findings to Rockwell Interviews with Robert Anderson and Gary Hillary.

163. Anderson meeting with Gen. Jones Interview with Anderson.

163. Carter's interest in B-1's ECM Betts, *Cruise Missiles*, p. 376.

163. B-1 study results and recommendations Betts, *Cruise Missiles*, pp. 374–75; also Staff Study for the Secretary of Defense: "Modernization of the Strategic Bomber Force" (unclassified version, Apr. 29, 1977).

163. Air Force resistance to cruise missiles Betts, *Cruise Missiles*, pp. 359–73.

164. Advice of Selin, York, and Ignatius Interview with Selin.

164. NSC studies of B-1 Interviews with White House officials.

165. Ohio Democrats write Carter for Cleveland Pneumatics Company Letter to Frank Moore (Office of Congressional Relations) from Rep. Mary Rose Oaker, Mar. 30, 1977, and Letter to the President from Sen. Howard Metzenbaum, Apr. 4, 1977 (Carter Presidential Library, White House Central File, Subject File, Box ND-1, Folder: Executive, National Defense 1).

165. Mann meeting with Utgoff Interview with Mann.

165. Labor unions lobbying Mondale Interview with Mondale.

166. Rockwell relations with Carter administration Interview with Anderson.

166. June 7 congressional meeting with Carter Diary notes of White House Aide Stuart Eizenstat for June 7, 1977.

167. June 10 congressional meeting with Carter Eizenstat diary notes for June 10, 1977.

167–168. Carter at Camp David Interviews; "Carter's Big Decision: Down Goes the B-1, Here Comes the Cruise," *Time*, July 11, 1977, pp. 8–12; Jimmy Carter, *Keeping Faith: Memoirs of a President* (New York: Bantam, 1982), pp. 80–83.

168. "This Bomber Is a Bummer" Stephen Chapman, "This Bomber Is a Bummer: Dump the B-1," *New Republic*, May 28, 1977, pp. 16–18.

168. "Have Blue" program for stealthy cruise missiles Bill Sweetman, *Stealth Aircraft: Secrets of Future Airpower* (Osceola, Wis.: Motorbooks International, 1986); also interviews.

169. June 20 discussion of congressional relations Eizenstat diary notes for June 10, 1977.

169. *Lance recommendations to Carter* Memorandum to the President from Bert Lance, Subject: B-1 Bomber, June 17, 1977 (Executive Office of the President, Office of Management and Budget, Washington, D.C.); "1979 Spring Planning Review, Department of Defense, Issue #2: B-1 Bomber," May 1977 (internal OMB paper).

170. *Mondale's recommendation* Interview with Mondale; also Stubbing, *The Defense Game*, p. 348.

170. *June 27 cabinet meeting* Eizenstat diary notes for June 27, 1977.

170. *Carter informs aides of his decision* Eizenstat diary notes for June 27, 1977.

170. *Diary note on Brown* Carter, *Keeping Faith*, p. 82.

171. *Carter announcing his decision* Carter, *Keeping Faith*, pp. 80–83; Charles Mohr, "Carter in the Role of Manager," *New York Times*, July 1, 1977, p. 11; "The President's News Conference of June 30, 1977," *Public Papers of the Presidents: Administration of Jimmy Carter, 1977* (Washington, D.C.: Government Printing Office, 1978), pp. 1197, 1199.

171. *Cheers in the White House* Interview with Mondale.

171. *Position of Carter aides* Interviews with Eizenstat, Jody Powell, and Hamilton Jordan.

171. *Jordan on Carter decision* Hedrick Smith, "Problems of a Problem Solver," *New York Times Magazine*, Jan. 8, 1978, p. 30.

171. *Dornan and McGovern reactions* "Carter's Big Decision: Down Goes the B-1, Here Comes the Cruise," *Time*, July 11, 1977, pp. 8–12; Haynes Johnson, "Only a Handful Knew Which Way Carter Was Going on B-1," *Washington Post*, July 1, 1977, p. A16.

171. *Whipple's reaction* Muriel Dobrin, "B-1 Politics and Statistics Turn into Personal Tragedies at Rockwell," *Baltimore Sun*, July 10, 1977, p. 10.

172. *Mary Turner's reaction* "Rockwell's Bombshell," *Newsweek*, July 11, 1977, pp. 61–62.

172. *Bingham letter to Carter* Letter to the President from Jonathan Bingham, July 12, 1977 (Carter Presidential Library, White House Central File, Subject File, Box ND-1, Folder: Executive, National Defense 1).

172. *Halperin views* Interview with Halperin.

172. *Jones-Chappell telephone conversation* Interview with Chappell.

172. *Jones's views on Carter decision* Interviews with Jones and others; also Letter to the Hon. George H. Mahon from Gen. David C. Jones (Air Force Chief of Staff), Feb. 21, 1978 (Department of the Air Force, Office of the Chief of Staff, United States Air Force).

174. *Chappell's role in B-1 fight* Interviews with Chappell and others.

175. *Beckel heading lobbying effort* Interviews with Beckel and Defense Department and congressional sources.

175. *White House playing on expectations* Interviews with Herschell Harris (assistant director of the Office of Management and Budget) and others.

176. **Anderson's B-1 vote** Mary McGrory, "The Costly B-1 Bomber Dies Many Hard Deaths in Congress," *Washington Star*, Dec. 13, 1977, p. 3.

176. **Burke vote on B-1** Interview with Mondale; Telegram to President Carter, June 30, 1977 (Carter Presidential Library, White House Central File, Subject File, Box ND-1, Folder: Executive, National Defense 1).

176. **Sen. Bellmon on B-1** Interviews with Bellmon and David Blankenship; also "Senate Backs Research on the B-1 as 'Insurance,' " *Washington Post*, July 20, 1977.

177. **Conversation at Trader Vic's** Interviews with Chappell and Rane.

178. **Brzezinski on Carter's "pristine decisions"** Interview with Brzezinski.

178. **O'Neill on B-1: "because voting for such"** Quoted in *The Congressional Record—House*, Feb. 22, 1978 (Washington, D.C.: Government Printing Office, 1978), p. H1362.

179. **Mahon: "We are looking at national"** Quoted in *The Congressional Record—House*, Oct. 20, 1977 (Washington, D.C.: Government Printing Office, 1977), pp. H34715–16.

14 THE SECRET WAR TO SAVE THE B-1

181. **Anderson telephone call to Hello** Interview with Anderson.

181. **Rockwell strategy to keep B-1 alive** Interview with Anderson; Stratford Sherman, "How Rockwell Kept the B-1 Alive," *Fortune*, Nov. 2, 1981, p. 107–112; Robert Lindsey, "Builder of the B-1 Bomber," *New York Times*, Oct. 11, 1981.

181. **Rockwell bookkeeping of B-1 charges** John Hanrahan, "Whistle-blower," *Common Cause*, March–April 1983, pp. 17–23.

183. **Hans Mark's views on and role in the B-1** Interview with Mark.

183. **Zeiberg's views on and role in the B-1** Interview with Zeiberg.

183. **Role of generals Burke and Stafford** Interviews with Air Force and Defense Department sources; Frank Greve, "Is the B-1 a Plane Whose Time Has Come?" *Philadelphia Inquirer Magazine*, Mar. 19, 1984.

184. **New leadership skills** Nick Kotz, Nancy Nathan, and Cathy Donohoe, "Where Have All the Warriors Gone?" *Washingtonian*, June 1984.

184. **$450 million injection into the bomber program** Greve, "Is the B-1 a Plane Whose Time Has Come?" p. 9; Fred Kaplan, "The Plane that Wouldn't Die," *Boston Globe Magazine*, May 16, 1982.

185. **Role of Battista** Interview with Battista; Kaplan, "The Plane That Wouldn't Die."

186. **Role of Ichord** Interview with Ichord and others.

186. **Role of Dickinson** Interview with Dickinson and others.

186. **Hello's meeting with Ichord** Interviews with John Rane and Ichord.

187. **California meeting between Rockwell and congressmen** Interviews with Watson, Rane, and Ichord.

187. **B-1 competition with the C-X** Kaplan, "The Plane that Wouldn't Die"; "Rockwell Awarded $5 Million to Evaluate B-1 as ALCM Car-

rier," *Defense-Space Daily,* Jan. 9, 1980, p. 33; "Air Force sees CX as Future Cruise Missile Carrier Option," *Defense-Space Daily,* Mar. 6, 1980, p. 28.

188. Boeing warned on B-52 Interviews with Pentagon and industry officials.

188. Rockwell strategy Interviews with Anderson, Watson, and others.

188. Mark's CMCA proposal and Carter's rejection Interview with Mark; Kaplan, "The Plane that Wouldn't Die"; Richard A. Stubbing, with Richard A. Mendel, *The Defense Game* (New York: Harper and Row, 1986), p. 102.

189. Perry commenting on Mark being "dangerously close to a forbidden line" Interview with Mark.

189. Mark pushes ahead on B-1 "Mark Wants Funds Early Next Year for Follow-On Bomber," *Defense-Space Daily,* Sept. 19, 1980, p. 101; Winston Williams, "Dogged Rockwell Bets on Reagan," *New York Times,* Sept. 30, 1984.

189. Burke's LRCA speech Remarks by Lt. Gen. Kelly H. Burke (deputy chief of staff for research, development, and acquisition) to the National Security Industrial Association, Dec. 12, 1979 (News Release, U.S. Air Force, speech entitled: "The Air-Breathing Leg of the Triad in the 1980s and Beyond").

191. Maxwell Air Force Base meeting Interviews with Mark and other Air Force participants; letter to author from Secretary of Defense Caspar Weinberger.

192. B-52 flights to Indian Ocean and around the world Interview with Mark; "Shorter Hops for B-52," *New York Times,* June 8, 1980, p. E3; John J. Fialka, "High-Altitude Bombers Gaining New Favor," *Washington Star,* Jan. 27, 1980, p. 4.

192. Monterey meeting Letter to author from Weinberger; interview with Mark and other participants; Charles A. Robinson, Jr., "Multipurpose Bomber Advances," *Aviation Week and Space Technology,* Aug. 4, 1980, pp. 16–18; Edgar Ulsamer, "The Tortuous Road Toward a New Bomber," *Air Force Magazine,* Sept. 1980, pp. 17–21.

193. Dornan House statement on SWL "House Approves Measure to Resurrect B-1 Bomber," *Baltimore Sun,* May 15, 1980, p. 6.

193. Carter letter to Stennis Letter to Chairman Stennis from Jimmy Carter, May 15, 1980 (Carter Presidential Library, White House Central File, Subject File, Box ND-1, Folder: Executive, National Defense 1).

194. Glenn press release on B-1, and quote: "Some estimates indicate" "Senate Approves Glenn Amendment for Multi-Role Bomber Development," July 2, 1980 (Press Release, office of Sen. Glenn, Washington, D.C.), p. 2; Robinson, "Multipurpose Bomber Advances," p. 16.

195. Republican platform quote: "accelerated development" *1980 Republican National Convention Platform* (Washington, D.C.: Government Printing Office, 1980), p. 32.

195. Republican Defense Advisory Board Interview with Gen. Dougherty.

195. **Reagan's B-52 anecdote** Ronald Reagan, "For B-52 Bombers Mission Impossible," *Citizens for the Republic Newsletter,* Oct. 30, 1979, pp. 1–3. [Citizens for the Republic was a Reagan political-action committee.]

195. **Reagan speech before the Veterans of Foreign Wars** Lou Cannon, *Reagan* (New York: Perigee, 1982), p. 271.

196. **Sindlinger and Company poll on B-1** *National Security Record,* Heritage Foundation, Feb. 1981, p. 4.

196. **Military leaders meeting Tower** Stubbing, *The Defense Game,* p. 359.

196. **Carter: "treat me like an enemy"** Eizenstat diary notes for Dec. 5, 1979.

196. **Carter on Brown, and quote: "Harold's been a horse's"** Eizenstat diary notes for Dec. 22, 1979.

197. **Stennis meeting with White House aides** Eizenstat diary notes for June 18, 1980.

197. **White House political strategy meeting, and Carter quote: "We're behind on MX"** Eizenstat diary notes for Aug. 12, 1980.

197. **Nuclear war plan and PD 59** Herbert Scoville, *MX: Prescription for Disaster* (Cambridge, Mass.: MIT Press, 1981), p. 57; Clarence A. Robinson, Jr., "Carter Strategic Policy Under Scrutiny," *Aviation Week and Space Technology,* Aug. 11, 1980, p. 21.

197. **Stealth stories leak** Interviews with Jody Powell and others; George C. Wilson, "Carter to Support New Bomber," *Washington Post,* Aug. 14, 1980, pp. A1, A17.

197. **Reagan criticism and previous public disclosures of Stealth program** "Stealth Had 1964 Counterpart," *Baltimore Sun,* Oct. 19, 1980, p. K2; Craig Covault, "Advanced Bomber, Missile in Definition," *Aviation Week and Space Technology,* Jan. 29, 1979.

198. **Ichord and Wilson as lobbyists** Interviews with Ichord and Wilson; records of Clerk, House of Representatives.

198–199. **Deaver connections with Rockwell and Reagan** Greve, "Is the B-1 a Plane Whose Time Has Come?" p. 2.

199. **Deaver arranging for Anderson and Hello to meet with the Reagan Defense Transition Team** Interviews with Reagan administration officials.

15 THE DEMOCRATIC BOMBER AND THE REPUBLICAN BOMBER

200. **Reagan: "margin of safety"** Michael Krepon, *Strategic Stalemate: Nuclear Weapons and Arms Control in American Politics* (New York: St. Martin's, 1984), p. 39.

200. **Weinberger: "must prevail and be"** Richard Halloran, "Pentagon Draws Up First Strategy for Fighting a Long Nuclear War," *New York*

Times, May 30, 1982, p. 1; "Weinberger Denies Plans for 'Protracted' War," *New York Times,* June 21, 1982, p. A5.

200. Pipes: "country better prepared" Krepon, *Strategic Stalemate,* p. 54.

201. Gray: "the U.S. may have no" Colin Gray, "Presidential Directive 59: Flawed but Useful," *Parameters* (journal of the United States Army War College), March 1981, p. 33.

201. Rowney: "we have put too much" Krepon, *Strategic Stalemate,* p. 34.

201. Views of the conservative ideologues: "the Russians as the problem" Krepon, *Strategic Stalemate,* p. 15.

201. Reagan defense budget David A. Stockman, *The Triumph of Politics: Why the Reagan Revolution Failed* (New York: Harper and Row, 1986), pp. 105–109; Richard A. Stubbing, with Richard A. Mendel, *The Defense Game* (New York: Harper and Row, 1986), p. 29.

201–202. Weinberger and Carlucci meeting with Air Force generals Interviews with Carlucci and Air Force officers.

203. Reagan's choice of Weinberger for secretary of defense Lou Cannon, *Reagan* (New York: Perigee, 1982), pp. 308, 386.

203. Hardliners annoyed with Carlucci Cannon, *Reagan,* p. 386; Gordon Adams, *The Politics of Defense Contracting: The Iron Triangle* (New Brunswick: Transaction Books and Council on Economic Priorities, 1981), p. 24.

204. DeLauer meeting with Air Force generals Interviews with Defense Department sources and Air Force officers.

204. Origins of Stealth bomber Interviews with Air Force officers; see also Bill Sweetman, *Stealth Aircraft: Secrets of Future Airpower* (Osceola, Wis.: Motorbooks International, 1986).

205. Air Force's desire and need for two bombers Interviews with Gen. Thomas Stafford and others.

206. Burke's role in B-1 Frank Greve, "Is the B-1 a Plane Whose Time has Come?" *Philadelphia Inquirer Magazine,* Mar. 19, 1984.

206. Relative costs of B-1, B-52, and Stealth "Strategic Bomber Proposals," *Hearings of the House Appropriations Defense Subcommittee on the Department of Defense Authorization for Fiscal Year 1982, part 6, July 8, 1981* (Washington, D.C.: Government Printing Office, 1981), pp. 1098–99.

206. Stealth lobbying activities of Jones, Wilson, and Thayer Interviews with Robert Anderson, Anthony Battista, William Chappell, and others.

207–208. Weinberger meeting with Rockwell Interviews with Anderson and others.

208. Anderson's reasons for not accepting a fixed-price contract Interviews with Anderson.

209. General Ellis's opposition to B-1 "Gen. Ellis Makes Case for 'Two-Bomber Program,'" *Aerospace Daily,* Feb. 19, 1981, pp. 250–51; Howard Silber, "Air Force Wants Stealth-like B-1," *Omaha World-Herald,* May 20, 1981, p. 1.

209. **Ellis takes his case to Congress**   Interview with Rep. John Seiberling; "Gen. Ellis Makes Case for 'Two-Bomber Program,' " p. 251.

209. **Weinberger orders generals back to Pentagon**   Walter Pincus, "Air Force in a Dogfight Over Its New Bomber," *Washington Post*, June 20, 1981, p. A14.

209. **Weinberger on his dilemma, and quote: "If you knew right now"**   Robert C. Toth, "Weinberger to Rule Soon on Bombers," *Los Angeles Times*, June 8, 1981, p. 1; Robert C. Toth, "Odds Favor Stealth Bomber Despite Flaws," *Los Angeles Times*, June 28, 1981, p. 1.

209–210. **Arguments of B-1 advocates**   "Strategic Bomber Proposals," *Hearings of the House Appropriations Defense Subcommittee on the Department of Defense Authorization for Fiscal Year 1982, part 6, July 8, 1981* (Washington, D.C.: Government Printing Office, 1981), pp. 1081–1135.

210. **Rockwell meeting with the Air Force on B-1 price**   Interview with Anderson.

210. **DeLauer's appeal to Weinberger for fixed-price contract**   Interviews with Defense Department officials.

210. **DeLauer telephone call to Anderson**   Interview with Anderson.

211. **Anderson's letter agreeing to fixed price**   Interviews with Anderson and Hillary; letter to Anderson from General Skantze (Air Force Systems Command), June 3, 1981, and letter to Skantze from Anderson, June 9, 1981 (information obtained during interview with Anderson).

211. **Jones lobbying at Paris Air Show**   Interview with Battista.

211. **Jones's relationship with Reagan**   Ralph Nader and William Taylor, *The Big Boys: Power and Position in American Business* (New York: Pantheon, 1986), p. 382.

211. **Anderson lobbying Meese**   Interview with Anderson.

211. **Addabo on the B-1**   Interviews with congressional sources.

212. **Frost on the B-1**   Interview with Frost.

212. **The religious right and the B-1**   Interview with former Rep. David Bowen (D-Miss.).

213. **Metzenbaum's switch on the B-1**   Interviews with Metzenbaum and UAW officials.

213. **Decline in value of Rockwell stock**   Greve, "Is the B-1 a Plane Whose Time Has Come?" p. 22.

213. **Dickinson advice to Reagan, and quote: "bird in the hand"**   "At 'A Minimum $200 Million a Bird,' B-1 Bomber Debate Begins," *New York Times*, Oct. 11, 1981, p. E5.

213. **Chappell's promise to deliver forty votes**   Interviews with Rane and congressional sources.

214. **Baker message to Reagan**   Interviews with congressional and industry sources and Air Force officers.

214. **AVCO's use of Baker**   Interview with Henry Ritter (former vice-president for marketing, AVCO, Nashville, Tenn.).

214. *Reagan's political problems with MX*   Cannon, *Reagan*, pp. 389–94.

215. *Reagan announces decision to Weinberger, and quote: "People vote for you"*   Interviews with Weinberger aide and Reagan White House aide.

215. *Reagan's public announcement of B-1 and MX decisions*   Cannon, *Reagan*, pp. 392–93; "Remarks and a Question-and-Answer Session with Reporters on the Announcement of the United States Strategic Weapons Program," Oct. 2, 1981, in *Public Papers of the Presidents: The Administration of Ronald Reagan, 1981* (Washington, D.C.: Government Printing Office, 1982), p. 879.

216. *Weinberger testimony on B-1 limitations*   George C. Wilson, "Reagan's Defense Plans Shelled from All Sides," *Washington Post*, Nov. 6, 1981, p. A20; Richard Halloran, "House Armed Services Committee Hears Weinberger and Jones," *New York Times*, Oct. 7, 1986.

216. *Weinberger: "unless someone wants to"*   Wilson, "Reagan's Defense Plans Shelled from All Sides."

216. *CIA testimony on B-52 capability to penetrate*   Richard Halloran, "Senator Cites CIA Data in Challenging B-1 Plan, " *New York Times*, Oct. 29, 1981, p. A17.

216. *GAO and CBO reports on B-1 costs*   "Costs of 100 B-1 Bombers Figured at Double the Air Force Estimate," *New York Times*, Nov. 10, 1981; George C. Wilson, "Cost of B-1s Estimated at $39 Billion," *Washington Post*, Nov. 10, 1981, p. 1.

217. *Weinberger-Casey letter to Congress*   Michael Getler, "Pentagon Disputes $40 Billion Hill Estimate for New B-1 Bomber," *Washington Post*, Nov. 11, 1981, p. 3.

217. *The "synergistic effect"*   "B-1B, ATB Seen as Synergistic Penetrators," *Aerospace Daily*, Oct. 16, 1981, p. 249.

217. *Reagan letter to Stevens, and quote: "a dangerous and misleading"*   Steven Y. Roberts, "Senators Reject Plan to Drop B-1," *New York Times*, Dec. 4, 1981.

16   BUT DOES IT FLY WELL ENOUGH?

223. *Rockwell B-1B production statistics*   Interview with Sam Icobellis (Rockwell vice-president).

223. *Problems with the B-1B*   "The B-1B: A Program Review," *Report of the Panel on the B-1B, Subcommittee on Research and Development, and Subcommittee on Procurement and Military Nuclear Systems of the Committee on Armed Services,* Mar. 30, 1987, House of Representatives (Washington, D.C.: Government Printing Office, 1987).

224. *Odgers quote*   Molly Moore, "B-1 Bomber Repair Fund Is Requested," *Washington Post*, Feb. 26, 1987 p. A7.

225. *Aspin: "The biggest problem"*   "B-1 Report Faults Air Force Management," *House Armed Services Committee News Release*, Mar. 30, 1987, p. 3.

225. **Welch: "The central fact is"** *Congressional Record—Senate,* Jan. 16, 1987 (Washington, D.C.: Government Printing Office, 1987), p. S884.

226. **Air Force complaints of media treatment** Gen. John T. Chain, Jr. (commander of SAC), "To the Critics of the B-1B: Bah!" letter to the editor, *Washington Post,* May 2, 1987, p. A21.

228. **"The B-1B Fiasco"** *New York Daily News,* Sept. 30, 1987.

228. **"Fly before you buy"** John H. Cushman, Jr., "Build-Now-Finish-Plane-Later-Plan," *New York Times,* Mar. 4, 1987.

229. **Stealth competition against B-1B** Richard Halloran, "3-Year Advance of Stealth Plane Rejected by U.S.," *New York Times,* Aug. 4, 1982, pp. A1, A8.

230. **Deaver hired by Rockwell and investigated** David Hoffman, "Deaver Met with OMB Chief on Behalf of B1 Contractor," *Washington Post,* Apr. 1, 1986, pp. A1, A10; David Hoffman, "Reagan Defends Deaver on Lobbying," *Washington Post,* Apr. 10, 1986.

230. **Burke, Stafford, and Hecker hired by Rockwell** Greve, "Is the B-1 a Plane Whose Time Has Come?" *Philadelphia Inquirer Magazine,* Mar. 19, 1984.

231. **Stealth secrecy, and Hello quote: "I can't make a comparison"** George C. Wilson, "B-1, Stealth Dogfight in Congress," *Washington Post,* Feb. 18, 1986, p. A8.

231. **Amalie on the Stealth program** Tim Weiner, "Secret Ledger Hides Military Projects," *Detroit Free Press,* Feb. 8, 1987, pp. 1A, 6A.

232. **Goldwater on Stealth** Letter to author from Sen. Barry Goldwater, Dec. 17, 1986.

17 OUT OF CONTROL

239. **Jones's views on military special interests, and quote: "A great problem is that"** Interview with Jones.

239. **Packard's views on defense procurement, and quote: "There are strong perverse"** Interview with Packard; David Packard, "A New Blueprint for Defense Management," *Washington Post,* April, 1986.

240. **Allen on B-70 fight, and quote: "I was a young officer"** Interview with Allen.

241. **Dickinson: "The window of vulnerability"** Interview with Dickinson.

243. **Goodpaster: "I've seen history repeating"** Interview with Goodpaster.

244. **Goodpaster on the "balance of terror"** Interview with Goodpaster.

244. **Kennan: "like men in a dream"** George F. Kennan, *The Nuclear Delusion: Soviet-American Relations in the Nuclear Age* (New York: Pantheon, 1983), p. 176.

246. **Eisenhower: "You can't have that"** Jerome B. Wiesner, "Why We Need a Tough National Science Advisor," *Washington Post,* May 24, 1987, pp. D1, D4.

246. *Wiesner: "increased technological complexity* Wiesner, "Why We Need a Tough National Science Advisor," p. D4.
248. *Watkins: "We have to get this whole"* Nick Kotz, Nancy Nathan, and Cathy Donohoe, "Where Have All the Warriors Gone?" *Washingtonian*, June 1985, p. 135.
249. *Mills: "succeeded within the American"* C. Wright Mills, *The Power Elite* (New York: Oxford University Press, 1959), p. 361.

BIBLIOGRAPHY

Adams, Gordon, *The B-1 Bomber: An Analysis of Its Strategic Utility, Cost, Constituency, and Economic Impact* (New York: Council on Economic Priorities, 1976).
———, *The Politics of Defense Contracting: The Iron Triangle* (New York: Council on Economic Priorities, 1981).
Adams, Sherman, *Firsthand Report: The Story of the Eisenhower Administration* (New York: Harper, 1961).
Ambrose, Stephen E., *Eisenhower: Soldier, General of the Army, President-Elect: 1890–1952*, vol. 1 (New York: Simon and Schuster, 1983).
———, *Eisenhower: The President*, vol. 2 (New York: Simon and Schuster, 1983).
———, *Rise to Globalism: American Foreign Policy Since 1938*, 3d ed. (New York: Penguin, 1983).
Atwood, John Leland, *North American Rockwell: Storehouse of High Technology* (Princeton: Princeton University Press, 1970).
Baker, Robert Gene, *Wheeling and Dealing: Confessions of a Capitol Hill Operator* (New York: Norton, 1978).
Ball, Desmond, *Politics of Force Levels: The Strategic Missile Program and the Kennedy Administration* (Berkeley: University of California Press, 1980).
Baritz, Loren, *Backfire* (New York: Morrow, 1985).
Barrett, Archie, *Reappraising Defense Organization* (Washington, D.C.: National Defense University Press, 1983).
Beckett, Brian, *Weapons of Tomorrow* (New York: Plenum, 1983).

Bertch, Kenneth, and Linda S. Shaw, *Nuclear Weapons Industry* (Washington, D.C.: Investor Responsibility Research Center, 1984).

Beschloss, Michael R., *Mayday: Eisenhower, Khrushchev and the U-2 Affair* (New York: Harper and Row, 1986).

Betts, Richard K., ed., *Cruise Missiles: Technology, Strategy, Politics* (Washington, D.C.: Brookings Institution, 1981).

Borawski, John, ed., *Avoiding War in the Nuclear Age: Confidence-Building Measures for Crisis Stability* (Boulder: Westview, 1986).

Brendon, Piers, *Ike: His Life and Times* (New York: Harper and Row, 1986).

Broder, David S., *Changing of the Guard: Power and Leadership in America* (New York: Simon and Schuster, 1980).

Brown, Harold, *Thinking About National Security: Defense and Foreign Policy in a Dangerous World* (Boulder: Westview, 1983).

Bundy, William P., *The Nuclear Controversy: A Foreign Affairs Reader* (New York: Meridian, 1985).

Burns, James, *To Heal and to Build: The Programs of Lyndon Baines Johnson* (New York: McGraw-Hill, 1968).

Campbell, Christy, *Weapons of War: Present and Future Weapons Systems and Strategies* (New York: Peter Bedrick, 1983).

Cannon, Lou, *Reagan* (New York: Perigee, 1982).

Carter, Ashton B., John D. Steinbruner, and Charles A. Zraket, eds., *Managing Nuclear Operations* (Washington, D.C.: Brookings Institution, 1987).

Carter, Jimmy, *Keeping Faith: Memoirs of a President* (New York: Bantam, 1982).

Coates, James, and Michael Kilian, *Heavy Losses: The Dangerous Decline of American Defense* (New York: Viking Penguin, 1985).

Cockburn, Andrew, *The Threat: Inside the Soviet Military Machine* (New York: Random House, 1983).

Coffey, Thomas M., *Iron Eagle: The Turbulent Life of General Curtis LeMay* (New York: Crown, 1986).

Collins, John M., *U.S.-Soviet Military Balance: Concepts and Capabilities, 1960–1980* (New Jersey: McGraw-Hill, 1980).

Cook, Blanche Wiesen, *The De-Classified Eisenhower: A Divided Legacy of Peace and Political Warfare* (New York: Penguin, 1981).

Cummings, Milton C., Jr., ed., *The National Election of 1964* (Washington, D.C.: Brookings Institution, 1966).

DeGrasse, Robert W., Jr., *Military Expansion, Economic Decline: The Impact of Military Spending on the U.S. Economic Performance* (New York: M. E. Sharpe, 1983).

Divine, Robert A., *Blowing in the Wind: The Nuclear Test Ban Debate: 1954–1960* (New York: Oxford University Press, 1978).

Dorfer, Ingemar, *Arms Deal: The Selling of the F-16* (New York: Praeger, 1983).

Drew, Elizabeth, *Portrait of an Election: The 1980 Presidential Campaign* (New York: Simon and Schuster, 1981).

———, *Senator* (New York: Simon and Schuster, 1979).

Dunnigan, James F., and Austin Bay, *A Quick and Dirty Guide to War* (New York: William Morrow, 1985).

Dyson, Freeman, *Weapons and Hope* (New York: Harper and Row, 1984).

Eisenhower, Dwight D., *Waging Peace* (Garden City, N.Y.: Doubleday, 1963).

Enthoven, Alain, and K. Wayne Smith, *How Much Is Enough: Shaping the Defense Program, 1961–1969* (New York: Harper and Row, 1971).

Ethell, Jeff, and Joe Christy, *B-52 Stratofortress* (New York: Scribner's, 1981).

Evans, Rowland, and Robert Novak, *Lyndon B. Johnson: The Exercise of Power* (New York: New American Library, 1966).

Fallows, James, *National Defense* (New York: Vintage, 1982).

Ford, Daniel, *The Button* (New York: Simon and Schuster, 1985).

Futrell, Robert Frank, *Ideas, Concepts, Doctrine: A History of the Basic Thinking in the United States Air Force, 1907–1964* (New York: Arno, 1980).

Garthoff, Raymond L., *Détente and Confrontation: American-Soviet Relations from Nixon to Reagan* (Washington, D.C.: Brookings Institution, 1985).

Germond, Jack W., and Jules Witcover, *Blue Smoke and Mirrors: How Reagan Won and Why Carter Lost the Election of 1980* (New York: Viking, 1981).

Gold, David, with Christopher Paine and Gail Shields, *Misguided Expenditure: An Analysis of the Proposed MX Missile System* (New York: Council on Economic Priorities, 1981).

Greenwood, Ted, *Making the MIRV: A Study of Defense Decision-Making* (Cambridge, Mass.: Ballinger, 1975).

Hadley, Arthur T., *The Straw Giant: Triumph and Failure: America's Armed Forces* (New York: Random House, 1986).

Halberstam, David, *The Best and the Brightest* (New York: Random House, 1969).

Halperin, Morton H., *Bureaucratic Politics and Foreign Policy* (Washington, D.C.: Brookings Institution, 1974).

Hart, Gary, with William S. Lind, *America Can Win: The Case for Military Reform* (Bethesda, Md.: Adler and Adler, 1986).

Hartung, William D., *The Economic Consequences of Nuclear Freeze* (New York: Council on Economic Priorities, 1984).

Hoeber, Francis P., *Slow to Take Offense: Bombers, Cruise Missiles, and Prudent Deterrence* (Washington, D.C.: Georgetown University Center for Strategic and International Studies, 1977).

Holland, Lauren H., and Robert A. Hoover, *The MX Decision: A New Direction in U.S. Weapons Procurement Policy* (Boulder, Colo.: Westview, 1985).

Hopkins, J. C., *The Development of Strategic Air Command* (Omaha: Office of the Historian, Headquarters Strategic Air Command, 1982).

Howe, Russell Warren, *Weapons: The Shattering Truth about the International Game of Power, Money and Arms* (London: Sphere, 1980).

Hudson, George E., and Joseph Kruzel, eds., *American Defense Manual (1985–86)* (Lexington, Mass.: Heath, 1985).

Hughes, Emmet, *The Ordeal of Power: A Political Memoir of the Eisenhower Years* (New York: Atheneum, 1963).

Johnson, Lyndon Baines, *The Vantage Point: Perspectives of the Presidency, 1963–1969* (New York: Popular Library, 1971).

Kaplan, Fred, *The Wizards of Armageddon* (New York: Simon and Schuster, 1983).

Kaufmann, William W., *A Reasonable Defense* (Washington, D.C.: Brookings Institution, 1986).

————, *The McNamara Strategy* (New York: Harper and Row, 1967).

Kennan, George F., *The Nuclear Delusion: Soviet-American Relations in the Atomic Age* (New York: Pantheon, 1983).

Kennet, Lee, *A History of Strategic Bombing: From the First Hot-Air Balloons to Hiroshima and Nagasaki* (New York: Scribners', 1982).

Kistiakowsky, George B., *A Scientist at the White House: The Private Diary of President Eisenhower's Special Assistant for Science and Technology* (Cambridge, Mass.: Harvard University Press, 1976).

Kolko, Gabriel, *Anatomy of a War: Vietnam, the United States, and the Modern Historical Experience* (New York: Pantheon, 1985).

Krepon, Michael, *Strategic Stalemate: Nuclear Weapons and Arms Control in American Politics* (New York: St. Martin's, 1984).

Kronenberg, Philip, *Planning U.S. Security* (New York: Pergamon, 1981).

Kwitny, Jonathan, *Endless Enemies: The Making of an Unfriendly World* (New York: Penguin, 1984).

Lavalle, Major A. J. C., ed., *Airpower and the 1972 Spring Invasion* (Washington, D.C.: Government Printing Office, 1976).

LeMay, General Curtis E., with MacKinlay Kantor, *Mission with LeMay* (Garden City, N.Y.: Doubleday, 1965).

LeMay, General Curtis E., with Major General Dale O. Smith, *America Is in Danger* (New York: Funk and Wagnalls, 1968).

Leutze, James R., ed., *The Military in a Democracy* (Atlanta: Southern Newspaper Publishers Association Foundation, 1970).

Loory, Stuart H., *Defeated: Inside America's Military Machine* (New York: Random House, 1973).

Luttwak, Edward N., *On the Meaning of Victory: Essays and Strategy* (New York: Simon and Schuster, 1986).

————, *The Pentagon and the Art of War* (New York: Simon and Schuster, 1984).

Manchester, William, *The Glory and the Dream: A Narrative History of America, 1932–1972*, vols. 1 and 2 (Boston: Little, Brown, 1973).

Martinusen, Janet, *Aerospace Facts and Figures 1984–85* (New York: Aviation Week and Space Technology, McGraw-Hill, 1984).

Mayers, Teena Karsa, *Understanding Nuclear Weapons and Arms Control: A Guide to the Issues* (New York: Pergamon-Brassey's, 1986).

McDougall, Walter A., *The Heavens and the Earth: A Political History of the Space Age* (New York: Basic, 1985).

McNamara, Robert, *Blundering into Disaster: Surviving the First Century of the Nuclear Age* (New York: Pantheon, 1986).

——, *Essence of Security: Reflections in Office* (New York: Harper and Row, 1968).

Melman, Seymour, *Pentagon Capitalism: The Political Economy of War* (New York: McGraw-Hill, 1970).

Momyer, General William W., *Air Power in Three Wars: World War II, Korea, and Vietnam* (Washington, D.C.: Government Printing Office, 1986).

Morgan, Anne Hodges, *Robert S. Kerr: The Senate Years* (Norman, Okla.: University of Oklahoma Press, 1977).

Nieburg, H. C., *In the Name of Science* (Chicago: Quadrangle, 1966).

Ornstein, Norman J., and Shirley Elder, *Interest Groups, Lobbying, and Policymaking* (Washington, D.C., Congressional Quarterly Press, 1978).

Paret, Peter, ed., *Makers of Modern Strategy: From Machiavelli to the Nuclear Age* (Princeton: Princeton University Press, 1986).

Parmet, Herbert S., *JFK: The Presidency of John F. Kennedy* (New York: Penguin, 1983).

Parton, James, *Air Force Spoken Here: General Ira Eaker and the Command of the Air* (Bethesda, Md.: Adler and Adler, 1986).

Power, General Thomas S., *Design for Survival* (New York: Coward-McCann, 1965).

Presser, Senator Larry, *Star Wars: The Strategic Defense Initiative Debates in Congress* (New York: Praeger, 1986).

Pringle, Peter, and William Arkin, *SIOP: Nuclear War from the Inside* (London: Sphere, 1983).

Quanbeck, Alton H., and Archie L. Wood, *Modernizing the Strategic Bomber Force* (Washington, D.C: Brookings Institution, 1976).

Rasor, Dina, ed., *More Bucks, Less Bang: How the Pentagon Buys Ineffective Weapons* (Washington, D.C.: Fund for Constitutional Government, 1983).

Raymond, Jack, *Power at the Pentagon* (New York: Harper and Row, 1964).

Rearden, Steven L., *The Formative Years: 1947–1950: History of the Office of the Secretary of Defense* (Washington, D.C.: Government Printing Office, 1984).

Rees, Ed, *The Manned Missile: The Story of the B-70* (New York: Duell, Sloan, and Pearce, 1980).

Rice, Berkeley, *The C-5A Scandal: An Inside Story of the Military-Industrial Complex* (Boston: Houghton Mifflin, 1971).

Richelson, Jeffrey T., *The U.S. Intelligence Community* (Cambridge, Mass.: Ballinger, 1985).

Robertson, James, *The Sane Alternative: A Choice of Futures* (St. Paul, Minn.: River Basin Publishing, 1978).

Rovner, Mark, *Defense Dollars and Sense: A Common Cause Guide to the Defense Budget Process* (Washington, D.C.: Common Cause, 1983).

Scheer, Robert, *With Enough Shovels: Reagan, Bush, and Nuclear War* (New York: Random House, 1982).

Schlesinger, Arthur M., Jr., *A Thousand Days: John F. Kennedy in the White House* (Boston: Houghton Mifflin, 1965).

Schram, Martin, *Running for President, 1976: The Carter Campaign* (New York: Stein and Day, 1977).

Scoville, Herbert, *MX: Prescription for Disaster* (Cambridge, Mass.: MIT Press, 1981).

Seiler, George J., *Strategic Nuclear Force Requirements and Issues* (Maxwell AFB, Ala.: Air University Press, 1983).

Sherry, Michael S., *The Rise of American Air Power: The Creation of Armageddon* (New Haven: Yale University Press, 1987).

Smith, Gerard, *Doubletalk: The Story of the First Strategic Arms Limitation Talks* (Lanham, Md.: University Press of America, 1985).

Sorensen, Theordore C., *Kennedy* (New York: Harper and Row, 1965).

Spector, Ronald H., *Eagle Against the Sun: The American War with Japan* (New York: Free Press, 1985).

Stacks, John F., *Watershed: The Campaign for the Presidency* (New York: Times Books, 1981).

Stockman, David A., *The Truimph of Politics: Why the Reagan Revolution Failed* (New York: Harper and Row, 1986).

Stokesbury, James L., *A Short History of Air Power* (New York: William Morrow, 1986).

Stubbing, Richard A., with Richard A. Mendel, *The Defense Game* (New York: Harper and Row, 1986).

Summer, Col. Harry G., Jr., *On Strategy: A Critical Analysis of the Vietnam War* (New York: Dell, 1982).

Swanborough, Gordon, *North American: An Aircraft Album* (London: Ian Allan, 1974).

Sweetman, Bill, *Stealth Aircraft: Secrets of Future Airpower* (Osceola, Wis.: Motorbooks International, 1986).

Talbott, Strobe, *Deadly Gambits* (New York: Vintage, 1985).

————, *Endgame: The Inside Story of SALT II* (New York: Harper Torchbooks, 1979).

Taylor, Gen. Maxwell D., *The Uncertain Trumpet* (New York: Harper and Brothers, 1960).

Twining, Gen. Nathan F., *Neither Liberty nor Safety: A Hard Look at U.S. Military Policy and Strategy* (New York: Holt, Rinehart, and Winston, 1966).

Tyroler, Charles, Jr., ed., *Alerting America: The Papers of the Committee on the Present Danger* (Washington, D.C.: Pergamon-Brassey's, 1984).

Watts, Lt. Col. Barry D., *The Foundations of U.S. Air Doctrine: The Problem of Friction in War* (Maxwell AFB, Ala.: Air University Press, 1984).

Weisberger, Bernard A., *Cold War, Cold Peace: The U.S. and Russia Since 1945* (Boston: Houghton Mifflin, 1984).

White, Theodore H., *The Making of the President, 1960: A Narrative History of American Politics in Action* (New York: Atheneum, 1961).

————, *The Making of the President, 1964: A Narrative History of American Politics in Action* (New York: Atheneum, 1965).

————,*The Making of the President, 1968: A Narrative History of American Politics in Action* (New York: Atheneum, 1969).

————, *The Making of the President, 1972: A Narrative History of American Politics in Action* (New York: Atheneum, 1973).

Witcover, Jules, *Marathon 1972–1976: The Pursuit of the Presidency* (New York: Viking, 1977).

Wooten, James, *Dasher: The Roots and the Rising of Jimmy Carter* (New York: Summit, 1978).

York, Herbert, *Race to Oblivion: A Participant's View of the Arms Race* (New York: Simon and Schuster, 1970).

INDEX

A-7 attack plane, 115
A-10 attack plane, 120, 212
Aaron, David, 164–65
ABM (antiballistic missile defense system), 84, 97, 105
Acklin, James T., 227
Addabbo, Joseph, 211–12
aerospace industry, 49, 51, 52, 90, 133, 168, 230
Afghanistan invasion, 190–91
Agnew, Spiro T., 97
AIL Corporation, 224, 225, 229
aircraft carriers, 45, 234
Air Force, U.S.:
  budget of, 119–20
  congressional voting records on, 20–21
  legislative liaison office of, 20–21, 124
  lobbying efforts by, 5, 7, 12, 20–23, 27, 36, 123–34, 137–38, 156–57, 160, 172–73, 240
  Navy vs., 45–46, 190
  Scientific Advisory Board of, 192–93
  Strategic Air Command (SAC) of, 11, 31, 37, 44, 45, 111, 118
  "strategic air power" doctrine of, 35, 37–47, 238–39
  Systems Command of, 108–10, 112, 115, 116, 210
  Tactical Air Command of, 190
Air Force Association, 125, 130, 132
Albert, Carl, 50, 176
ALCM (air-launched cruise missile), 149
Aldridge, E. C. (Pete), 161, 162
Allen, Genevieve (Ginger), 124, 160, 177
Allen, James, 111–12, 116, 130, 240
Allen, Lew, Jr., 210, 213
Allen, Richard, 211
Amalie, Thomas, 231
Ambrose, Stephen E., 66
America Is in Danger (LeMay), 43–44
American Friends Service Committee (AFSC), 140–41, 142, 143
AMSA (advanced manned strategic aircraft),79–80, 81, 84, 85, 92, 161
Anderson, John, 176
Anderson, Kenneth, 20–21
Anderson, Robert, 94, 95, 98, 105, 116–17, 124, 137–38, 156, 157, 162–63, 166, 181, 199, 207–11, 237
Andrews, Robert, 194, 198

Apollo space capsule, 50, 54, 90, 112
arms control:
  defense strategy and, 28, 33, 35–36,
    43, 46, 57–58, 59–61, 64–66, 77, 89,
    105–6, 158, 242, 243–44
  political impact of, 6, 8, 84, 152, 161,
    217, 244–45
  test-ban treaties and, 44, 77, 246
Aspin, Les, 5, 136, 225
Atwood, John Leland (Lee), 48–49, 51,
  52, 53, 54, 90, 94, 127–28
AVCO Corporation, 214, 222

B-1 bomber:
  aerodynamic design of, 121
  air bases for, 10–23
  altitude of, 113, 115, 227–28
  appropriations for, 16, 126–27, 131,
    137, 147, 155–56, 177, 180–81
  avionics of, 128, 155, 181, 185, 222,
    223–25, 226–27, 229
  as B-1B, 201–2
  B-52 compared with, 5, 92, 110–11,
    113, 116, 133, 153–54, 161–62, 163,
    187–88, 195, 202, 226, 229
  B-70 compared with, 8, 117, 121, 122,
    147, 244, 249
  as backup weapon, 233
  cancellation of, 16, 158–79, 180–82,
    183–84, 204, 214, 230
  as CMCA, 188
  competitive bids on, 94–96, 112
  computers of, 4
  congressional debate on, 8, 97–98,
    106, 113, 126–27, 131–32, 145–56,
    160, 166–69, 174–77, 180, 194,
    212–13, 216–17, 241
  costs of, 3, 5–6, 18, 100, 112–13, 116,
    118, 119–21, 133, 152, 154, 161,
    171, 210, 216, 228, 229, 249, 250
  crashes of, 227–28
  criticism of, 5, 109–10, 208–9
  cruise missile compared with, 93,
    166–67, 168, 171, 173, 217
  defects of, 223–29
  economic impact of, 11, 17–18,
    128–29, 133–34, 156–57, 165,
    171–72, 222
  electronic countermeasures (ECM) of,
    163
  engines of 222, 228
  environmental impact of, 144
  escape capsule for, 116, 117, 121
  fixed-price contract for, 208, 210–11,
    223
  "goldplating" of, 108, 114, 116, 121,
    228, 239
  "grass-roots" support for, 11–12,
    136–37
  ICBMs compared with 7, 115, 166,
    179, 184, 189–90, 195, 232
  initial proposal for, 92–93
  jobs generated by, 128–29, 133,
    156–57, 165, 171–72
  Jones-Allen proposal for, 111–12, 116
  lobbying for, 5, 7, 12, 20–23, 27, 36,
    50–51, 123–38, 156–57, 160, 166,
    172–73, 176, 231–32, 240
  as LRCA, 189–90, 191, 194
  media coverage of, 3–4, 96, 151, 152,
    168, 172, 209, 228
  missiles carried by, 3
  in "mixed" nuclear force, 92, 166,
    170, 171, 232–33
  models of, 16
  "multiple bird strikes" and, 227–28
  navigation system of, 113, 115, 229
  as nuclear deterrent, 6, 7, 131
  opposition to, 8, 58, 97–98, 99, 118,
    127, 140–50, 152–55, 217–18
  as penetrating bomber, 3, 4, 132–33,
    184, 209–10, 217, 223, 229, 232–33
  political impact of, 7, 8, 100–106,
    121–22, 138, 140, 143, 144, 151,
    155, 157, 173, 178, 205, 216, 225,
    229, 244
  presidential decisions on, 7–8, 218
  production of, 3, 12, 16, 146–47,
    149–50, 155–56, 221–26, 229
  public opinion on, 191, 243
  radar detection of, 223–24
  as "Republican" bomber, 205, 225
  research and development of, 94–96,
    100, 102, 107–17, 126–27, 146, 157,
    172, 177, 180–82, 206, 207–8,
    221–23, 230
  secret funding of, 16, 180–99
  Soviet response to, 97–98, 166–67
  spare parts for, 182, 227
  specifications for, 108, 111–12, 116,
    121, 223, 228–29

B-1 bomber (*cont.*)
  status reports on, 108–10
  Stealth compared with, 6–7, 12, 16,
    184, 194, 197, 205–17, 229, 230,
    231, 232, 233
  as "stealthy," 185
  strategic importance of, 16–17, 119,
    132–33, 153–54, 162–63, 183,
    189–90, 215–16, 224–25, 232–33,
    244, 248–49
  studies of, 161–62, 164–65, 168, 209
  supersonic speed of, 98, 113, 114, 117,
    202, 228
  support for, 16, 96, 99–106, 199, 203,
    207, 213–16, 218, 223, 228–29
  swing wings for, 114, 187
  as SWL, 186–87, 193
  as symbol, 8, 234
  "synergistic effect" of, 217
  technical problems of, 4–5, 112,
    113–16
  variable air inlet for, 114
"B-1 Bomber—Nixon's TFX, The"
  (Slocombe), 99–100
B-17 bomber, 39, 40, 92
B-25 bomber, 53
B-29 bomber, 40–41, 71
B-36 bomber, 45
B-52 Superfortress bomber:
  B-1 compared with, 5, 92, 110–11,
    113, 116, 133, 153–54, 161–62, 163,
    187–88, 195, 202, 226, 229
  B-70 compared with, 35, 42, 43, 62, 97
  cruise missiles for, 16, 97, 133, 135,
    149, 153–54, 162, 163, 164, 165,
    166–67, 171, 176, 187–90, 202, 233
  fleet of, 11, 33, 55, 72, 85, 183, 204,
    206
  production of, 55, 63, 176, 187–88
B-58 Hustler bomber, 57, 62, 63, 85,
  110–11
B-70 Valkyrie bomber:
  altitude of, 60
  B-1 compared with, 8, 117, 121, 122,
    147, 244, 249
  B-52 compared with, 35, 42, 43, 62,
    97
  cancellation of, 48–49, 57, 127, 147
  as "canard–shaped," 31–32
  criticisms of, 58, 97–98
  human control of, 42–43

ICBMs compared with, 32, 34, 38, 46,
    48, 59
  LeMay's support for, 42, 46, 47, 61,
    72–73, 93, 118, 173, 240
  opposition to, 34–36, 38, 47, 48, 55,
    64, 69, 73–77, 102, 147, 153
  political impact of, 50, 61–64, 75–76,
    244
  prototypes of, 31
  research and development of, 30–33,
    48–49, 50, 54, 58, 73, 74, 86, 90,
    110–11
  as RS-70 bomber, 73–74
  as strategic bomber, 27, 30–36
  supersonic speeds of, 31, 72, 86, 112
B-747 transport, 95, 102
Baker, Bobby Gene, 51
Baker, Howard, 18, 123–24, 214
bases, military, 10–17, 19, 23, 226,
  236
Battista, Anthony, 185–86, 187, 188,
  193, 211
Beall, Donald, 207–8
Bean, Ricky M., 227
Beckel, Bob, 165, 175, 178
Bellmon, Henry, 176–77
Bingham, Jonathan, 145, 172
Blankenship, David, 176–77
Boeing Corporation:
  B-1 avionics developed by, 128, 155
  B-52 built by, 55, 63, 176, 187–88
  B-70 developed by, 30, 31
  Rockwell vs., 55, 94, 96, 99, 206–7
"bomber gap," 30, 61, 242
Boren, David, 157
Boswell, Marion, 124–25, 136
Bowen, David, 212
Boyd, James, 5, 114
Brammer, Bob, 140, 143–44, 145, 146,
  150, 154, 159
Brezhnev, Leonid, 191
"brinkmanship," 28
Brodie, Bernard, 243
Brown, George, 159
Brown, Harold, 19, 159, 160–62, 164,
  166, 167, 169, 170, 182, 188, 189,
  196, 202
Brzezinski, Zbigniew, 159, 170, 178
Bumpers, Dale, 19, 20
Bundy, McGeorge, 81, 150
Burke, Arleigh, 46

Burke, Kelly, 132, 182, 183, 184, 187, 188, 189–90, 192, 201, 204–5, 206, 210, 213, 230
Byrd, Robert, 149–50, 155

C-5 transport plane, 99, 186
C-5A transport plane, 6, 102, 149
C-17 troop carriers, 19–21
Caddell, Patrick, 151
Callahan, Daniel, 132
Carlucci, Frank C., III, 201, 203
Carter, Jimmy:
  arms control supported by, 158, 242
  B-1 as election issue for, 140, 143, 144, 151, 155, 157
  B-1 cancelled by, 16, 158–79, 180–82, 183–84, 204, 214, 230
  budgets examined by, 185, 188–89
  defense policy of, 190–91, 193–94, 195–98, 201
  electon of, 139–40, 143, 144, 151–52, 155, 157
Case, Clifford, 167
Casey, William, 217
Central Intelligence Agency (CIA), 59, 60
Chain, John T., 226
Chapman, Kenneth, 120
Chappell, William V., 172–75, 177, 193, 211, 213
Clark, Joseph, 152
Clausewitz, Carl von, 72–73
Cleveland Pneumatics Company, 165
Clifford, Clark, 85, 150
CMCA (cruise-missile-carrier aircraft), 188
Coffey, Thomas, 83
Cohen, David, 145
Cold War, 27, 61, 69
Cole, Mike, 145
Common Cause, 143, 154–55
Conahan, Frank L., 226
Congress, U.S.:
  B-1 as issue in, 8, 97–98, 106, 113, 126–27, 131–32, 145–56, 160, 166–69, 174–77, 180, 194, 212–13, 216–17, 241
  defense strategy and, 74–76
  micromanagement" by, 126, 241

military appropriations by, 51–52, 55–56, 126–67, 241–42
  seniority system in, 127
Congressional Budget Office, 216
Conte, Silvio, 138
Convair 440 aircraft, 99
Convair Corporation, 57, 63
Cooper, Tom, 187
Corona Quest, 119–21, 161
Costanza, Midge, 160
Covert, Eugene, 192
Covington, Carl, 111
Cranston, Alan, 131, 166, 194
Cross, Carl, 86
cruise missile:
  air-launched (ALCM), 149
  B-1 compared with, 93, 166–67, 168, 171, 193, 217
  for B-52, 16, 97, 133, 135, 149, 153–54, 162, 163, 164, 165, 166–67, 171, 176, 187–90, 202, 233
Cuban missile crisis, 77
Culver, John, 145, 148, 149, 150, 155, 167
Currie, Malcolm, 135
C-X transport, 187

Daniell, James, 104, 135, 136
David, Edward, 100
Dawson, Rhett, 211
Deaver, Michael K., 198–99, 211, 230
defense budget:
  "black programs" in, 231
  Carter's examinations of, 185, 188–89
  economic impact of, 56–57, 58, 247, 248, 249–50
  increases in, 32, 77, 133–34, 201, 203, 217
  reductions in, 89, 145–46, 150, 159
  research and development funds in, 184–85, 239
defense contractors:
  contracts of, 237
  economic impact of, 96, 100–103
  lobbying by, 126, 135, 172, 230, 237
  "peace conversion" of, 58, 98, 172
  strategic role of, 23, 55, 91, 95–96, 99, 101–3, 126, 135, 172, 230, 237
Defense Department, U.S.:
  decentralization of, 91–92, 93

Index

Defense Department, U.S. (*cont.*)
  interservice rivalry in, 7, 32, 45–47, 56, 173, 238–41
  procurement system of, 5, 6, 227, 234–50
  reorganization of, 32
  war plan of, 4, 38, 44, 45, 47
Defense Reorganization Act (1986), 248
defense strategy:
  arms control and, 28, 33, 35–36, 43, 46, 57–58, 59–61, 64–66, 77, 89, 105–6, 158, 242, 243–44
  congressional approval of, 74–76
  control of, 235–36, 244–50
  for conventional wars, 238–39
  cost-effectiveness of, 70, 238, 249, 250
  decision-making process in, 239–41, 246, 250
  dissenting opinions and, 240, 241–42
  economic impact of, 236, 237–38
  fear of Soviets and, 28–30
  military-industrial complex and, 9, 51, 64–65, 91, 126, 138, 152, 237, 245, 249
  "multiple," 46
  for nuclear wars, 6, 28, 77, 84, 85, 242–44, 246–47
  politics of, 8, 14–15, 16–17, 20–21, 22, 23, 50, 106, 124, 204, 235, 248
  presidential decisions on, 65–66, 218, 240, 246–47
  role of defense contractors in, 23, 55, 91, 95–96, 99, 101–3, 126, 135, 172, 230, 237
  Soviet vs. U.S., 28–29, 43–44
  special interests and, 8, 235, 236–37, 242–43, 245–46
  systems analysis and, 70–72, 76, 85, 86, 92
DeLauer, Richard, 204, 208, 210, 212
Dickinson, William, 186, 187, 193, 213, 241
Divad antiaircraft gun, 6
Dodson, Ed, 15
Dole, Robert, 17–18
Doolittle, Jimmy, 53, 192
Dornan, Robert, 171, 193, 231
Dougherty, Russell E., 132, 154, 195
Douglas, Donald, 52
Douglas Aircraft Company, 56

Douhet, Giulio, 38, 39
Downey, Thomas, 136–37, 153, 217–18, 241–42
Duberstein, Kenneth M., 230
Dulles, John Foster, 28
Duncan, Charles, 166
Dyess Air Force Base, 15–17, 19, 226

Edwards, Jack, 230
Ehrlichman, John, 101, 103
Eisenhower, Dwight D.:
  arms control supported by, 28, 33, 35–36, 43, 46, 57–58, 59–61, 64–66, 77, 243–44
  B-70 opposed by, 34–36, 38, 47, 48, 55, 64, 102, 153
  defense policy of, 9, 18, 27–36, 42, 62, 245–46
  foreign policy of, 28
  LeMay and, 42, 43
  "massive retaliation" strategy of, 27–28, 45, 65, 68
  military-industrial complex as viewed by, 64–65
  summit meeting of, 59–60
  U–2 shootdown and, 59–61
Eizenstat, Stuart, 151–52, 155, 156, 168
Ellis Richard H., 119, 192, 209
Engle, Clair, 55–56
Enthoven, Alain, 70, 73
Evans, William (Broadway Bill), 120

F-4 fighter–bomber, 45
F-15 fighter, 94, 120
F-16 fighter, 120
F-18 fighter, 170
F-20 fighter, 211
F-86 Sabre, 54
F-100 Super Sabre fighter, 90
F-111 fighter, 99, 100, 114, 209
Falwell, Jerry, 212
FB-111 fighter-bomber, 85, 175, 194
Fifth Avenue Compact, 63
"first-strike capability," 6, 76
Fitzgerald, Ernest, 102
Flanigan, Peter, 100, 101
Ford, Gerald, 117, 136, 150–51, 156–57, 159
Foster, John, 100

308

Frost, Martin, 212
Fulbright, J. William, 19, 105

Gates, Thomas S., Jr., 36
General Accounting Office, 18, 112,
    118, 216, 227
General Dynamics, 77, 94, 95, 99, 182
General Electric Company, 86, 112, 130,
    131, 141, 170, 182, 228
Gilpatric, Roswell, 67, 71
Glasgow Air Force Base, 18–19
Glenn, John, 131, 194, 213, 231
Glenn L. Martin Company, 50, 52
Glosser, Otto, 110, 114–115, 117
Goldwater, Barry, 55–56, 80, 81, 121,
    147, 149, 154, 166, 211, 232, 236,
    248
Goodpaster, Andrew, 30, 243, 244
Gray, Colin, 201
Gray, John, 125
Grumman Corporation, 105, 174

Haldeman, Robert, 103
Halperin, Morton, 172
Hannaford, Peter, 199
Harris, Fred, 144
Hebert, F. Edward, 127
Hecker, Guy, 230
helicopters, 234–35
Hello, Bastian (Buzz), 113, 119, 121, 122,
    124, 138, 147, 180–82, 186, 189,
    195, 199, 205–7, 210, 223, 231
Herter, Christian, 35
Hillary, Gary, 91, 162, 211
Hitch, Charles, 70
Hoag, Earl A., 109
Hobbs, Thomas H., 109–10
Holland, Spessard, 51
Hollings, Ernest, 166
Holum, John, 145
Hoover, J. Edgar, 81
House Armed Services Committee, 5, 43
Huffstutler, Robert, 216
Hughes, Fred Lee, 19
Humphrey, Hubert H., 90

ICBM (intercontinental ballistic
    missile):

B-1 compared with, 7, 115, 166, 179,
    184, 189–90, 195, 232
B-70 compared with, 32, 34, 38, 46,
    48, 59
Soviet, 28, 29, 34, 67, 68
U.S., 32, 33, 42, 52, 54, 56, 69, 72, 183
Ichord, Richard, 186, 187, 188, 193, 198
Icobellis, Sam, 223
Ignatius, Paul, 164

Jackson, Henry (Scoop), 30, 55, 128, 144,
    149, 151
Javits, Jacob, 167
Jewell, Chris, 13
Johnson, Lyndon B., 19, 30, 43, 49, 51
    defense policy of, 79–84
    Great Society programs of, 80
    in Senate, 61–62
    Vietnam War and, 80, 81–84, 86
Jones, David C., 111–12, 116, 118–21,
    125, 129, 160, 161, 163, 172–73,
    211, 239, 240
Jones, Thomas V., 206, 207, 211
Jones, W. Alton (Pete), 63
Jordan, Hamilton, 171
Jupiter missile, 56

Kassebaum, Nancy, 17
Kaufmann, William, 70
Kennan, George F., 244
Kennedy, Edward, 167, 170
Kennedy, John F.:
    arms control and, 77
    assassination of, 77–78, 80
    B-70 opposed by, 69, 73–77, 147, 153
    defense policy of, 67–69, 75–78, 216,
        242
    election campaign of, 30, 62–64
    "flexible response" strategy of, 68–69
    McNamara and, 67–68, 76
    "missile gap" issue and, 62–64, 67–68
    New Frontier programs of, 72
    Nixon vs., 63–64
Kent, Glenn, 58, 114, 115–16, 117, 189,
    193
Kerr, Gordon, 145
Kerr, Robert, 49–51
Khrushchev, Nikita, 29, 33, 35, 69, 71,
    186

Killian, James, 32
Kindelberger, James Howard (Dutch), 52–54, 127–28
Kissinger, Henry, 89
Kistiakowsky, George, 34, 35, 46–47, 48, 57, 60
Korean War, 44–45, 54, 83

L-1011 passenger jet, 99, 186
Lace bomber, 33
Laird, Melvin R., 91–92, 95, 100, 105, 115, 116, 164, 202
Lance, Bert, 159, 164, 169
Laxalt, Paul, 215
Leahy, Patrick, 130
LeMay, Curtis E., 31, 39, 40, 41, 84, 85
  B-70 supported by, 42, 46, 47, 61, 72–73, 93, 118, 173, 240
  Eisenhower and, 42, 43
  as head of Air Force, 79–81, 111
  as head of SAC, 41–47
  McNamara vs., 69, 71–72, 74, 80, 83, 84, 111
  as military strategist, 37–38, 43–44, 71–73, 76, 81–82
Levin, Carl, 11–12, 13–14, 23
Lipscomb, Glennard, 95
Little Rock Air Force Base, 19–21
Lockheed Corporation, 99, 132, 149, 176, 204
Lousma, Jack, 13
LRCA (Long Range Combat Aircraft), 189–90
LTV Corporation, 128, 130, 206–7, 212

M-1 tank, 13–14
McCarthy, James P., 20–21
McClellan, John, 19
McCloy, John J., 56
McConnell, John P., 85, 114
McDonnell Douglas Corporation, 94, 99
McElroy, Neil, 30, 34, 57
McGovern, George, 97, 98, 106, 126–27, 137, 145, 149, 167, 171
McIntosh, Robert, 15
McIntyre, Thomas, 130
McNamara, Robert Strange:
  B-70 opposed by, 73–74, 76
  as defense analyst, 69–72, 76, 244

Kennedy and, 67–68, 76
LeMay vs., 69, 71–72, 74, 80, 83, 84, 111
as Secretary of Defense, 67–77, 85–86
Vietnam War and, 82
"whiz kids" of, 69–70, 71, 79, 91, 115
Magnuson, Warren, 128, 155, 177
Mahon, George, 166, 179, 233
Mann, Michael, 144, 165
Mansfield, Don, 97, 145, 154
Mansfield, Mike, 19, 149
Mark, Hans, 182–83, 184, 188, 189, 191, 192, 209
Marshall, George, 38
Martin, Abner, 121
Martin, Glenn L., 52
Meese, Edwin, 211
Members of Congress for Peace through Law (MCPL), 97, 145, 147
Metzenbaum, Howard, 213
military-industrial complex, 9, 51, 64–65, 91, 126, 138, 152, 237, 245, 249
Miller, Grant, 123, 125, 129, 175
Mills, C. Wright, 249
Minuteman missile, 56, 68, 70, 76, 77, 84
MIRV (multiple, independently targetable reentry vehicles), 84, 106
"missile gap," 61–64, 67–68, 196, 216, 243
Mitchell, John, 103
Mitchell, William, (Billy), 38–39
Mohr, Charles, 151
Mondale, Walter, 156, 165, 169, 170, 176
Moore, John R., 98
Moore, Molly, 224
Moorer, Thomas, 135
Murphy, George, 95
"mutual assured destruction," 84, 85
MX missile, 13, 133, 167, 169, 172, 183, 191, 197, 214–15, 218, 241

National Campaign Against the B-1 Bomber, 143, 144, 152–53, 157, 159, 172
Navy, U.S., 45–46, 90, 234
Nelson, Douglas, 109
Nitze, Paul, 195

Nixon, Richard M.:
  arms control and, 89, 105–6
  B-1 supported by, 96, 99–106, 203,
    218
  campaign funds of, 103–4, 105, 137
  defense policy of, 63–64, 86
  economic policies of, 101
  election campaigns of, 90–91,
    100–106, 137
  Kennedy vs., 63–64
  secret political operations of, 100–106
  Vietman War and, 89, 91
  Watergate scandal and, 104, 106, 117
Northrop, Jack, 52
Northrop Aviation, 204, 206–7, 208,
  210, 230
nuclear weapons:
  "counterforce" capability of, 68, 77,
    84
  defense strategy for, 6, 28, 77, 84, 85,
    242–44, 246–47
  "flexible response" strategy for,
    68–69
  "massive retaliation" strategy for,
    27–28, 45, 65, 68
  "mixed" force of, 42, 62, 92, 166, 170,
    171, 232–33
  "mutual assured destruction" by, 84,
    85
  "window of vulnerability" for, 195,
    201, 209, 214, 216, 224–25, 241,
    242, 243
Nunn, Sam, 5, 131, 132, 149, 248

Odgers, Peter W., 4–5, 224
Office of Systems Analysis, 92, 99
O'Loughlin, Earl, 10–12, 13, 14
O'Neill, Thomas P. (Tip), 170, 177, 178
Operation Common Sense, 134–35, 137

P-51, Mustang, 53, 54, 112
Packard, David, 91, 92, 100, 117, 239
Pearlman, Steve, 144, 145, 154
Perry, William, 183, 189, 202
Pershing missile, 191
Pipes, Richard, 200–201
Polaris submarine, 46, 68, 70
political-action committees (PACs),
  136, 177, 237

Powell, Jody, 171
Power, Thomas S., 32, 46, 76
Power Elite, The (Mills), 249
Powers, Francis Gary, 60
Preemptive strikes, 37–38, 39
Provance, Terry, 142, 143, 144, 145, 146,
  154, 157, 159
Proxmire, William, 137, 145, 146, 147,
  149, 155, 161
Pryor, David, 19–21

Rane, John, 104, 124, 133, 135–36, 160,
  177, 187
Rather, Dan, 3–4
Reagan, Ronald, 11, 15, 95, 133, 150,
  194
  B-1 supported by, 16, 199, 207,
    213–16, 218, 223, 228–29
  defense policy of, 195–96, 200–201,
    203, 215–16, 242
  election campaigns of, 195–98
Reuther, Walter, 148
Riegle, Donald, 11–12, 13
Roche, James, 230
Rockefeller, Nelson, 63
Rockwell, Willard, Jr., 90, 96, 103, 104,
  105, 124, 135
Rockwell International:
  B-1 developed by, 94–96, 100, 102,
    107–17, 172, 177, 180–82, 206,
    207–8, 221–23, 230
  B-70 developed by, 31, 48–49, 50, 54,
    58, 73, 74, 86, 90
  Boeing vs., 55, 94, 96, 99, 206–7
  bookkeeping by, 182
  campaign contributions by, 90–91,
    96, 103–4, 137
  company retreats of, 135, 137–38
  congressional support for, 49–51
  demonstrations against, 142–43
  formation of, 90
  growth of, 52–55
  lobbying by, 50–51, 124, 127–29,
    133–38, 156–57, 166, 176, 231–32
  space shuttle built by, 103, 105, 138
  stock of, 213, 223
  subcontractors of, 128–29, 130, 207,
    222, 228
Rose, John, 101
Rowny, Edward, 201

Russ, Martin, 23
Russell, Richard, 51–52, 75, 96
Ryan, John, 92–93

SALT I, 105, 150, 166–67, 168, 169, 178
SALT II, 191, 204
SAM (surface-to-air missile), 38, 58, 60, 72
SCAD (subsonic cruise armed decoy), 163–64
Schlesinger, James, 100, 118–19, 121, 132
Scientific Advisory Committee, 32, 246
Scowcroft, Brent, 216
SCUD (subsonic cruise unarmed decoy), 163–64
Seamans, Robert, 92, 117
Seiberling, John, 97–98, 145, 146–47, 154, 155
Selin, Ivan, 93, 164
Senate Armed Services Committee, 13, 43, 126
Short, Dewey, 51
Shrum, Robert, 151
Shultz, George, 100
Sieberling, John, 133
Skantze, Lawrence, 3, 210, 211
Skybolt missile, 76–77
Slocombe, Walter, 99–100
Smathers, George, 51
space shuttle, 103, 105, 138
Sputnik, 28–30, 61, 244
SS-7 missile, 67
SS-20 missile, 191
Stafford, Thomas, 182, 183–84, 187, 195, 198, 204, 213, 230
Stans, Maurice, 103
Star Wars, 235, 247–48
Stealth bomber:
   B-1 compared with, 6–7, 12, 16, 184, 194, 197, 205–17, 229, 230, 231, 232, 233
   as "Democratic bomber," 205, 231
   development of, 204–6, 231–32
   as "invisible aircraft," 205, 210
   nonclassified information on, 197–98
Stennis, John C., 166, 177, 179, 193, 197
Stetson, John, 183
Stevens, Ted, 217
Stevenson, Charles, 145

Stone, Jeremy, 145, 150
Stop the B-1 Bomber/National Peace Conversion Campaign, 142–50, 152–55, 157, 159–60, 172
Strategic Air Command (SAC):
   LeMay as head of, 41–47
   as part of Air Force, 11, 31, 37, 44, 45, 111, 118
   war plan of, 44, 45
Strategic Bombing Surveys, 41
Strategic Defense Initiative (SDI), 235, 247–48
Sunstrand Aviation Corporation, 130, 222
SWL (Strategic Weapons Launcher), 186–87, 193
Symington, Stuart, 30, 61
Synar, Mike, 231
systems analysis, 70–72, 76, 85, 86, 92

Tactical Air command, 190
Taft, William Howard, IV, 101–2
Tammen, Ron, 145, 147, 155, 175
Taylor, Maxwell, 73–74, 150
Teller, Edward, 160, 183, 192
TFX fighter, 6, 77, 85, 99–100
"This Bomber Is a Bummer," 168
Titan missile, 17, 18, 19, 56
Tobin, Pat, 144
Toth, Robert, 209
Tower, John, 16, 128, 196, 198, 213–14
Trenchard, Hugh, 38
Tressolini, Roger, 144, 145
Trident submarine, 6, 95, 105, 106
Trident II missile, 191, 215
Truman, Harry S., 45, 247
TRW Corporation, 52, 204
Twining, Nathan F., 34, 45, 57, 62

U-2 spy plane, 59–61, 244
Udall, Morris, 144, 151
unions, labor, 129, 131, 148, 165, 168
United Automobile Workers, 129, 131, 148
Utgoff, Victor, 164–65, 168

Vance, Cyrus, 159
Vanguard satellite, 42, 46

Vietnam War, 79, 80, 97
  limited-war strategy in, 82, 85–86
  strategic bombing campaign in,
    81–84, 106
Vinson, Carl, 74–76, 96
Vogt, John, 120

Walker, Joseph A., 86
Watergate scandal, 104, 106, 117
Watkins, James D., 248
Watson, Ralph J. (Doc), 96, 123, 124,
    135–36, 138, 160, 177, 187
Webb, James, 50
Weinberger, Caspar, 4, 102, 103, 229,
    231
  as Secretary of Defense, 200, 201,
    202–8, 210, 213–17
Welch, Jasper, 114, 117
Welch, Larry, 5, 225–26
Whipple, Gerry, 134, 171–72
White, Thomas D., 34–35, 36, 38,
    70–71

Whitlock, Wayne D., 227
"whiz kids," 69–70, 71, 79, 91, 115
"Who's on Who" strategy, 123–24,
    137–38
Wiesner, Jerome, 76, 246
Wilson, Pat, 19–20
Wilson, Robert, 193, 198
"window of vulnerability," 195, 201,
    209, 214, 216, 224–25, 241, 242,
    243
Wood, Archie, 153
Woodcock, Leonard, 129, 148
Wright, Jim, 128
Wurtsmith Air Force Base, 10–15, 23

Yatron, Gus, 146
York, Herbert, 29, 56, 164

Zeiberg, Seymour, 182, 183, 184, 189,
    192
Zuckert, Eugene, 76

ABOUT THE AUTHOR

As a reporter for the *Des Moines Register* and the *Washington Post*, and as a freelance writer, Nick Kotz has won many of journalism's most important honors, including the Pulitzer Prize for national reporting, the Sigma Delta Chi Award for Washington correspondence, the Raymond Clapper Memorial Award, and the first Robert F. Kennedy Memorial Award. His study of American military leadership won the 1985 National Magazine Award for public service. This is his fourth book examining American history and public policy.

As a Distinguished Adjunct Professor at the American University School of Communication, Kotz was honored in 1985 as the university's outstanding adjunct professor. His teaching includes a semester as Senior Journalist in Residence at Duke University.

A magna cum laude graduate of Dartmouth College, Kotz did graduate study in international relations at the London School of Economics. After college, he served as a lieutenant in the U.S. Marine Corps. He is married to Mary Lynn Kotz, a journalist and author; their son, Jack Mitchell Kotz, is a photographer.